# 797,885 Books

are available to read at

# Forgotten Books

## www.ForgottenBooks.com

Forgotten Books' App
Available for mobile, tablet & eReader

ISBN 978-1-332-23178-2
PIBN 10301788

This book is a reproduction of an important historical work. Forgotten Books uses state-of-the-art technology to digitally reconstruct the work, preserving the original format whilst repairing imperfections present in the aged copy. In rare cases, an imperfection in the original, such as a blemish or missing page, may be replicated in our edition. We do, however, repair the vast majority of imperfections successfully; any imperfections that remain are intentionally left to preserve the state of such historical works.

Forgotten Books is a registered trademark of FB &c Ltd.
Copyright © 2015 FB &c Ltd.
FB &c Ltd, Dalton House, 60 Windsor Avenue, London, SW19 2RR.
Company number 08720141. Registered in England and Wales.

For support please visit www.forgottenbooks.com

# 1 MONTH OF FREE READING

at

www.ForgottenBooks.com

By purchasing this book you are eligible for one month membership to ForgottenBooks.com, giving you unlimited access to our entire collection of over 700,000 titles via our web site and mobile apps.

To claim your free month visit:

www.forgottenbooks.com/free301788

\* Offer is valid for 45 days from date of purchase. Terms and conditions apply.

# Similar Books Are Available from
# www.forgottenbooks.com

The History of Medieval Europe
by Lynn Thorndike

The Dark Ages, 476-918
by Charles Oman

The Universities of Europe in the Middle Ages, Vol. 1 of 2
Salerno - Bologna - Paris, by Hastings Rashdall

The Franks
by Lewis Sergeant

History of the Reign, Ferdinand and Isabella the Catholic, Vol. 1
by William H. Prescott

Handbook of Mediaeval Geography and History
by Wilhelm Pütz

Europe in the Middle Ages
by Ierne Arthur Lifford Plunket

History of the Moorish Empire in Europe, Vol. 1 of 3
by S. P. Scott

The Empire and the Papacy, 918-1273
by T. F. Tout

Mediæval Popes, Emperors, Kings, and Crusaders, Vol. 1
Or, Germany, Italy and Palestine, from A.D. 1125 to A.D. 1268, by Mrs. William Busk

Charles the Great
by Thomas Hodgkin

Mediaeval Rome, from Hildebrand to Clement VIII, 1073-1600
by William Miller

History of Prussia to the Accession of Frederic the Great, 1134-1740
by Herbert Tuttle

Medieval France
A Companion to French Studies, by Arthur Augustus Tilley

Italy in the Thirteenth Century, Vol. 1
by Henry Dwight Sedgwick

The Feudal Age
by Roscoe Lewis Ashley

Medieval Europe from 395 to 1270
by Charles Bémont

The End of the Middle Age, 1273-1453
by Eleanor C. Lodge

Germany in the Later Middle Ages, 1200-1500
by William Stubbs

The History of Charlemagne
by G. P. R. James

# THE BEAUTIFUL QUEEN

## JOANNA I. OF NAPLES

By
FRANCESCA M. STEELE

AUTHOR OF
"*The Village Blacksmith,*" "*The Story of the English Pope,*"
"*St. Bridget of Sweden,*" etc.

WITH SEVENTEEN ILLUSTRATIONS,
INCLUDING TWO PHOTOGRAVURE PLATES

New York
DODD, MEAD AND COMPANY
1910

PRINTED IN GREAT BRITAIN

# CONTENTS

| CHAP. | | PAGE |
|---|---|---|
| I. | INTRODUCTORY | 1 |
| II. | JOANNA'S CHILDHOOD | 17 |
| III. | PETRARCH'S FIRST VISIT TO NAPLES | 33 |
| IV. | THE LAMB AMONG WOLVES | 48 |
| V. | PLOTS AND COUNTER-PLOTS | 66 |
| VI. | THE MURDER OF ANDREW | 80 |
| VII. | WHAT FOLLOWED THE MURDER | 96 |
| VIII. | JOANNA MARRIES A SECOND TIME | 112 |
| IX. | THE KING OF HUNGARY'S VENGEANCE | 128 |
| X. | JOANNA PLEADS BEFORE THE POPE AND CARDINALS | 142 |
| XI. | JOANNA'S ACQUITTAL AND ITS RESULTS | 158 |

## Contents

| CHAP. | | PAGE |
|---|---|---|
| XII. | PEACE IS PROCLAIMED | 172 |
| XIII. | THE CORONATION OF JOANNA | 187 |
| XIV. | JOANNA'S SECOND WIDOWHOOD | 204 |
| XV. | THE DEATH OF ACCIAJUOLI | 222 |
| XVI. | URBAN V. RETURNS TO ROME | 236 |
| XVII. | JOANNA AND CHARLES OF SWEDEN | 247 |
| XVIII. | JOANNA'S FOURTH MARRIAGE | 263 |
| XIX. | THE BEGINNING OF THE GREAT SCHISM | 276 |
| XX. | JOANNA IS EXCOMMUNICATED | 292 |
| XXI. | JOANNA IS BESIEGED | 303 |
| XXII. | THE CAPTIVE QUEEN | 315 |
| XXIII. | THE FINAL TRAGEDY | 327 |
| | GENEALOGICAL TABLE | *facing* 336 |
| | SOURCES OF INFORMATION AND BOOKS CONSULTED IN WRITING THIS BIOGRAPHY | 337 |
| | INDEX | 339 |

# ILLUSTRATIONS

| | | |
|---|---|---|
| QUEEN JOANNA | *Photogravure Frontispiece* | |
| | | FACING PAGE |
| PETRARCH | . . . . . . . . | 34 |
| PORTRAIT OF A LADY (FORMERLY ATTRIBUTED TO LEONARDO DA VINCI) . . . *Photogravure* | | 44 |
| BOCCACCIO . . . . . . | | 106 |
| PONT BÉNÉZET . . . . . . . | | 148 |
| CLEMENT VI. . . . . . . . | | 154 |
| AVIGNON . . . . . . . | | 164 |
| QUEEN JOANNA (WOODCUT) . . . . . | | 200 |
| QUEEN JOANNA . . . . . . | | 226 |
| URBAN V. . . . . . . . | | 244 |
| ST. BRIDGET ON HORSEBACK . . . . | | 260 |
| GREGORY XI. . . . . . . . | | 272 |
| ST. BRIDGET DELIVERING HER RULE . . . | | 286 |
| URBAN VI. . . . . . . . . | | 298 |
| CHARLES III. OF NAPLES . . . . . | | 312 |
| CASTEL D'OVO . . . . . . . | | 324 |
| TOMB OF QUEEN JOANNA . . . . . | | 330 |

# THE BEAUTIFUL QUEEN
## JOANNA OF NAPLES

### CHAPTER I

### Introductory

> "For she was beautiful; her beauty made
> The bright world dim, and everything beside
> Seemed like the fleeting image of a shade."
> SHELLEY.

THE subject of this biography was, according to all accounts, one of the loveliest women of all time, but there is much difference of opinion among historians about her character. Some of her biographers regard her as a saint and a martyr, a victim to calumny; others have cast the vilest reproaches against her, even suggesting that she was, as her detractors maintained, one of the conspirators in the assassination of her first husband; but all are agreed that she was supremely beautiful and exceedingly talented.

Joanna I. of Naples, whose romantic story resembles in many respects that of Mary Queen of Scots, with whom she is often compared, is said to have been the most beautiful Queen that ever lived. The theme of poets, whose friend and liberal patroness she was, all Europe rang with her praise in the middle of the fourteenth century, when she was known in all the foreign courts of Europe as "la douce Reine." Her own court was magnificent and highly civilised and refined; it attracted the principal men of genius of the age, poets, of whom Petrarch was the first, and writers, with Boccaccio as chief, frequented it.

If it be true that the women and the countries that have no history only are happy, we may rightly infer that intensely unhappy must have been the "sweet Queen" whose story is related in the following pages, and the kingdom over which she ruled, for their history during the whole of her reign, from 1343 to 1382, was most exciting and often dramatic in its interest.

The scene is constantly changing from the luxury of the most brilliant court in Europe to the hardships of the battle-field, from the gay songs of the troubadour to the war-cry of the barbarian invader, from palace to prison, from the ballroom to the torture-chamber, from the love-stories of brave men and lovely women to the devastating ravages of the Plague, from that "fragment of Heaven vouchsafed to earth, Naples," to the fiends that inhabited it.

The mysteries of history are more enthralling

than the mysteries of fiction, which only remain mysteries to the end of the volume, while most of the former remain unsolved to the end of time. The central event of the reign of Joanna, the murder of Andrew of Hungary, is one of the unguessed mysteries of history: we look " down the long arches of the years," and we see historians attempting to solve it, some accusing Joanna—who was certainly innocent of consenting to it; others fixing the guilt upon Louis of Taranto, Joanna's second husband; others on Charles of Durazzo; others again on Philippa the Catanese, and her grand daughter Sancha; and yet others on the Countess of Durazzo,—all of whom are *dramatis personæ* in the drama we are about to describe; but the actual murderers will never be known—probably they were some hired assassins. One thing is certain: there was a plot to assassinate Andrew the Hungarian, and it succeeded; but who all the chief conspirators were can never be certainly affirmed, though we may be able to fix upon them with a high degree of probability.

Just as difficult is it to get a true picture of a Queen whose biographers vary so much in their estimation of her character, and this from reasons national, political, and religious. The fact that in her later years Joanna was unfortunately the partisan of the anti-pope Clement VII. prejudiced some writers so deeply against her that their judgment of her character was completely warped. The gentle, learned, and refined Pope Clement VI. was her best friend and a firm believer in her innocence, while the haughty, passionate Urban VI., although a Neapolitan himself, was one of her bitterest enemies.

It is greatly to be regretted that neither of her celebrated contemporaries, Petrarch and Boccaccio, ever wrote her biography, for both knew her intimately, and were in a position to throw light on her character, and on the mystery which darkened her youth and cast a shadow on the whole of her life. Both of these men of genius had a great admiration for her, especially Petrarch, who was one of her domestic chaplains. One of the later biographers of this "famous princess—as famous as ever lived"—Giannone, calls her "the wisest of princesses, the Light of Italy, and the Jewel of the World."

Before we begin to tell the story of her life, it will be as well to clear the ground by giving a brief sketch of her immediate predecessors on the throne, and, to help to the better understanding of subsequent events, to show the relation in which she stood to Andrew of Hungary and the princes of Taranto. As many readers dislike retrospective writing, this shall be done as shortly as possible.

The crown of Naples passed from the house of Swabia to the house of Anjou in 1269, when

# Introductory

Charles of Anjou was invested with the Two Sicilies—that is, the island of Sicily and the kingdom of Naples—by Pope Clement IV.

Manfred, the illegitimate son of Frederick II. of Swabia, was then acting as Regent for his nephew Conradine, at that time a minor, and he sent ambassadors to Charles I. to try to avert the loss of the Neapolitan throne. Charles's reply was more forcible than polite. "Go," he said, "and tell the Sultan of Lucera from me, that I will either send him to hell, or he will send me to Paradise."

Manfred was subsequently slain at the battle of Benevento, and Charles I., after being crowned in Rome, proceeded without further opposition to Naples; but young Conradine now attempted to retain possession of his throne, aided by the Duke of Austria, and falling into Charles's hands was executed with seven or eight of his followers on a scaffold covered with crimson velvet and erected in the market-place of Naples.

Charles of Anjou, a bold and ambitious king, was succeeded by his son, Charles II., Prince of Salerno, who at the time was a prisoner in Spain and only obtained his liberty two years after his father's death, on condition of leaving his three elder sons as hostages in Spain, where they were compelled to remain twelve years.

Charles II. was a true father to his people, and administered the government of his kingdom with a strict sense of justice, not suffering the Neapolitans to be oppressed by Provençal adventurers, as they had been in his father's reign.

In the fourteenth century kings transferred their rights to kingdoms, just as fathers divided their property among their children—by will; and Charles II., whose wife, Maria of Hungary, had brought him the Hungarian crown, left Hungary to the heirs of his eldest son, Charles Martel. His second son, St. Louis, the Bishop of Toulouse, died in his father's lifetime, at the age of twenty-three, and was afterwards canonised. To his third son, Robert, he left the Two Sicilies—that is, the island of Sicily and the kingdom of Naples—and also the duchies of Provence and Piedmont. To his fourth son he left the principality of Taranto, which embraced nearly half the kingdom of Naples, and to his fifth son, afterwards the Duke of Durazzo, a considerable part of the remaining half, so that the King of Naples was really only the chief of princes who, if they combined against him, were as powerful as himself.

Charles Martel's descendants never liked the disposition of Charles II.'s dominions, and the great tragedy of Joanna's life was due in a large measure to the fact that the Hungarians were ever endeavouring to gain possession of Naples. Thus we find Canrobert of Hungary, son of Charles Martel, claimed the throne of the Two Sicilies as his right

# Introductory

on Charles II.'s death, and the case was pleaded before Pope John XXII., who decided in favour of Robert, granting him also Provence and Piedmont.

The Neapolitans had cause to be very grateful to the Pope for this decision, for Robert proved an excellent king, and earned the titles of the Wise and the Good from his subjects, by whom he was greatly beloved. In 1309, the year of Charles II.'s death, Pope Clement V. transferred the Papal See and the Curia or Papal court from Rome to Avignon, which being in Provence was within the dominion of the King of Naples : this move very much weakened the temporal power of the Popes in Italy, and left Rome forlorn and deserted, a prey to her turbulent inhabitants.

Robert, with his two brothers, Charles and St. Louis, had only been liberated from their captivity in Spain a few years before he came to the throne. During his imprisonment he had acquired studious habits, and a great love of literature which never afterwards forsook him, and which made him a great patron of learning and learned men, so that his court became the most intellectual in Europe, and the resort of men of genius, who found in Robert the Wise a liberal and powerful protector.

He gathered together at enormous expense the richest library in Europe, and placed it under the care of Paul of Perugia, one of the greatest scholars of his age. He was indeed almost too passionately fond of books for a sovereign in those warlike times, and used to read even in his walks. He was a philosopher, a theologian, and a physician, but he had his limitations, for he despised poetry and was unacquainted with the works of his great contemporary, Dante. He was also a brilliant soldier, and is said to have been an excellent orator.

He married, at the age of eighteen, Violante, Princess of Aragon, by whom he had an only son, Charles Duke of Calabria, the father of Joanna, to whom he was most tenderly attached, and whom he treated more as a brother than a son, making him his companion and confidant, and entrusting him from his earliest youth with the government of Naples, from which he was himself often called away on military business.

The Duke of Calabria was neither so learned a student nor so celebrated a soldier as his father, but, like his grandfather Charles II., he was distinguished for his justice—a quality which he transmitted to his daughter Joanna in an eminent degree. Two anecdotes are told of him in connection with this virtue.

He was in the habit of visiting all his dominions once a year, to see that his humbler subjects were not oppressed by the great barons, and on one occasion he discovered that a certain Count had taken an estate by force from a vassal, because it afforded a pleasant site for his own residence.

## Introductory 9

Charles sent for the Count, and praising the lovely view and beautiful situation of his house, begged him as a friend to give it up to him, that he might build a royal palace there, promising to pay the full price for the property. The Count angrily refused to do anything of the kind; but said if the Duke chose to take it by force he must do so, but, as he was famed for his justice, he did not fear this alternative.

The Duke replied, "Now you know what your vassal must feel; and unless you restore his lands immediately, I will take your head as well as your estates." Needless to say, the Count at once made restitution to his vassal.

Another of the Duke's customs was to sit every day in the palace of justice, in front of the Castel Nuovo, which his father built, and hear the pleas of all his subjects who had any grievances; and lest the servants should prevent the poor from having access to him, he had a large bell placed at the outer gate for the applicants to ring, that he might hear it.

One day an old horse, that belonged to a knight named Marco Capece, which was straying about the city, rubbed itself against the wall, and inadvertently rang the bell. The Duke ordered the porter to bring in the complainant, and amid the laughter of the court the man returned to announce that it was only Marco Capece's old horse.

Charles, however, said that a horse deserved

justice as well as his other subjects, and sent for the owner and rebuked him severely for his neglect of an old and faithful servant, and ordered him to take better care of it, under pain of losing the pension he in a measure owed to it.

It is a pity the Neapolitans do not take this old story to heart, for there is perhaps no city in Europe in which horses are worse treated than in Naples.

In 1326 Charles left Naples for Florence, which he had agreed to govern for ten years at the request of the inhabitants, taking with him his wife, Maria of Valois, his uncles, the princes of Taranto and Durazzo, sixteen of the great Neapolitan barons, and two hundred other knights with golden spurs, their wives and children.

The princes and knights travelled on richly caparisoned horses, wearing cloaks of cloth-of-gold of various colours over their brilliant armour: the ladies wore dresses and mantles of cloth-of-gold or silver, or velvet or silk, either violet, crimson, purple, or green, both material and colour being determined by their rank. They travelled either on horseback or in litters, or in springless chariots covered with the gayest coloured velvet or some other costly material. Both knights and ladies wore for travelling long silk hoods embroidered with grotesque devices, these were fastened under the chin with jewelled clasps, and hung down

## Introductory

behind in two long points almost reaching to the ground.

Each knight had at least three squires, one of whom carried his master's arms on high. Hence the expression "With a high hand." Another carried his helmet on his saddle, and the third led his charger.

This cavalcade is said to have been the most magnificent which had travelled through Italy since the fall of the Roman Empire. In its train were 1,500 sumpter-mules of the barons, followed by large numbers of other animals carrying the baggage of the knights, and a large body of infantry. They started on May 31st from Naples, but stayed some weeks at Sienna, so they did not reach Florence until July 31st. Here they received a splendid reception, the streets being brilliantly decorated and their path strewn with flowers.

The court of Joanna's mother, Maria, Duchess of Calabria, at Florence was famed for its magnificence and for the sumptuous entertainments, both banquets and balls, given by the Duke and his wife. Maria appears to have won the hearts of the Florentine ladies, by a policy calculated to appeal to the feminine mind in all ages. It seems that the Florentine men had forbidden their wives and daughters to wear what they considered a disreputable ornament of thick tresses of white and yellow silk, which they arranged round their faces instead of their hair. In December, 1326, the Florentine dames petitioned the Duchess to get her husband to repeal the sumptuary law which forbade them to wear this hideous head-dress, and the Duchess prevailed upon her husband to do so. The Duke probably thought in this fourteenth century that "wilful woman must have her way," just as it is allowed her as generally in the twentieth.

In the spring of 1327 Maria of Valois, Duchess of Calabria, gave birth to a prince, who died a few days after his public baptism, to the great grief of all the royal family, for he was the heir to the throne of the Two Sicilies. The following December the Duke was recalled by his father, Robert, to Naples to assist in repelling an invasion of Louis the Bavarian, Emperor of Germany. The next March Joanna was born.

It must be remembered that in the fourteenth century the year began on March 25th, instead of on January 1st, so that the date of the future Queen's birth was 1327 according to the old style of reckoning, 1328 according to the Gregorian or new style—which, by the way, England was the last country in Europe to adopt.

It will not be uninteresting perhaps to pause for a moment to describe briefly the apartments of the Duchess of Calabria upon this interesting occasion.

There was a suite of three apartments. The first was called "the chamber of parade," and was hung

# Introductory 13

with crimson satin, embroidered with gold; the floor was covered entirely with crimson velvet. This room contained one bed, curtained with crimson satin, and with a counterpane of the same material. The bed was only used to accommodate Joanna upon the day of her baptism. A low chair and a buffet, under a canopy of crimson cloth-of-gold, completed the furniture of this apartment. The shelves of the buffet were covered with the finest white linen, and on them stood flagons, cups, and vases of gold and silver.

This ante-chamber opened into the bedroom of the Duchess, the walls of which were completely draped with white silk damask hangings; curtains of the same material were festooned over the windows and doors and between and round the two beds, which stood five feet apart under one tester or canopy, similarly draped. The counterpanes of these beds were of ermine.

This apartment also contained a huge buffet, which stood under a canopy of crimson cloth-of-gold; the shelves were covered with the finest damask cloths, and on them were placed crystal vessels, ornamented with gold and jewels, and never used except upon these august occasions. Massive gold candlesticks stood at each end of the buffet, and the huge wax-candles in them were only lighted upon the entrance of visitors, but two smaller tapers were kept burning day and night for fifteen days after the birth, during which period it was not étiquette to admit daylight.

The innermost room, which was assigned to the new-born infant, was also draped in white silk, but of an inferior quality.

Immediately Joanna was born she was placed in the hands of Philippa the Catanese, who was destined to play a tragic part in the drama of which Joanna was the heroine.

In the same year that Joanna was born her father founded the celebrated monastery of San Martino, between Naples and the Castle of St. Elmo. It was one of the last acts of his life, for before the year was ended Robert the Wise and the Neapolitans were overwhelmed with grief by the death of the Duke, caused by a fever while engaged in his favourite sport of hawking. During Charles's last illness Robert sat day and night by his son's bedside, endeavouring to prolong his life by his own skill as a physician. When all remedies failed, and the unfortunate Duke, still in the prime of life, passed away, the King exclaimed: "The crown has fallen from my head. Woe to me, woe to you!"

Charles had always been the darling of the people and the support of the throne, and his death was a great blow to the nation, as well as to the King, who idolised his only son and the heir to his kingdom. The late Duke was a handsome man, of fine figure, courageous, though not fond of war; his abilities were inferior to those of his father and daughter, but he was of an amiable disposition which endeared him to every one.

He was buried in the church of St. Clare, founded by his father in 1310. A story is told of the Duke and his father with regard to this church, on which Robert had expended immense sums of money, both in building and ornamenting it. When finished he took Charles to see it, and pointed out its beauties to him; then, suspecting from the Duke's manner that he did not particularly admire it, he asked him what he thought of it. The Duke with more candour than tact said he thought it was more like a stable than a church.

"May it please God, my son, that you are not the first to eat in this stable," said Robert, irritated at Charles's criticism. As it happened, the poor Duke was the first member of his family to be buried in this church, which the Neapolitans took to be the meaning of the rebuke.

There was still a hope that Charles might be succeeded by a son, for Maria of Valois was expecting an addition to her family when her husband died; but a few months after his death she gave birth to another daughter, who was named Maria, and from that time Joanna was recognised as her grandfather's heiress and successor.

The Duchess only survived her husband three years. She died in 1321, leaving the two little princesses, Joanna and Maria, to the care of their grandfather and his second wife, the devout Queen Sancha. Maria, whose brother Philip of Valois, the first King of France of the house of Valois, came to the throne in 1328, left half her fortune of sixty thousand francs, which she received from her father, and half her lands in Naples, to each of her daughters, but to Joanna she left the largest share of her jewels, clothes, and personal effects.

Little is known as to her character, beyond the fact of her popularity in Florence; but she is believed to have been a good and virtuous princess, whose early death is to be lamented as it deprived her children of a mother's care.

## CHAPTER II

## Joanna's Childhood

A MINOR mystery in the life of Joanna I. is why so wise a man as Robert the Good should have chosen Philippa the Catanese, whom historians speak of as "a woman sprung from the dregs of the people, originally a laundress," as the most fitting person to have charge of the heiress to the Neapolitan throne. Whether Philippa was worthy of the confidence reposed in her by the King and Queen or not, it was an unwise choice Philippa's low origin afterwards reflected injuriously upon her royal charge, and roused at the time the envy of her contemporaries, who, prejudiced by the favour shown her, were ready to attribute every vice to Joanna's governess.

Philippa was a native of Catania in Sicily, the wife of a Sicilian fisherman and herself a laundress, who was called in by Violante of Aragon to act as wet-nurse to her son Charles, the Duke of Calabria, when she was in Sicily with her husband, who was engaged in an expedition against the Sicilians. Philippa was not only beautiful and graceful, but intelligent also, and she soon acquired courtly manners, and took such tender care of her foster-son that Violante henceforth heaped honours upon her.

Robert's seneschal, Raymond de Chabannes, had at this time a favourite Moor who acted as his cook and steward, and pleased his master so well that he gave him his own names in baptism, and set him free, and when he resigned the seneschalship recommended Robert to take the Moor in his place. Raymond the Moor soon became as great a favourite with the King as Philippa was with Violante, and when the Catanese's first husband died they arranged a second marriage for Philippa with the new seneschal, now raised to the rank of a knight.

Before Violante died she begged Robert to be good to Philippa, and when he married Sancha, another Aragon princess, he gave Philippa to her as one of her ladies of the bed-chamber, and Sancha grew equally fond of her. When the Duke of Calabria, her foster-son, married Catherine of Austria, Philippa was made first lady of the bed chamber to her; and when his second wife, Maria of Valois, went with him to Florence, the Catanese accompanied her in the same office.

The Angevine princes were celebrated for their fidelity in rewarding the attachment of their subjects, in no matter how low a station, by bestowing upon them high posts in their household, which may account for the affection and gratitude of so many of the Neapolitan royal family to Philippa. Her contemporaries, with the credulity of their age, however, attributed it to magic potions, in which the Sicilian women were said to be very clever. Boccaccio made a much shrewder guess at the source of her influence, attributing it to her skill in making cosmetics and confectionery.

She succeeded in winning Joanna's affection also, and is believed to have lavished a mother's care upon her; and when the young Queen came to the throne she was the first lady in her court, and was treated with the greatest respect.

It is impossible that Philippa could have risen to so high a position, from so lowly an origin, unless she had had great talent as well as personal gifts to recommend her, for she was a trusted servant of Robert for forty-five years, and the devout Queen Sancha had such regard for her that it was due to her influence that Joanna was placed under her charge.

Both Robert and Sancha must have had solid reasons for this choice, for we read in Carracciola's Life of Joanna how particular they were in choosing the little Princess's attendants. The King took special care that nothing should be said or done in the child's presence from which she could learn evil, and to that end he confided her to chaste matrons; moreover, he took some nuns out of their convents, with the permission of the Pope, to instruct her in all Christian duties and in the religious ceremonies at which she would have to assist, and to train her in industrious habits. Indeed, so strictly did Robert and Sancha bring their little grandchild up that they would not allow any one to be seen in her company who wore rouge or paint or the hair of any dead person.

It was a custom in the fourteenth century, when gross ignorance was the rule in all ranks of life, to entrust the education of royal princes and princesses to the religious orders, whose members were generally more cultivated, and for this purpose, as in the case of Joanna, nuns were permitted by dispensation from the Pope to leave their enclosure and live in the palace where their services were required. Thus it was quite in accordance with the spirit of the age for Robert to send for two nuns to come to court, and try to form the character of the future Queen on religious principles, and it was particularly acceptable to Sancha.

This unworldly Queen desired to leave the world and join the Poor Clares, the strictest order of the Church, for whom she had built a convent in Naples; and she was only deterred from taking this step by Pope John XXII., who very wisely told her she would be neglecting her duty as a wife if she did so, and thereby rendering herself displeasing to Almighty God, instead of her proposed sacrifice being acceptable to Him. The pious Queen therefore remained in the world until the death of her husband.

As Joanna grew older, still more elaborate rules were laid down by her grandfather with regard to her bringing up. None of those who dressed her were to be of low birth, or unpolished manners; her court was to be presided over by a man of the highest prudence and authority, whom the nobles and their sons who frequented it would obey. He who gave the future Queen water for her hands at table, as was then the custom, must be a knight or greater than a knight, and so must those who bore the dishes to her, and who tasted them to see that they were not poisoned before they were handed to her. The cupbearer must do his duty with the greatest fidelity, lest any harm, designed or inadvertent, should come to the young Princess. The major-domo was to observe at supper that she did not eat anything greedily or ask for it arrogantly, and if he detected her in this he was to advise her secretly, not publicly, as that would be indecorous and exceedingly disagreeable to the King, and he was not to do it a second time if she amended at the first reproof.

The King also ordered that the most illustrious doctors should assist at supper and dinner always, lest any unwholesome food should be offered the child, and to see that she only took as much as was necessary for health. It seems quite clear from all these minute directions that there could have been nothing objectionable in Philippa the Catanese, except her lowly origin, or Robert, who took such elaborate pains to shield his grandchild from moral and physical evil, would never have selected her as the governess and confidante, and we may say foster-mother, of the Princess.

We have dwelt at some length upon these details, because some historians laid all Joanna's faults, real and imaginary, at Philippa's door.

Her education included Latin and French, both of which languages she read and wrote as well as her own; and besides the study of theology and philosophy, she was taught to sew and to cook, and used to exult girlishly over her cousins, the young princesses of Taranto and Durazzo, who were brought up with her and her sister Maria, when she excelled in any of these things.

In the year 1331 Robert caused the oaths of allegiance to be taken to Joanna, with the reversion to Maria in the event of the death of the elder child. This was necessary to secure, in those turbulent times, the peaceable succession to the throne on his death. The following year the Prince of Taranto died without male issue, and he left the principality of Taranto to Joanna; by preferring

## Joanna's Childhood

her to the prince of the house of Durazzo, he made her claim to the throne of Naples and Sicily much more secure. As the heiress of all the rights and estates of her father, she was now styled the Duchess of Calabria and the Countess of Provence.

As soon as Robert had decided to make Joanna his heiress, he took care to let her, child as she was, receive the principal men of the State, that she might hear them speak and learn how to answer them; and she so pleased the King by her manners that he frequently presented the Ambassadors of foreign courts, who came to Naples to see him, to her, and let them know she was his heiress. As she grew older her cultivated mind and her remarkable talents and great charm of manner, as well as her extraordinary beauty, which increased daily, made the death of her father less grievous to the King, who saw his granddaughter promised to make a good queen, and be a worthy successor to his throne.

Unfortunately Robert's anxiety on Joanna's account did not stop here. To make her succession still more secure, as he thought, he arranged a marriage for her when she was only five years old, with Andrew, Prince of Hungary, the third son of Canrobert, King of Hungary. In this matter Robert is said to have acted on the advice of Pope John XXII., who desired thus to unite the opposing claims of the two elder branches of the Angevine family to the crown of Naples.

As we saw in the last chapter, the eldest and Hungarian branch of the Anjou line had never liked the disposition of Charles the Lame, in leaving the throne of the Two Sicilies to his second son, Robert; and the Pope hoped a marriage with Canrobert's third son, Andrew, with the heiress to the Neapolitan throne would prevent Canrobert and his heirs from attempting to wrest the crown from the reigning branch.

Accordingly Robert arranged this unfortunate marriage between Andrew, then a little boy of seven, and Joanna, a child of five. These child-marriages among royal families were not uncommon. A dispensation had to be obtained from the Pope, and sometimes, as in the case of Joanna's contemporaries, Magnus II. of Sweden and Blanche of Dampierre, the marriage was celebrated by proxy. It is true Magnus was eighteen at the time of his marriage, but the little Belgian Princess Blanche was only ten. The great Queen Margaret of Sweden, the Semiramis of the North, as she was called, was only ten when in 1363 she married Haquin and was brought to the Swedish court to be educated. Another of these child-marriages was that of Prince John of Bohemia—he was like Andrew of Hungary, of feeble intellect—who when only nine years old was married in 1330, just three years before Joanna, to Margaret, daughter of Prince Henry, Count and ruler of Tyrol. Margaret, who is known to history as "Mucklemouthed Meg," was a few years older than her husband, and her marriage turned out more disastrous, if less tragic, than that of Andrew and Joanna.

Robert, however, determined that Andrew should come to Naples, and, after the wedding of these two children had been celebrated there with all possible pomp, decided that the young prince should remain at the Neapolitan court, and be educated there and subjected to the influence of its culture, for the Hungarians were at this time a semi-barbarian nation, rude and uneducated. By his attempt to conciliate the Hungarian branch of the Angevins with this alliance, Robert disappointed the elder princes of Taranto and Durazzo, both brave, talented youths, who hoped their uncle would bestow the hand of the heiress of the Two Sicilies upon one of them, or on one of their younger brothers, all of whom were well known to Joanna, and constant frequenters of the Neapolitan court.

It was unfortunate for every one concerned that Robert's choice fell upon Andrew, whom he had not seen, instead of on one of the other attractive cousins of Joanna. The boy was so young, when he arrived in Naples to celebrate his marriage, that the King could not possibly tell what time and education might do for him, or how his character would develop; but he seems to have been almost, if not quite, imbecile. It was, however, too late to retract now, and Robert received the child-bridegroom and his father, Canrobert, the King of Hungary, with every sign of joy.

Canrobert was attended by a number of Hungarian barons, who were as astonished at the magnificence, culture, and refinement of the Neapolitan court as the Neapolitan princes and nobles were at the barbarian appearance and rude, uncultivated manners of the Hungarians.

This marriage, which was destined to turn out so disastrously, was celebrated with the utmost pomp and splendour. The subsidiary courts of Taranto and Durazzo, with their princes, were all present as well as the Hungarians. Ambassadors from all the other states and principalities of Italy were there, and among these the most numerous and the most gorgeously attired were the Florentines, whose staff bore the arms and wore the liveries of the Duke of Calabria, as though he were still their ruler. This was considered the most delicate compliment they could possibly have paid to his memory.

The Neapolitan nobility vied with the princes and members of the royal family in the splendour of their costumes in an age when extravagance in dress was carried to an extent never since surpassed either in costliness of material, brilliancy of colour, or absurdity in fashion. In all these particulars the men equalled, if they did not surpass, the women. Among other ridiculous fashions affected by the younger men were their parti-coloured clothing, one leg being clad in blue velvet and the other in pink knee-breeches and silk stockings, or else one in green and the other in red brocaded damask, or cloth-of-gold, while their shoes had long points turned up at the toe and fastened to the knee with a gold or silver chain. Men of fashion all wore long hair hanging in ringlets over their shoulders. The old men had long beards and long, flowing robes like Orientals.

For a long time after this great function Florentine, Roman, Venetian, Sienese, and other Italian ladies endeavoured to follow at their weddings, on a mitigated scale, the fashions set at Joanna's, which seems to have been the subject of court-gossip all over Europe.

The infant-bride was resplendent in gold and pearls and other jewels; and little did Robert think, as the two children—who, we are told, were delighted with all this fuss and splendour—knelt before him for his blessing, that they were both doomed to be the subjects of violent and tragical deaths.

At the end of October in this same year Canrobert went back to Hungary, leaving behind him a suite of Hungarians, with one Nicholas at their head as the governor of Andrew—who, by the way, was a mere nonentity—and one Friar Robert, in whom was vested all authority over the young prince, as his tutor.

This is another instance of a member of a religious order being chosen as tutor to a prince. Unfortunately Friar Robert, upon whom Italian historians heap every kind of abuse—and even Petrarch can hardly speak of him without animosity—was not only unsuitable for the office, but by his ambition was, to a large extent, responsible for the tragedy that followed. He was a Franciscan friar, and was evidently highly obnoxious to the Neapolitans, but whether he was really such a sink of iniquity as he is described by his contemporaries to have been may be doubted.

He lived in an age when neglect of bodily cleanliness was considered a great mark of holiness, as it certainly is the greatest of all the bodily mortifications practised by the saints, and there is no doubt Friar Robert, from all accounts, gave convincing proofs of one meaning, and that not the highest, attached to the "odour of sanctity" This is attributed to him as hypocrisy, and Petrarch calls him "worse than a serpent," who is said to have concealed under his dirty habit vice and cruelty; he is also accused of having wilfully brought up Andrew in ignorance, in order to gain a pernicious influence over his mind. This may or may not be true. Andrew was apparently so stupid, if not actually imbecile, that Friar Robert may have found it impossible to impart any knowledge to him.

## Joanna's Childhood

He certainly hated the Neapolitans as much as they hated him, and he tried all he could to exalt his pupil at the expense of Joanna, and the Hungarians at the cost of the Neapolitans, but he did not appear in his true character until after the death of King Robert.

About a month after Joanna's marriage the city of Florence was nearly destroyed by a most disastrous flood, which Villani, the historian, and some of the Florentines themselves, looked upon as a judgment from Heaven for their sins. King Robert shared this opinion, and in a long Latin letter, which he as chief of the Guelphs wrote to the citizens on this occasion, he exhorts them to repentance.

The view that it was a chastisement was strengthened by a vision seen on the night of the deluge by a hermit who lived above the monastery of Vallombrosa. He heard a terrific noise as he was praying, and, going to the door of his hermitage, saw a troop of armed horsemen, all black and terrible in aspect, ride furiously past, who, in answer to his question as to where they were going, said they were going, please God, to drown the city of Florence for its wickedness.

Florence was at this time a very licentious city, and the scene of frequent bloodshed caused by encounters between the Guelphs and Ghibellines, the former of whom espoused the part of the Pope, the latter the part of the Emperor; they were also called the Neri and Bianchi, as the followers of the Pope's party and the King of Italy's are to this day in Rome.

During this century all the Italian republics and cities were divided between rival factions. In Rome the constant battles between the adherents of the Colonnas and the Orsini, and the absence of the controlling power of a residential Pope, made the Eternal City a prey to murder, assassination, and rapine, and unsafe to live in, for even the churches were in ruins.

No incident of importance happened in Joanna's life for five or six years after her early marriage. The child made such progress in her studies, and had such excellent abilities, that by the time she was twelve years old Costanzo and other writers say of her " that she already surpassed in understanding not only every child of her age, but many women of mature years." Moreover, by her generous and affectionate disposition and charming manners, she endeared herself to all around her. She was most obedient to Robert, whose heart was torn with remorse when he saw his beautiful grandchild growing daily more accomplished and more fit to fill the high dignity in store for her, while, on the other hand, her semi-idiotic consort learned nothing from his Hungarian teachers except their unpolished manners and the hatred they felt for the

Neapolitans, with which Friar Robert endeavoured to inspire him.

As the children grew up, the contrast became more striking between the beautiful Joanna and the unfortunate and boorish Andrew, who, Petrarch says, was "from all eternity ugly and contemptible."

Joanna, as she entered her girlhood, is said to have been saddened at the terrible prospect of spending her life yoked to so uncongenial a companion, especially when she saw herself surrounded by many handsome, brave, and attractive princes, her constant companions, who paid her homage, worshipped at her shrine, and would gladly have died for her, who was one of the richest heiresses of her time, and endowed with extraordinary beauty as well as with such exceptional talents.

Robert dimly foresaw some of the temptations to which his own want of discretion would expose his grandchild, and when Pope John XXII. died, and was succeeded in 1334 by Benedict XII., he might have obtained a dispensation from the new Pope to annul this infantine marriage, on the ground of Andrew's unfitness; but, instead of doing this, he contented himself with calling a general assembly of the nation, at which he caused the oaths of allegiance to be taken to Joanna alone. This step excluded Andrew, or rather his ambitious and barbarian followers, from any share in the government of the kingdom, and all Robert's Italian subjects joyfully took the oath of exclusive allegiance to the popular Joanna.

Apart from all national jealousy, the Neapolitans hated the Hungarians on account of their drunkenness and other low, coarse vices, and insolent, barbarian manners. The Neapolitans were themselves by no means immaculate—and indeed in the matter of licentiousness there was not much to choose between them and the Hungarians. But the Neapolitans were sober and polished and refined in manner, and of the careless, happy, joyous disposition which still characterises them; while the Hungarians, in spite of their boorish inferiority, were haughty and ambitious, and impudently aimed at gaining the ascendency in the kingdom for themselves.

By this oath the political union between Andrew and Joanna was dissolved, but their marriage contract was still unfortunately religiously and civilly binding, in spite of their youth when it was made.

King Robert, however, was to a great extent absorbed in his books, for he remained a scholar to the end of his days, and during the last year or two of his life was much taken up with Petrarch, whom he succeeded in getting crowned with laurels at Rome, and induced to pay his first visit to the court of Naples, the year before Robert died—to see, as the poet said, " the only King who could judge of anything more important than a ragout or a flight of birds."

## CHAPTER III

## Petrarch's First Visit to Naples

ONE of Joanna's many claims to fame is, she was the friend of Petrarch and Boccaccio, the two greatest geniuses of her time, both of whom have eulogised her in enthusiastic terms in their immortal writings. She was only thirteen when Petrarch paid his first visit to the court of Naples, in 1341, to submit his writings to the learned King Robert for examination before he accepted the crown of laurel, although he was already so famous that this examination was unnecessary.

Francis Petrarch was now thirty-seven, and so strikingly handsome and of so fine a presence that wherever he went he attracted attention, and he was an ornament to any court. He was tall and very manly in appearance, with fine features and eyes full of fire; he had a clear, ruddy complexion and a countenance that betrayed the genius and imaginative power which distinguished his writings. A highly accomplished scholar, he was a philosopher and a theologian as well as a poet of the first water ; but he was more and higher than all this, as the following words of his will show.

"I love truth," he says, "and not sects. I am something of a Peripatetic, a Stoic, or an Academician, and often none of them, but *always a Christian.* To philosophise is to love wisdom : and the true wisdom is Jesus Christ. Let us read the historians, the poets, and the philosophers, but let us have in our hearts the gospel of Jesus Christ, in which alone is perfect wisdom and perfect happiness."

He was the intimate friend of Cardinal James Colonna, who was one of his greatest patrons, and introduced him to his family, the noblest and most prominent in Rome. After leaving the university of Bologna, Petrarch had spent a year in Avignon, and amid all the beauties of the magnificent and brilliant court there had remained heart-whole : in his own words, he was "free and wild as an untamed stag," though of a most passionate nature. But before he left Avignon he was destined to meet his fate.

On Palm Sunday, 1327, he went to Mass in the monastery of St. Clare, and for the first time saw Laura, dressed in a green robe embroidered with violets. Her wondrous beauty, as we learn from the Sonnets of Petrarch, at once captured the poet's heart, and she became the idol of his adoration and the inspiration of his verse. But alas! she

*From a print by Raffaelle Morghen, after a picture by Tofanelli.*
PETRARCH.

was already the wife of another. Possessed of a handsome dowry, her mother had married her when very young to one Hugh de Sades, who held a high position in Avignon, Laura's native city.

She was an honourable woman, a faithful wife, and neither an allegorical myth nor the mistress of Petrarch, as some romancers have said in an age when calumny was rife Equally false was another report, that Urban V. had granted Petrarch, who was in holy orders, a dispensation to marry Laura and that Petrarch had refused it, saying "the conjugal tie would sully his affection." Urban V. did not come to the throne till after the death of Laura.

Laura, on discovering the poet's passion for her, treated him with chaste severity, avoiding him if they met by accident, and when forced to meet him in any public place or social gathering she wore a veil, against the use of which he laments in one of his sonnets. She also terrified him by the austerity of her expression.

When he went to Naples Petrarch was still under the spell of Laura's fascinations, and indeed he desired the honour of the laurel crown more for her sake than his own. The custom of crowning a genius with a laurel crown in Rome had been abandoned for a thousand years, and there was now a question as to whether Petrarch should receive this honour in Rome or in Paris; but he ultimately decided to go to Rome, if Robert, King of Naples, pronounced him worthy of such an honour.

The King entertained the poet by showing him the wonders of his beautiful capital, and especially by taking him to visit the supposed tomb of Virgil at the entrance to the Grotto of Posilipo, which was then darker and narrower even than it is now; but it was held so sacred, Virgil having been supposed to have made it so by incantations, that no robbers dared to infest it.

Then Robert held a public examination of the poet, which lasted for five days, during which the king questioned Petrarch on all kinds of subjects, scientific and philosophic; Petrarch lectured on poetry and history, astonished the King by his wisdom and learning, and almost converted him to become in his old age a lover of poetry, which he had hitherto scorned. At the close of this examination the King in the presence of the Queen, Joanna, and all the princes and princesses of the court, pronounced a sort of panegyric on the genius of the poet, and declared him worthy of the laurel crown.

Robert desired that the ceremony of coronation should take place at Naples, but Petrarch preferred to be crowned in Rome, where, as he explained to the King, Virgil, Horace, and so many other poets had received this honour. Accordingly Petrarch left Naples in the beginning of April for Rome; but before he left, Robert took off the robe he was wearing, and, giving it to him, begged him to wear it at his coronation.

During his stay in Naples Petrarch read his " Africa," an epic poem which he was then writing, to King Robert, who was so pleased with it that he begged it might be dedicated to him. Petrarch promised that it should be, and fulfilled this promise after the King's death. He was crowned in Rome on April 8th, 1341, wearing the King's robe of state, and accompanied by twelve young Roman men clad in scarlet robes and wearing crowns of flowers on their heads. The ceremony was performed in the Capitol by the Senator of Rome.

Among the learned men Petrarch met at the court of Naples were John Barrili and Barbatus Sulmone, whom he compared to Homer and Virgil; another celebrated man was the King's librarian, Paul of Perugia, a friend of our Richard de Bury, Bishop of Durham, said to have been the wisest man in England, and the author of a charming little essay on the "Love of Books." Petrarch had met de Bury at the court of Avignon, and was on friendly terms with him. He is said to have possessed the largest library in Europe. Boccaccio, with whom Petrarch was destined to become very intimate on a later visit to Naples, had not yet written the Decameron, nor won the fame he afterwards enjoyed, and was at this time living in obscurity in that city, and through the favour of Paul of Perugia coming to the palace to visit the King's library. Here he met the beautiful Maria of Sicily, Robert's natural daughter, who became to Boccaccio what Beatrice and Laura were to Dante and Petrarch.

Maria, who was witty and accomplished as well as beautiful, had married a Neapolitan nobleman named d'Aquino, but she was the constant companion of her father, whether he was at Castel Nuovo or at one or other of his summer residences, either in the Bay of Baiæ, or Sorrento, or Amalfi, or some other lovely spot in that land of beauty.

Three days after Petrarch left Naples Boccaccio met Maria for the first time, and under precisely similar circumstances to those under which Petrarch, who probably told him the story, first met Laura, namely, in church—and, oddly enough, in the church of St. Clare in Naples instead of St. Clare's at Avignon—and meeting, he straightway fell in love with her. Through Maria he became acquainted with Joanna, then nearly fourteen, "whose cultivated mind," says Guinezelli, "appreciated all his merit."

It was the fashion at that time for every married woman of rank to have some celebrated military or literary man in her train as her lover, and he was considered as indispensable an appendage as her coronet: if a soldier, he fought for her and wore her favour on his shield; if a poet, he dedicated his poems to her exclusively. How far this devotion went depended upon the character of the woman; in Maria of Sicily's case it is believed to have gone very far, for in those days Boccaccio had the reputation of being somewhat lax in his morals. But we must never forget that calumny was one of the besetting sins of the age, and all stories of intrigues require to be taken with the proverbial pinch of salt.

Giovanni Boccaccio, who was the natural son of a Florentine merchant, was born in 1313, and is believed to have written his first works, "The Rime," "The Filocolo," a very prolix effusion, "The Fiammette," etc., under the direct inspiration of Maria, who also suggested the "Decameron," on which his claim to immortality rests, for in this he appears as the maker of Italian prose.

One more most celebrated figure among King Robert's courtiers we must not omit to mention, for he is accused by some writers of playing the assassin's part in the murder of Andrew of Hungary, that ghastly tragedy which left a stain never yet effaced on the most brilliant court of the fourteenth century.

This was Nicholas Acciajuoli, whom Petrarch called his second Mæcenas. He was the son of one of the very richest merchants of Florence, and originally came to Naples to negotiate a loan between his father and the King. He was very good-looking, highly accomplished, and endowed with such charming manners that the Princess of Taranto made him the tutor and governor of her son, Louis of Taranto, Joanna's second husband, and his younger brother Philip. Acciajuoli was not only a conspicuous figure in Robert's court, but also one of the most important personages in Joanna's reign, for his influence over Louis was supreme, and the friendship which grew up between them most intimate.

In the beginning of January, 1343, Robert felt his strength was fast failing, and, judging death to be near, he made his will, dictating it in the presence of his counsellors. He made Joanna his universal heiress, not only of the kingdom of Naples, but also of the counties of Provence and Piedmont. If Joanna died without issue, her sister Maria was to succeed, and she was bequeathed a marriage dowry of 30,000 ounces of gold, with some lands for which she had to do homage to Joanna. To Andrew, in case he survived Joanna, he left the principality of Salerno, for which he was to do homage to the then reigning King and Queen. According to an agreement he had made with his nephew Canrobert, King of Hungary, he left Maria's hand in marriage to the eldest brother of Andrew, Canrobert's eldest son Louis, who had just ascended the throne of Hungary.

This marriage, if it ever came off, could only increase the difficulty of Joanna's succession, because the elder member of the Neapolitan family was already married to the younger son of the King of Hungary, and his elder son was by this will to be united to the younger sister of Joanna. Robert the Wise did not display his wisdom in the disposition of his two grandchildren. Not content with marrying Joanna to an idiot, he now proposed to marry Maria to a semi-barbarian king, who was destined to become her sister Joanna's deadliest enemy.

Robert would fain have made his Queen, Sancha, Regent of the kingdom during the minority of the young King and Queen, but she refused to accept the charge, being bent on entering a convent at her husband's death. He therefore appointed a council of regency with Sancha at the head of it; the other members were Philip of Cabassole, Bishop of Cavaillon and Chancellor of the Kingdom of Naples, Philip of Sanguineto, Seneschal of Provence, Geoffrey, Count of Squilazzo, High Admiral, and Charles Artus, Grand Chamberlain of the kingdom. Joanna and Andrew, and also Maria, were not to attain their majority till they reached the age of twenty-five, and until that time all their edicts, gifts, and sales were to be considered null and void without the consent of the Council.

Finally Robert recommended the Queen, his

grandchildren, and his dominions to the protection of the Pope and the College of Cardinals. The Pope at this time was Clement VI., who was a good friend to Joanna after Robert's death. He was a great Pope, clement by nature as well as by name, and one of the most profound scholars of his age, to whom Italian historians have not done justice, because of his preference for Avignon, where his court was celebrated for its luxury and magnificence.

As soon as his will was duly sealed and attested, Robert called Joanna and Andrew to his bedside and endeavoured to impress upon them the solemn responsibilities of their position, warning them of the dangers with which they were surrounded on all sides, and apparently frightening them, for we are told they wept so bitterly that he gently reproved them for their grief. Three days before his death, though very weak, he had himself carried to the church of St. Clare, which he had founded, and there was invested with the habit of the Third Order of St. Francis, in which humble garb he died. He was only sixty-four at the time of his death. Petrarch says of him: " He died as he had lived, speaking and acting in the same manner. If Heaven had positively decreed that he should not prevent the misfortunes which were to follow his death, it was the greatest happiness that could have happened to him, and I believe no man ever died at a more fortunate moment for himself."

With a poet's prescience of coming evil, and with a keen sense of his own prophetic powers, which the sequel justified, he wrote to his friend Barbatus Sulmone, on hearing of the death of Robert, as follows:

"What I have so much dreaded has happened, our great King has left us! What an affliction for me, my dear Barbatus! I fear to see his death followed by the calamities I have predicted. My mind is but too good a prophet when it announces sinister events. The youth of the Queen and her husband, the age of the Queen Dowager, her projects, the dispositions and manners of the courtiers, make me fear everything. God grant that I may be deceived in my sad forebodings! But I see two lambs in the midst of wolves, a monarchy without a monarch—for can we thus term a child in tutelage?" The lambs alluded to were Joanna and Maria, the wolves Friar Robert and the Hungarians.

Joanna, who was now in her sixteenth year, was "fair and goodly to look upon," says Boccaccio, who enlarges at great length on her intellectual gifts and her generous and fine disposition. Brantôme, the celebrated French chronicler who accompanied Mary Queen of Scots to Holyrood, says that Joanna's beauty far exceeded that of Petrarch's Laura. "Her portrait, which is still to be seen," he writes, "shows that she was more angelic than human. I saw it at Naples in a number of places where it is treasured with the greatest care. I have seen it also in France, in the cabinet of our kings and queens and of many of our noble ladies. Certainly this was a beautiful princess, whose countenance displayed great sweetness with a beautiful majesty. She is painted in a magnificent robe of crimson velvet, loaded with gold and silver lace and embroidery. On her head she wears a bonnet on a cushion. In brief, this fine portrait of this lady represents her as all beauty, sweetness, and true majesty so well that one becomes enamoured of her mere image."

This portrait was taken when the terrible tragedy of her life had added majesty to the beauty of youth, the *beauté du diable* with which at the time of Robert's death Joanna was sparkling; but we find all her admirers speaking of the sweetness and majesty of her beauty, which was evidently of a very high type, though unfortunately none of the portraits of her which have come down to our time do justice to her.

One of the most beautiful pictures in the world is said to be a painting of Joanna by Leonardo da Vinci copied from an old portrait, now in the Doria Gallery at Rome. From it she would appear to have been of the fair Italian type, for her eyes and hair are brown, her hair pale enough to be called golden: her face is a perfect oval, her forehead high, her chin beautifully rounded, her lips

Portrait of a Lady;
formerly described as Queen Joanna I.

full with a sweet smile playing round them, her nose slightly aquiline with delicately formed nostrils, and her eyes large, soft, and full. Joanna's beauty and intellectual gifts only made her boy husband's deficiencies the more striking, and it is no wonder that one of Robert's dying regrets was having made such a sacrifice of the future Queen's happiness to political expediency.

He saw the two children grow up under his eyes, Joanna taking part in all the amusements of the court, and delighting him with her intelligence, entering into his love of learning, and developing her natural gifts of wit and eloquence, for which she was afterwards so famed; while Andrew remained ignorant and loutish, interesting himself in nothing except eating and drinking, in which he took too much pleasure.

The principal amusements of the Neapolitan Court in the fourteenth century were music and singing, and telling thrilling tales of love and adventure, in which art both men and women excelled. Cards were not introduced until the end of the century, when they were invented in Paris. Chess and backgammon were much played.

The dancing was slow and stately, and the so-called *ballade* was the favourite Italian dance; this was a dance accompanied by a chant, the dance illustrating the subject of the words sung. At great festivals, not only the King and Queen engaged in these solemn dances, but likewise legates, prelates, and even cardinals.

The fashionable drive round the Mole of Naples, in which Joanna and the other young princes and princesses daily took part, to the delight of the people, was also very slow and impressive, though the cavalcade of horses and chariots, princes and princesses, knights, courtiers, and ladies-in-waiting was magnificent.

The troubadours were a conspicuous feature at Robert's court, for the Counts of Provence and Toulouse had always been the chief patrons of these Provençal court-poets, and singers of war and love and adventure; they were one of the typical romantic figures of French and Spanish and Italian courts, from the beginning of the twelfth to the end of the fourteenth century.

Entertainment was also provided by the court-jugglers and tumblers, who came into the banqueting-hall between the courses, at the *entremets*, to perform various feats of jugglery. At public banquets, pageants, mock-battles, and various other scenes were represented during these interludes, for the amusement of the guests, and perhaps also to give them time to get up an appetite for the next course.

These banquets lasted an interminable time, and the tables groaned under the weight of the dishes, which consisted among other things of peacocks, cranes, venison, sturgeon, herons, seal, porpoises, and roast swan, besides various kinds of meat, cut up into small pieces before brought to table, which in England were called gobbets, and were conveyed to the mouth by the fingers as a rule, although spoons were then in use, but forks did not become general until the middle of the sixteenth century.

An amusing incident is recorded of the introduction of forks into Europe. The first of these now indispensable table-appointments is said to have been a golden prong brought by a Byzantine princess to Venice, when she came there as a bride in the eleventh century. St. Peter Damien, then Bishop of Ostia, hearing of what he deemed such extravagant luxury, preached a sermon in which he denounced her for her wicked extravagance in conveying her food to her mouth with a golden prong, instead of using her fingers, which Almighty God had given her for that very purpose! "Autres temps, autres mœurs." The preacher who inveighs to-day against the wicked speed of motor-cars and the presumption of airships will probably strike our descendants as quite as fanatical and uncivilised as St. Peter Damien appears to us of the twentieth century.

In the outdoor sports of hawking, fishing, and hunting, in which men then delighted, Italian ladies took no part, and in tournaments they were only spectators of the achievements of the knights.

# CHAPTER IV

## The Lamb among Wolves

JOANNA and Andrew were proclaimed Queen and King as soon as King Robert's funeral was over. The Neapolitans received Joanna with the greatest joy, and ambassadors from all the Italian courts visited her, to condole with her on her grandfather's death and to congratulate her on her accession, and she received them all with grace and befitting dignity.

For a brief period only the Council of Regency was permitted to govern, and during this time Joanna possessed influence over them, and astonished them by her wisdom and prudence. She and the Dowager Queen Sancha took the first opportunity of promoting their favourite, Philippa the Catanese, and her family to higher dignities than they enjoyed in the reign of the late King.

Philippa was still Joanna's governess; she was now made Countess of Montoni. Her granddaughter

## The Lamb among Wolves

Sancha, the Dowager Queen's godchild, was married to the Count of Murzano; Philippa's son, the Count of Evoli, was made seneschal of the kingdom, a rank inferior only to that of the Sovereign: by virtue of this appointment he became one of the seven great officers of the Crown. Philippa was now at the zenith of her prosperity, little irking of the terrible fate in store for her. But let us not anticipate evils, where an armed band of troubles was close at hand.

That "serpent," as Petrarch calls him, Friar Robert, began immediately to appear in his true character. He prompted his pupil Andrew to declare the crown of Naples was not Joanna's dowry, but his by right, and no sooner was the proclamation of the new King and Queen pronounced than he demanded admission to the Council of Regency for himself and for Nicholas the Hungarian, the governor of Andrew. Unfortunately the Council, after some hesitation, made the fatal mistake of admitting them, thereby compassing the very evil the late King had endeavoured to ward off from the kingdom, to which end all his measures for many years had been directed. Not content with this first successful move, Friar Robert went on to obtain places of trust and influence for the Hungarians, intending ultimately to seize the reins of government for himself.

Pope Clement VI. then interfered, partially cancelling the Regency appointed by King Robert, and nominating a legate to govern in its place ; whereupon the most ambitious among the Neapolitan nobles seized the opportunity to promote their own ends, and refused to obey either the legate or the Regency, playing off one against the other. Meanwhile Friar Robert's hypocrisy imposed upon the people, who, judging his external poverty, as shown in his dirty habit and slovenly appearance, to be a sign of supernatural sanctity, were ready to obey and support him. He won the more mercenary nobles over by promises of promotion, and soon found himself at the head of a party powerful enough to defy the Pope himself.

He treated both Joanna and the Queen Dowager with the greatest insolence, and claimed everything in the right of Andrew alone, making Joanna practically a State prisoner, while the Hungarians pressed themselves everywhere, to the exclusion of the Neapolitan princes and nobles.

The princes of the blood, banished from court by the haughtiness of the Hungarians, retired to their own castles, leaving Joanna to the mercy of these barbarians—the lamb among wolves, as Petrarch so aptly called her. The lamb, however, was not altogether unprotected. Philippa was with her, and, for the first year after King Robert's death, the Dowager Queen remained at Castel Nuovo, where Joanna and Maria resided with her.

The Princess of Taranto also continued to live in Naples with her daughters, whilst her eldest son Robert was absent fighting for her real or supposed rights as the titular Empress of Constantinople. This princess, seeing that Andrew was a mere tool in Friar Robert's hands, and utterly incapable of appreciating either Joanna's beauty or her talents, or of doing anything except eat and drink, began, it is said, to plan a marriage with Joanna and her second son, Louis, trusting, if she succeeded in winning Joanna's affection for Louis, to persuade the Pope to annul her marriage with Andrew.

There seems no doubt that the Princess of Taranto did try to divert the young Queen's affections from her boorish, idiotic husband to her own handsome, learned, brave, and attractive son, and in all probability it is equally true that Philippa the Catanese aided and abetted her in this to the best of her power; but that Nicholas Acciajuoli joined in this vile conspiracy to tempt Joanna to be unfaithful to her first husband, as some historians assert, is believed by Costanzo, whom we are following, to be a libel on so upright and honourable a man. Acciajuoli owed everything to Robert, and common gratitude to the late King would prevent him from joining in a plot to compromise Joanna's honour, in days when the marriage-tie was not so easily broken as now.

Louis, as the sequel will show, was by no means

so blind to his cousin's charms as was her husband Andrew, but there is not a scrap of evidence to show that the young Queen at this time had any but a cousinly affection for Louis; on the contrary, she was so watched and guarded by the Hungarians, that had she shown any preference for Louis, Friar Robert and his creatures would have been only too glad to seize upon any pretext to get rid of her and secure the throne for Andrew alone. Joanna was too fond of her grandfather, to whose commands and wishes, both before and after his death, she showed implicit obedience, and too innocent, to think of such a thing as abandoning her lawful husband for another more attractive one.

In the October following Robert's death Petrarch again visited Naples for two purposes. He was deputed by the Pope to assert his right to administer the government of the kingdom during the minority of the King and Queen, and further charged by his friend and protector, Cardinal Colonna, to obtain the release from perpetual imprisonment of the Pipini brothers, the Counts of Minervino, Lucera, and Potenza. They had been sentenced to life-long imprisonment in the castle of Capua by King Robert, for besieging Count Marra in his castle of that name. The Pipini were friends of the Colonna family, whom they assisted in their quarrels with the Orsini, their hereditary enemies, and the municipal authorities of Rome. Soon after his arrival in Naples, Petrarch wrote to Cardinal Colonna, and in his letter gives such a graphic description of Naples that we cannot do better than quote parts of it, for Petrarch was a very effusive correspondent, and his epistle is too long to be quoted in full.

He says: " Immediately on my arrival in Naples I visited the two Queens, and went to treat with the council on the subject of my coming. But oh infamy of the world, what a monster! May Heaven rid the soil of Italy of such a pest. . . . I mourn for thee, Naples, my beloved! that thou art rendered like to one of these Saracens—no pity, no truth, no faith, a horrible animal, with bald head and bare feet, short in stature, swoln in person, with worn-out rags torn studiously to show his naked skin, who not only despises the supplications of thy citizens, but from the vantage ground of his feigned sanctity treats with scorn the embassy of the Pope. Yet this is not marvellous, because his pride is founded upon the treasures he accumulates, for from what is reported it appears that his caskets full of gold do not accord with the rags he wears. Perhaps you would know his name: he is called Robert, succeeding, in this place, to that Robert lately dead who was as much the honour of our age as this is its eternal infamy."

Having enlarged on this theme, he continues

further on: "He wears nor crown nor brocade nor silk, but with a squalid mantle, filthy and torn, which covers but half his swollen body, and with a crouching gait, bent not by age, but by hypocrisy, he rules with unutterable arrogance and tyranny the courts of both Queens, oppresses the weak, treads justice under foot, confounds all things human and divine, and like a new Palinurus or Tiphys[1] sits at the head of this great vessel, which from what I can discern will quickly go to the bottom, as all the mariners are like himself, except the Bishop of Cavaillon, who as much as he can takes the side of justice, abandoned by all the others."

He goes on to tell the Cardinal to relate these things to the Pope, and to add that the Apostolic embassy would have been received with more reverence by the Saracens than it was in Naples. He also says he has been three or four times to visit the Capuan prisoners, who place all their hope of release in the Cardinal. The old Queen has great pity on them, but can do nothing to help them, as Friar Robert was determined to keep them in prison; Joanna and Andrew might have mercy on them, if Friar Robert and Nicholas, the governor of the King, would permit them.

If Friar Robert had never done anything worse than refuse to release these turbulent Pipini, we should not have much to say against him, for they

---

[1] Palinurus and Tiphys were pilots

were not worthy of the interest Cardinal Colonna took in them; and their subsequent release, which Petrarch persuaded Andrew to grant, only hastened the catastrophe which was impending on this unhappy King.

Petrarch had many opportunities of conversing with Joanna during this visit, and was struck with her talents and learning. She would fain have attached him to her court; but as at that time she was a Queen in name only, without power to do good to any one, as she pathetically said of herself, this was impossible; but she was able to appoint him her domestic chaplain and almoner, an office only bestowed upon people of distinction.

Shortly before coming to Naples for the second time, Petrarch had received further preferment from Pope Clement VI., who made him Archdeacon of Parma, and at the end of 1342 conferred upon him the Priory of St. Nicholas, Pisa.

The deed by which Joanna appointed the poet her domestic chaplain was signed on the day of a most terrific tempest, which occurred while Petrarch was in Naples, and is described by him with his usual eloquence. This storm was caused by a violent sirocco, and was felt on all the shores of the Mediterranean, but spent its worst fury on Naples. It was predicted a few days before by the bishop of one of the neighbouring islands, as a scourge from God; he also prophesied that the city would be destroyed by an earthquake on November 25th, when the storm actually happened.

Happily this second part of the prophesy was not fulfilled, but it spread such terror through the city that the inhabitants prepared for death, leaving their business unattended to, and when the first signs of the storm broke women rushed half-clothed, with their babies in their arms, to the churches, where they prostrated themselves on the floor praying for mercy.

Petrarch, who confesses he was frightened by the general consternation, went to spend the night in the monastery of St. Laurence, where he went to bed shortly before midnight, the monks having retired at their usual hour.

"Scarce had I closed my eyes," he says in a letter he wrote the day after the earthquake, "when I was awakened by the loud rattling of my chamber-windows. I felt the walls of the convent violently shaken from their foundations. The lamp which I always keep lighted through the night was extinguished. The fear of death had fast hold of me.

"The whole city was in commotion, and you heard nothing but lamentations and confused exhortations to make ready for the dreadful event. The monks, who had risen for Matins, terrified by the movements of the earth, ran into my chamber armed with crosses and relics, imploring the mercy of Heaven. A prior whose name was David, and who was considered a saint, was at their head. We proceeded to the church, which was already crowded, and here we remained during the rest of the night, expecting every moment the completion of the prophesy.

"We all threw ourselves on the ground, and implored aloud the mercy of Heaven, expecting from time to time that the church would fall upon us.

"It is impossible to describe the horrors of that infernal night. The elements were let loose. The noise of the thunder, the winds, and the rain, the roarings of the enraged sea, the convulsions of the heaving earth, and the distracted cries of those who felt themselves staggering on the brink of death, were dreadful beyond imagination. Never was there such a night. As soon as we apprehended that day was at hand, the altars were prepared, and the priests vested themselves for Mass. Trembling we lifted up our eyes to Heaven, and then fell prostrate upon the earth.

"The day at length appeared. But what a day! Its horrors were worse than those of the night. No sooner were the higher parts of the city a little more calm, than we were struck with the outcries which we heard from the sea. Anxious to discover what was passing there, and still expecting nothing but death, we became desperate, and instantly mounting our horses we rode down to the shore.

"Heaven! What a sight! Vessels wrecked in the harbour; the strand covered with bodies, which had been dashed against the rocks, and appeared like so many eggs which had been broken in pieces. Nor were the shrieks of the men and women who inhabited the falling houses close to the sea less terrible than the roaring of the sea itself. Where the day before we had gone to and fro on the dusty path was now a sea more dangerous than the Straits of Messina. You could not pass in the streets without the risk of being drowned.

"More than a thousand Neapolitan knights came from all sides to the spot where we were, as if to assist in the funeral obsequies of their country. This splendid troop gave me a little courage. 'If I die,' I said to myself, 'I shall still be in good company.'

"Scarce had I made this reflection when I heard a dreadful clamour everywhere around me. The sea had sapped the foundations of the place where we were standing, and it was at this instant giving way. We fled therefore immediately to more elevated ground. Here we beheld a most tremendous sight. The sea between Naples and Capri was covered with moving mountains; they were neither green as in the ordinary state of the ocean, nor black as in common storms, but white.

"The young Queen rushed out of the palace barefooted, her hair dishevelled, and her dress in the greatest disorder. She was followed by a train of females, whose dress was as loose and disorderly as her own. They went to throw themselves at the feet of the Blessed Virgin, crying aloud, 'Mercy! Mercy!' and visited in turn all the churches of the Mother of God in the city.

"Towards the close of the day the storm abated, the sea was calm and the sky serene. Those who were upon land suffered now only the pains of fear, but it was otherwise with those upon the water. Some galleys from Marseilles and Cyprus were sunk before our eyes, nor could we give them the least assistance. Larger vessels from other nations met with the same fate, in the midst of the harbour. Not a soul was saved except one galley of four hundred criminals, under sentence of death, who had been reserved as a forlorn hope, to be exposed in the first expedition against Sicily. They were a hardy set of men, and struggled with the storm, and when the ship began to sink ran aloft and clung to the rigging. At this moment the tempest was appeased, and these poor convicts were the only ones whose lives were saved in the port of Naples. Lucan says, 'Fortune preserves the guilty.'"[1]

[1] "Life of Petrarch," by Mrs. Dodson (London, 1805).

This graphic description of the terrible scene, we may take it, does not in any way underestimate the horrors of this historical storm and earthquake, for Petrarch's style was picturesque; and at any rate both he and Joanna recovered sufficiently from their terror to sign the document making him her chaplain the same day, for it bears the date of November 25th, 1343. Petrarch concludes his letter by vowing that nothing shall ever make him risk his life on the sea after witnessing the destruction of that storm. "I will leave the air to the birds, and the sea to the fish, for I am a land animal, and to the land will I confine myself. I know very well the divines insist there is as much danger by land as by sea. It may be so. But I beseech you to permit me there to give up my life where I first received it. I like that saying of one of the ancients, 'He who is shipwrecked a second time cannot lay the fault upon Neptune.'"[1]

The state of Rome at this time was in the utmost disorder, for the quarrels of the barons and the insurrections of the populace made the Eternal City a constant scene of bloodshed. Naples, according to Petrarch, was not much better; for in another letter which he wrote on this visit he says the streets at night "are filled by young men of rank who are armed and attack all who pass, without distinction—they must fight or die. This evil is

"Life of Petrarch," by Mrs. Dodson (London, 1805).

without remedy; neither the authority of parents, the severity of the magistrates, nor the power of kings has been able to suppress it. But it is not surprising that such actions are committed by night, when they kill each other for diversion in open day."

Here Petrarch is alluding to combats resembling those of gladiators, which were at this time the favourite amusement of both sexes and all ranks in Naples. They took place in a part called the Carbonaria, amid the most brilliant and magnificent assemblage of nobility in Europe. Petrarch was induced to go to one of these entertainments, at which the young King and Queen were present; but he left in disgust after seeing a young nobleman expire at his feet, whereupon he put spurs to his horse and fled.

He used all his eloquence to try to disgust the Neapolitan nobles with these barbarous tournaments, but in vain; they would not be persuaded to give them up.

It was during this visit of Petrarch to Naples that Joanna, for her own amusement and that of her courtiers, established her "Court of Love," or "Parliament of Love," as these courts were called. They settled difficult questions on subjects connected with love and marriage, composed by their arbitration the quarrels of lovers, and awarded prizes to poets and other writers.

Joanna was chosen as President of the Court of

Love, which was organised this year for her birthday-feast, and a story is told in connection with it which throws a light on the relations of Andrew and Joanna. It seems that when Joanna took her seat under the canopy erected for her, there was another empty seat a little below hers, and Andrew tried to take it, but the young Queen waved him away from it, saying:

"Fair sir! I reign here alone; you cannot share my authority."

Andrew retired in a fury, and Petrarch unrebuked took the seat.

During the banquet it was the custom for presents to be brought in, and Joanna gave them to whom she pleased. These gifts were of various kinds—armour, hounds, falcons, jewellery, etc. On this occasion Joanna gave Louis of Taranto a steel mask for his face, and sent a falcon to Andrew, who angrily refused it.

"Take the bird to your mistress, and let her give it to whom she likes. I accept no constrained courtesy," he said.

Joanna, who saw Andrew's action if she did not actually hear his rude words—which in justice to him must be allowed to have had some provocation—was as angry as Andrew had been when she waved him away from the seat by her side, but said nothing.

Presently seeing her displeasure, Nicholas the Hungarian, Andrew's tutor, made some excuse for the young King, but Joanna angrily and haughtily told him that it was his evil counsels which had prompted Andrew's insult.

This glimpse at this Court of Love gives a better idea of the relations which existed between Joanna and her boorish husband than could be conveyed by pages which might be written upon the subject. The little scene is so natural: first Joanna smilingly waving the young King, who was seldom sober, away from the seat of honour to which he aspired; his subsequent sulky refusal of her gift given according to custom, and her girlish anger and pique at his rudeness; finally her royal rebuke of the Hungarian tutor, who was the cause of much of the friction between the young King and Queen.

Petrarch remained in Naples until the end of December, and before he left, Andrew went himself to the Castle of Capua, and by his own authority set free the Pipini brothers. This is the only act of vigour he ever performed, but he was probably prompted to it by Friar Robert, who wanted to attach these dangerous men to his party. Andrew acted apparently in this instance from compassion, and then took a great fancy to the three liberated prisoners, whom he could not bear out of his sight, and made great friends of them. The Pipini soon began to presume on his favour, and grew more violent and overbearing than before their imprisonment, and only increased the hatred which the

Neapolitans were beginning to feel for Andrew personally, dreading as they did the encroachments of the Hungarians; moreover, they now feared that the weakness of his mind would make him the tool of any one to whom he took a fancy.

While on the one hand the Neapolitans were dreading the ascendency of the Hungarians and their party, Friar Robert, who knew that his rule could only last during the extreme youth of Joanna, now eighteen, began to fear her great popularity with the people and the best of the nobility, the favour which she enjoyed of the Pope, and her superior abilities. To counteract all this, the wily friar wrote to Louis of Hungary, Andrew's eldest brother, begging him to come to Naples and marry the Queen's sister Maria, according to the testament of Robert, and to seize on the kingdom itself in his own right, as the heir of his grandfather, Charles Martel. Louis of Hungary was only too ready to fall in with these plans, but they were met by a counter-plot of the house of Durazzo, as we shall see directly.

The Dowager Queen Sancha remained only a year in the world after her husband's death, and about the first anniversary of it entered the convent of Poor Clares in Naples, which she had herself founded some years before. Sancha had always, as we have said before, hankered after the religious life, and now seized the first opportunity of retiring from a world she despised, to join the strictest Order in the Catholic Church and exchange the luxury of the most refined court in Europe for the coarse habit, and inclined board as a bed, of the Poor Clares. It turned out fortunate for her that she did so, before the impending tragedy which involved the ruin of so many.

Petrarch's epitaph on King Robert may fitly close this chapter. " Here lies the body of King Robert. His soul is in heaven. He was the glory of kings, the honour of his age, the chief of warriors, and the best of men. Skilful in the art of war, he loved peace. . . . His genius equalled his valour, he unravelled the holy mysteries, he read the events of Heaven. The Muses and the Arts mourn their protector. All the virtues lie buried in his tomb. No one can praise him as he deserves, but Fame shall make him immortal."

# CHAPTER V

## Plots and Counter-plots

THE Durazzos, it will be remembered, were the youngest branch of the Angevine family. King Robert's youngest brother, the Duke of Durazzo, had married Maria of Périgord, the sister of Cardinal Talleyrand—a name that became celebrated through the distinguished diplomatist who lived four hundred years later.

The Duchess of Durazzo was a widow at the time of King Robert's death. She was living in Naples with her three sons, Charles, Louis, and Robert, and her daughters, all of whom were well known members of the Neapolitan Court. Charles was a handsome man and a brave soldier, but unscrupulous and ambitious, and report said was very fond of his cousin Joanna, and certainly quite alive to the advantages of a marriage with her sister, Maria of Sicily, whom King Robert had assigned by his will to Louis of Hungary.

As soon as Maria was of marriageable age, the

Duchess of Durazzo set to work to win her affections for her son Charles, just as the widowed Princess of Taranto was endeavouring to estrange Joanna's affections from her husband Andrew in favour of her son Louis, but with this difference—that Maria was only betrothed to Louis of Hungary, while Joanna was actually the wife of Andrew.

The Duchess persuaded her brother, Cardinal Talleyrand, to induce Pope Clement VI. to grant Maria a dispensation to enable her to marry the Duke of Durazzo, who was her first cousin, once removed. Clement, who was always only too ready to oblige his friends, consented without in this case considering what the consequences would be of this marriage of the heir-apparent to the Neapolitan throne. Had he given it more thought, he would have seen that it not only threatened Joanna's interests, but might also prove dangerous to her crown.

Maria was living at Castel Nuovo with the Queen Regnant, and the Dowager Queen Sancha, who had not yet entered the monastery of Poor Clares; and the Duchess visited her constantly, and, having succeeded in setting Maria against the Hungarians, was soon able to persuade her to give up Louis of Hungary, whom she had not seen, for the Duke of Durazzo, whom she knew well. She then made all the necessary arrangements for the marriage · she seems to have had a genius for intrigue, and to have planned everything very cleverly, for she managed to get Maria out of the palace and married to Charles before the child (for she was only fifteen) was missed.

When it was discovered one fine day that the heir-apparent to the throne had been abducted and married to the Duke of Durazzo, thereby setting her grandfather's will at defiance, there was great consternation in the palace. The two Queens, Joanna and Sancha, were furiously angry, for Joanna, though so young, was old enough and wise enough to see what dangerous consequences might result to herself from it; for Louis of Hungary was not likely to submit quietly to being thus cheated of his bride, and would probably revenge himself by invading Joanna's kingdom. Moreover, the fact that the Duke of Durazzo's grandmother was a princess of Hungary increased the danger to Joanna's throne, as the Hungarians were only too ready to dispute her right to it; and from their point of view, this gave the Duke some claim to it himself, and was what he was aiming at secretly.

It was immediately after this elopement that the Queen Sancha retired to her convent, leaving Joanna under the care of Philippa the Catanese. She took the habit, and died before she had been more than a year in the monastery, being probably too old to stand the austerity of the rule : she was thus happily spared the knowledge of the terrible tragedy which was impending and its consequences.

Angry as Joanna was with Maria and Durazzo, she soon forgave them both, and was reconciled to them, perhaps feeling the need of her sister's society and sympathy in the midst of her own difficulties and troubles, surrounded as she was by Friar Robert's boorish and ambitious Hungarians.

Meanwhile the Princess of Taranto and Philippa seem to have been pursuing their infamous design of trying to undermine Joanna's loyalty to her young husband, trusting that as the Pope had been so accommodating in Maria's case as to give her the necessary dispensation to marry Durazzo, he would be equally obliging in Joanna's, and pronounce her marriage null and void. Whether Joanna was aware of these designs we cannot tell at this distance of time and among so many conflicting reports. She must have known of the daily increasing unpopularity of the Hungarians, and probably shared in the desire to get rid of the odious Friar Robert, but there is no evidence to show that she wished to be separated from Andrew.

In the course of 1344 Clement VI. appointed Cardinal Americus as his legate, to govern the kingdom during Joanna's minority; and on August 28th the beautiful young Queen received the investiture of the crown from his hands, and took the oaths according to the customary ceremonies, and on the same conditions as her predecessors, Andrew being only a spectator. It was the Cardinal's influence which achieved this stroke of policy, and he afterwards did his best to control the authority of Friar Robert, but he did not succeed very well, for he was a stranger in Naples, and therefore ignorant of the most important affairs of State, and all those who were opposed to his appointment withheld the necessary information from him.

Friar Robert was, as we have seen, popular among the lower orders, who believed in his reputed sanctity. Joanna, seeing everything going to ruin, now wrote to the Pope and begged him to allow her to govern for herself, without the interference of either legates or guardians. Clement, on account of her youth—for she was not yet seventeen—refused this request; and she then wrote another letter to him, begging him to recall Cardinal Americus, and appoint in his place Philip de Cabassole, the Bishop of Cavaillon, whom King Robert had in his will placed at the head of the Council of Regency with Queen Sancha, and with his last breath had committed the care of his kingdom and the charge of his grandchildren to him.

This good bishop, who was afterwards made a Cardinal and Patriarch of Jerusalem, was also a friend of Petrarch, who says of him "that he was a great man with a little bishopric," Cavaillon being only a small town near Avignon and also near Vaucluse, where Petrarch frequently retired when he wished to live in seclusion. Philip was of noble birth, and had been made a canon at the age of twelve, according to a mediæval custom of conferring these nominal preferments upon boys and youths, long before they were old enough to be ordained. The Cabassoles had always been attached to the Angevine family, who, with their usual generosity to their dependents and friends, had loaded them with benefits. The Bishop had remained at Naples after Robert's death, and had showed his anxiety to do all he could for the late King's family.

Clement VI. knew this, and, recognising the reasonableness and wisdom of Joanna's request, gave his consent immediately, and the result was some mitigation of the miseries of the people and of the indignities to which the royal family had been subjected by the Hungarians.

The tyranny and rapaciousness of these barbarians, whose object was to wrest the kingdom from Joanna in favour of the Hungarian family, had so roused the great barons and the princes of Taranto and Durazzo that they now determined not to consent to the coronation of Andrew on any terms. Louis of Hungary had already tried to obtain a Bull from Avignon for his coronation in right of his grandfather, Charles Martel, but the Neapolitans had refused to take the oaths of allegiance to him, except as the consort of Joanna, and now they refused to acknowledge him as king, dreading, as they had good cause to dread, the increase of any Hungarian influence.

The Duke of Durazzo, as the husband of Maria of Sicily, was peculiarly interested in this question, and no sooner was he married to Maria than he began to intrigue not only against Andrew, but against Joanna also. Through his uncle, Cardinal Talleyrand, he secretly represented to the Pope at Avignon the danger which would ensue for Naples if Andrew were crowned, in which case the Neapolitans feared their kingdom would become merely a province of Hungary. Clement considered their representations, and delayed to grant the Bull for the coronation for two years after Robert's death; then the court of Hungary is said to have sent the Pope's council a bribe of 100,000 florins, after which Clement issued a Bull for the coronation of Andrew and Joanna, but of Andrew only as the Queen's consort, without giving him any personal claim to the crown. The date for the coronation was fixed for September 20th, 1345.

Before coming to the events that occurred on the eve of this long-delayed coronation, it will be as well to take a glimpse at the condition of Europe at this time, and then briefly to recapitulate the conflicting interests in the Neapolitan court, so as to bring before our readers the principal *dramatis personæ* in what came perilously like an Adelphi drama.

Pierre Roger, who took the title of Clement VI. when he ascended the Papal throne in the year King Robert died, 1342, was, as his name implies, a Frenchman, and the fourth of the Avignon Popes. He loved magnificence and pomp, and the notoriously luxurious court of Avignon was never more luxurious than under his rule. He was fond of the society of ladies, and allowed them to frequent his court; he became a great friend of Joanna's, as will appear. He had many great qualities. He was frank, noble, and generous to a fault, and dispensed his favours with both liberality and grace. His failing, of which his detractors have made the most, was a love of luxury. On the other hand, his benevolence was equally great, and at the time of the plague, when in 1348 it visited Avignon, he not only gave most lavishly to the hospitals and sufferers, but enacted very wise laws for its suppression. Naturally highly gifted, he spent much of his time in study, and had such an excellent memory that Petrarch says he never forgot anything that he read: indeed if he had wished to do so he could not.

He admired Petrarch, and offered him the post of apostolic secretary; but nothing could induce the poet to accept it—probably because he disapproved of the luxury of the Avignon court and the licentiousness of the city, for it was never in a worse state than during the reign of this gentle and refined pontiff.

The struggle between the Empire and the Papacy was still going on when he came to the throne, though Louis the Bavarian, who for the last thirty years had troubled the peace of the Popes, had now pretended to submit. In 1344, however, he had the impudence to convoke a diet at Frankfort, which he induced to protest against, what they described as, the ambition and violence of the Pope.

Clement VI. thus provoked determined on the deposition of Louis in favour of Charles of Luxembourg, who was elected in 1346, and ascended the throne the following year under the title of Charles IV., when Louis died. Thus ended the long contests between the Papacy and the Empire.

Clement published two Bulls for the protection of the Jews from the persecutions to which they had been subjected under his predecessors, and he extended the Jubilee, which then only occurred every hundred years, to every fifty years. This was a very popular action with the Romans, for the year of the Jubilee brings an enormous number of pilgrims and other visitors to Rome, and the citizens made a good harvest out of it and also in the sale of pious articles, rosaries, medals, and other objects of devotion.

The year after Clement came to the throne, Cola de Rienzi, the great Roman patriot, came to Avignon at the head of a deputation of the Romans to urge the Pope to return to Rome; but they were unsuccessful, as Clement refused to leave Avignon for Rome, the scene of constant struggles between the rival barons and the people. On Rienzi's return to Rome he incited the citizens to rise against the nobles, his hatred of them having been excited by the assassination of his younger brother some years previously.

Rienzi's romantic career is so well known that we need only refer to it here, remembering that he was afterwards sent back to Avignon as prisoner and confined by Clement VI., and released by his successor Innocent VI., who sent him back to Rome to crush the nobles again. His tragic fate was due to his haughtiness, which disgusted the people who had formerly idolised him.

War between England and France was still going on when Clement came to the throne. Benedict XII., who for the time being had settled the quarrel between the Papacy and Louis of Bavaria, had also succeeded in getting a truce proclaimed between Edward III. of England and Philip VI. of Valois, but it only lasted for a year. Edward was disputing the throne of France with Philip on the ground that being a nephew of the deceased King Charles IV., through his mother Isabella, Charles's sister, he was therefore a degree nearer to the throne than Philip, who was only cousin-german to Charles. The Salic law, however, which excluded women from the succession, prevailed in France, so there was no real ground for Edward's pretensions. Friction between the two monarchs had further arisen, first by Edward having received Robert of Artois, who had been banished from France, and then Philip had returned the compliment by receiving David Bruce, who had been dethroned from Scotland by Edward Balliol, whom Edward III. supported.

Louis of Bavaria sided with the English, and had also declared war against Philip, while Edward was now expected to invade France. His first attempt at invasion through Flanders had failed; but all Europe was disturbed and suffering from this war between its two mightiest monarchs, and Clement did his best to make peace, but only succeeded so far as to get another truce proclaimed, but it was not long observed.

The robber bands of mercenaries which followed in the wake of both armies were a terror to all Italy, as well as to France, where they penetrated as far as Avignon, so that even a French Pope was annoyed by the depredations of the French King's forces.

If the state of France and Italy was such as to give great anxiety to the Holy Father, when he turned his eyes to Spain things were not much better there. A struggle was going on there which all Europe was watching with interest, between the Moors who had overrun the country and the Christians. Besides this religious strife, civil war was disturbing the Peninsula, between the nobles and priests on the one hand, and on the other the

## Plots and Counter-plots

members and representatives of a confederacy of towns which had joined together for mutual defence and had developed into a sort of Cortes.

It was really a struggle between the aristocracy and the democracy, and in 1350, when Pedro the Cruel came to the throne, the struggle was further complicated by England taking the side of Pedro and the people, and France that of the nobles under Henry of Trastevera, an illegitimate son of the late King Alphonso XI., and half-brother of Pedro.

In Italy, Florence was at the head of all the other cities in art and civilisation, but it was the scene of constant combats between the Guelphs and the Ghibellines. Naples, as we have said before, possessed the most refined and cultivated court in Europe. Rome was a prey to broils and insurrections, to robbers and assassins, which while they rendered expedient in some ways the exile of the Pope, were at the same time increased by his absence.

Venice was governed by a council of ten, with the Doge at their head, possessing terrible powers over the rest of the State ; and here and in Siena and all the Italian cities, which were all independent States, a constant struggle was going on, not only between rival nobles, but also between nobles and people, while the entire peninsula was to a large extent at the mercy of all those marauding bands of mercenaries which infested it, such as the White Company.

A celebrated contemporary of Joanna at Naples

was Marino Faliero, a distinguished military hero, who, after being at war for years with the Hungarians, finally defeated them in 1346, and some years later was made Doge of Venice. He had a beautiful young wife, whose romantic story and the subsequent tragic ending of the Doge's life have been the subject of Byron's drama "Marino Faliero," and of Swinburne's tragedy.

In Scandinavia, where the people were slowly emerging from the dark night of paganism into the glorious light of Christianity, there had arisen a celebrated prophetess and politician, a Swedish princess, afterwards a canonised saint of the Church— St. Bridget of Sweden, wife of Ulf, Prince of Nericia, who left her a widow in 1345. She afterwards became a friend of Joanna, whose court she visited several times, once under very romantic circumstances, as we shall presently see. St. Bridget played a great part in trying to induce Clement VI. to leave Avignon and return to Rome, but she did not succeed: it was left to the daughter of the dyer at Siena, St. Catherine, to accomplish finally the work of bringing back the Popes to the Eternal City.

But to return to Naples, where the beautiful young Queen and her boorish husband were surrounded by conflicting influences. On the one hand were Friar Robert in his dirty, ragged habit, and his insolent and semi-barbarian Hungarians, hated by all the Neapolitans, with an old nurse of Andrew's in the background; on the other side were Philippa the Catanese, still a very handsome woman, and her granddaughter Sancha, Charles, Duke of Durazzo, and his child-wife Maria, the Queen's sister, his mother, the Dowager Duchess of Taranto, the widowed Empress of Constantinople, Catherine of Valois, widow of Philip, Prince of Taranto, and her three sons, the Bishop of Cavaillon, the Queen's aunt, the Princess Maria of Sicily and her satellite and lover, Boccaccio, a frequent visitor at this brilliant court, and Nicholas Acciajuoli, the handsome Florentine, afterwards promoted by the Queen to be Grand Seneschal of the kingdom, for whom the Empress of Constantinople is said to have had more than a Platonic friendship. Indeed, it was her indifferent reputation and her intimacy with Nicholas which led to his being accused of being the actual murderer of Andrew.

Two other conspicuous personages at the Neapolitan court at this time were Charles Artus, Grand Chancellor of Naples, and a member of the Council of Regency, appointed by the late King Robert and his son, both of whom were also great friends of the Empress of Constantinople.

# CHAPTER VI

## The Murder of Andrew

IT was the custom of the Angevine Kings and Queens of Naples to leave the city during the summer, when the heat became intolerable, and take up their abode in one of their delightful summer residences, or more often in one of the monasteries which they had founded, in the neighbourhood of Naples, where the beautiful gardens and spacious apartments formed a pleasant retreat from the cares of State and the noise and sultriness of the city.

In 1345 Joanna had special reasons for desiring to get away from Naples, for she was expecting to become a mother at the end of the year; and in the month of August she and Andrew removed to the castle of Aversa, to enjoy the cool retreat of the gardens in the Celestine monastery close by, and to escape the preparations for their coronation in Naples next month. Aversa is situated about twelve miles north of Naples, in the enchanting scenery of the district known as "the happy Campania." In this fatal year, 1345, Aversa consisted of little more than its grand old castle, which belonged to the Crown, and a fine old Celestine monastery with lovely grounds, the town not having recovered from its demolition by Charles of Anjou, who destroyed it to punish the inhabitants for having sided with some barons who were averse to his policy. Hence its name, Aversa.

The castle was surrounded then by olive-woods, and orange-gardens, and dark forests of cedars and other trees; and in this delightful retreat, relieved from the presence of the odious Friar Robert, who remained behind to govern the kingdom, the young Queen enjoyed her *villeggiatura,* looking forward openly to her approaching coronation, and secretly dreaming of the fulfilment of her hopes of maternity at the close of the year.

But while Joanna, in her youthful innocence, dreamt of the splendour and pomp of her coronation, in which she took a girlish and natural pride and delight, and meditated upon the still more sacred and purer joys of motherhood, which the poorest of her subjects were also privileged to enjoy, these coming events were casting a shadow over the pages of history which time will never efface.

These two circumstances, the coronation and the birth of an heir to the throne, were the immediate causes of the murder of the young king; for the Neapolitans feared that when once Andrew was crowned, Friar Robert, who ruled him, would rule them, and tyrannise more than ever over the kingdom; and in the next place, they anticipated that the birth of an heir to the throne would endear Andrew to the Queen, and give him fresh claims upon the affection and loyalty of the people.

So while the young sovereigns were enjoying the combined pleasures of court and country life, of music and dancing, of the tales of the poet and the songs of the troubadour, of the outdoor sports of falconry and tournaments, a vile plot was being hatched among the courtiers for the assassination of Andrew.

Although Friar Robert was left in Naples, some of the Hungarian suite had accompanied Andrew to Aversa, and it is particularly noted that his old nurse, Isolda, who was passionately attached to him, was staying in the castle. At this distance of time it is impossible to fix the guilt of this odious murder of the young King upon anyone; but it is possible, judging from the known character of some who were accused of it, and in the knowledge of subsequent events, to acquit at least two of them of complicity in it.

We may dismiss at once as altogether improbable, if not impossible, the theory that Joanna had any part in it, and equally unlikely is it that a man of so fine a nature as Nicholas Acciajuoli was the actual murderer, as is stated by de Sade in his Life of Petrarch; and many other writers have copied him, without questioning what a little more knowledge of the man would have shown was at least highly improbable.

Acciajuoli's intimacy with the Empress of Constantinople seems to have been the cause of his being accused, for the probability seems to be in favour of the opinion that this princess, whose moral character would not bear investigation, was one of the principal conspirators against Andrew, her well-known desire being to see her son Louis in his place.

Philippa the Catanese is believed by some writers to have known of and sympathised with the plot, her motive being to deliver Joanna, whom she idolised, from her boorish husband, who appears to have been totally blind to her charms. But first and foremost of all the conspirators was undoubtedly the ambitious and unscrupulous Charles, Duke of Durazzo, who is frequently accused of being one of the actual assassins.

For six weeks the young Queen and her husband led a happy and gay life at Aversa, whose propinquity to Naples permitted the daily coming and going of all those courtiers who were not living at the Castle.

September 20th had been fixed as the date of the

coronation of Joanna as Queen and of Andrew as King-consort, and on the eve of that day a great banquet was given at the Castle to celebrate the great occasion fitly.

The sovereigns appear to have retired early to rest in view of the fatigue of the coronation on the following day; the Hungarian courtiers and attendants had as usual taken more than was good for them, and were sunk in too deep a sleep to hear the subsequent disturbance, but the conspirators were wide awake, bent on executing their fell purpose.

In the adjoining monastery the black-robed monks who had risen at midnight for matins, had gone to bed again, and all there was quiet when in the dead of the night, between one and two o'clock, one of the Queen's ladies of the bedchamber, Mabrice, sister of Andrew's chamberlain, Jacobo de Pace, entered the royal bed-chamber in haste, and told the King that a courier from Friar Robert had just arrived with dispatches of great importance, and desired to see him upon State business.

The poor, unsuspecting young King rose at once, and dressing hurriedly left the sleeping Queen, to proceed to another apartment at the end of a long gallery where, instead of the supposed courier being in attendance, the conspirators were assembled. These are believed to have been Charles Artus and his son, Jacobo de Pace, Michael de Mirazzano, Andrew's chamberlain, Philippa's son the Count of

Evoli, and her son-in-law the Count de Trelice, and Raymond of Catania, the Grand Seneschal.

Directly the King left the bed-chamber, some of the conspirators locked the door, either to prevent the Queen from coming out and raising an alarm, or to hinder Andrew from returning. When the unfortunate young man, who was not yet twenty, had reached the middle of the corridor, he was surrounded and seized by some of the conspirators. To muffle his cries one thrust an iron gauntlet into his mouth, another threw a rope round his neck to strangle him, others knelt upon his chest; and then they dragged him to the balcony and hanged him over it, while their accomplices in the garden below seized his feet and strangled him by pulling them. Not content with thus brutally murdering him, according to some accounts, they actually disembowelled him, and were about to bury his remains in a ditch in the garden, intending to say that he had left Italy for Hungary, when they were interrupted.

It appears that his faithful nurse, Isolda, slept in a room under the balcony, and was awakened by the sound of his falling body when they cut the cords which held it suspended. Whether she guessed who the victim was, or whether she saw it was the King, we do not know, but she managed to run to the monastery close by and awaken the monks, who hastened to the garden, where their arrival dispersed the murderers, who were now about to bury the body.

The tears and lamentations of Isolda were probably the most sincere that honoured the mangled corpse of the unfortunate victim of this foul murder, for, in spite of his unattractiveness, as to which all writers are agreed, his old nurse loved him passionately—perhaps because of those very weaknesses—and her faithful heart was torn with grief and horror at the marks of violence on his corpse as she prepared it for burial.

The monks carried the remains into the church of the convent, and watched it and prayed for the repose of his soul, until three days later he was taken to Naples to be buried.

There are many versions of the account of this murder, no two of which agree in detail with each other; but the above is taken from Costanzo, the most reliable of the biographers of Joanna. Some later Italian writers have given their imaginations play and concocted scenes which probably never occurred. For instance one, Rastrelli, says that the Hungarian Isolda, on entering the Queen's apartments in the morning according to her usual custom, found Joanna sitting up by the bedside, and when she asked where the King was the Queen, laughing, replied that she did not know. The nurse then went out, and, following a miraculous light, found Andrew's body lying on the ground below the balcony. Thinking that he was asleep, she returned to Joanna and said, " Your Majesty, the King sleeps in the garden"; to which the Queen answered, "Let him sleep there." Isolda, still unsatisfied, went down again to the garden, where her appearance put the murderers to flight and she discovered the truth.

Those who, like Muratori, suspected Joanna of complicity in this atrocious crime represent the Hungarian nurse as rushing into the Queen's room, after she had discovered the murder, and informing Joanna of it, and state that when others, drawn by her cries to the room, confirmed the report, " the Queen was so conscience-stricken, and so great was her confusion, that she could not even rise from the spot, but lay there until the morning was far advanced, and knew not how to raise her tearless eyes, or to look up at any one."

Thus does the malignant spirit of calumny interpret the poor young Queen's most natural behaviour upon hearing of such a terrible catastrophe as that which had just happened. Her tearlessness was no proof of guilt.; on the contrary, it is often a sign of the deepest feeling—of grief too deep for words, too bitter for tears. She was evidently paralysed with horror; tears would have been a blessed boon, but they were denied her, and the child was yet unborn who might have brought them "like a summer tempest." Nor could they praise the unfortunate victim, either "soft and low" or hard and high, for there seems to have been little to praise and much to blame in the late King. If Joanna's calumniators had nothing more incriminating to go upon than her behaviour on the morning following the murder, there would not be the slightest foundation for their accusations; on the contrary, her conduct was exactly what might have been expected from any young wife on such an occasion.

She says of herself, in a most touching letter which she wrote to Andrew's brother the King of Hungary: "Stunned by grief I had well-nigh died of the same wounds"; and there is not the slightest reason for doubting that this was the very truth.

Another historian says of her: "The Queen, who was only eighteen years old, trembled so that she did not know what to do with herself."

Later in the morning Joanna rose, and in a terrible state of agitation and fear left Aversa, and returned to Naples; and calling all her best friends around her, asked their advice in the horrible calamity which had befallen the royal house.

The first thing to be done was to send letters to inform the Pope and the King of Hungary, and messengers were at once dispatched with the ghastly news to Rome and Hungary. In the above-mentioned letter from the young widowed Queen to Louis of Hungary, Joanna implored the King's protection for herself and her unborn child. How Louis responded to this appeal will presently appear.

Another ridiculous charge brought against Joanna is that she left the body of Andrew unburied for three days, and that then it was brought to Naples and buried by the canons of the cathedral at their own expense. The facts were that the body was left in the charge of the Celestine monks in their church at Aversa until the necessary arrangements could be made in Naples for the funeral; and these for a king could not be completed sooner, for the funeral rites and ceremonies due to Andrew's rank were elaborate, and if he had been hurriedly buried the scandalmongers would have seen in this precipitation fresh proof of guilt and a desire of concealment.

At the end of the three days the body was brought to Naples, and laid in the chapel of St. Louis in the cathedral with many tears and lamentations. It is said that the Neapolitans showed the greatest horror of the crime, and Andrew's undeserved sufferings moved the hardest hearts to sympathy; this circumstance is recorded unanimously by all historians. Indeed, the murder of Andrew sent a thrill of horror all over Europe; there was not a court that was not horrified and scandalised by it.

The reproach brought against Joanna that she allowed the canons of the cathedral to pay for the funeral is absurd: it was their duty to perform the ceremony, for the Neapolitan sovereigns were always buried in the cathedral, and it was probably the custom for these canons to bear some of the expenses, just as the canons of St. Peter's at Rome had to pay for the greater part of the Popes' funeral expenses.

The faults of Andrew have probably been exaggerated by his contemporaries, for it was the policy of Joanna's friends and enemies alike to paint him as black as possible: her friends did so to excuse her if she were guilty of connivance in his assassination, her enemies to find a motive for the personal repulsion they supposed her to feel to such an extent as to make her an accomplice in his murder.

He is described as a ferocious boor, a glutton, a drunkard, and a semi-idiot, with low propensities and gross habits. On the other hand, Petrarch, who knew him personally, writing when the shock of his murder was fresh in his mind, to his friend Barbatus of Sulmone, calls him "the most gentle and inoffensive of men, a youth of a rare disposition, a prince of great hopes" The poet also says that he foresaw that some dreadful calamities threatened this unhappy kingdom, but that he did not imagine that a young and innocent prince would be the first victim sacrificed to barbarity.

Petrarch's praise must be discounted by the fact that Andrew's release of the Pipini had won his regard and gratitude, and also by the consideration that the poet's eloquence often led him to exaggerate.

## The Murder of Andrew

The just measure of Andrew's character is perhaps somewhere between Petrarch's praise and the blame of Italian historians.

Possibly Andrew, had he lived, might have developed later in such a way as to justify the hopes of which Petrarch speaks; but his culpable indolence and consequent gross ignorance made him a mere tool in the hands of Friar Robert and his tutor, Nicholas of Hungary, whose ambition and tyranny, by rousing the hatred of the Neapolitans against the Hungarians, had contributed to the deplorable calamity.

Another cause of the assassination was undoubtedly connected with the Pipini. When King Robert had imprisoned these counts, he enriched certain of the Neapolitan nobles with their spoils: when Andrew released them from their captivity, and took them into such great favour, these nobles feared they would fall into the hands of the Pipini, and be deprived by them of their fortunes and probably of their lives also.

Among them were the son and sons-in-law of Philippa the Catanese, and they were peculiarly obnoxious to Robert, and the probability is that they, being greatly interested in getting rid of Andrew, were among the conspirators. Philippa has been universally condemned as being implicated in the guilt of the Count of Evoli, her son, and her sons-in-law, but in her favour it must be said that neither she nor her grand-daughter Sancha was in the gallery or near the royal bed-chamber at the time of the murder.

The Duke of Durazzo may or may not have devised the plot against Andrew; but if we give him the benefit of the doubt in this case, it is certain that he cannot be acquitted of almost as cruel a crime in trying to destroy Joanna by openly accusing her of the murder of her husband, in order to rise himself on her ruin. He held her up to universal execration; and if he did not murder the King, he murdered the fair name and reputation of the young Queen.

Charles Artus and his son, whether innocent or not, behaved as if they were guilty, for they fled precipitately immediately after the murder had taken place, and took refuge with the Empress of Constantinople, who has in consequence been accused, with great presumption of truth, of being one of the conspirators. But if the letters which the King of Hungary afterwards alleged that the Duke of Durazzo wrote to Charles Artus were genuine, Durazzo was certainly one of the conspirators, for in this letter the murder was planned and arranged. In spite of his vile assertions against Joanna, not a particle of circumstantial evidence was ever forthcoming against her, or against Louis of Taranto, in all the inquiries which followed, and the only evidence against Nicholas

Acciajuoli was his intimacy with the Empress of Constantinople.

Much has been made by Joanna's enemies of the fact of the court going to Aversa. They allege that she inveigled Andrew there in order to get rid of him more easily, but we have already explained the reasons for this customary *villeggiatura*. We must now note that the only historians of any repute, contemporary with Joanna, who have accused her of complicity in the murder were the two Villanis, both very credulous men, and Matthew Villani was an intimate friend of Nicholas the Hungarian, the tutor of Andrew. It was, of course, to this man's interest to calumniate Joanna, for the only hope the Hungarians had of regaining their ascendency in the kingdom was by destroying Joanna's influence and reputation.

After the King of Hungary received the Queen's touching letter, containing the terrible news of Andrew's assassination, he issued a manifesto to all the sovereigns of Europe announcing the death of his brother; and it is very remarkable, in view of his subsequent conduct, that he makes no accusation against the Queen in this first document; later on, when he found that it might be practicable to seize her kingdom, he inculpated her. Then it was that Pope Clement VI., who was in a better position to know the truth than any one else in Europe, wrote a letter to Louis, in which he said, "As to the murder of Prince Andrew, Joanna can neither be convicted nor suspected of it, and still less has she confessed it."

Petrarch was convinced of her innocence, and, although he was not at Naples at the time of the murder, he obtained all his information from his intimate friend, the Bishop of Cavaillon, who was on the spot.

Boccaccio was also at the court when the tragedy occurred; and he and two of the most celebrated lawyers of the day, Angelo and Baldus of Perugia, not only believed in Joanna's innocence, but also in her incapability of such a crime, Angelo calling her " a most holy Queen, the honour of the world and the light of Italy " And here we may mention that Joanna is known to this day among Neapolitans as " the good Queen Jane "; and as the boatmen row past the grim castle of Muro, in which she was eventually imprisoned and murdered, they raise their caps in honour of " the good Queen."

But the most conclusive piece of negative evidence in favour of Joanna is the fact that her great and cruel enemy, Pope Urban VI., himself a Neapolitan, once Archbishop of Bari, when he fulminated his Bull of excommunication and deposition against Joanna, never breathed a word of reproach or accusation of her having consented to the murder of her first husband. Lastly, all the best Neapolitan and Provençal historians, and all the most enlightened

## The Murder of Andrew

of her contemporaries, have entirely exonerated her in this matter.

One of Villani's assertions against Joanna, prompted no doubt by Nicholas the Hungarian, is that she showed little or no concern at the death of her husband; but this is flatly contradicted by the repeated declarations of Pope Clement VI., that she always expressed the greatest horror at the murder of Andrew, and deplored his tragical fate with the deepest grief.

## CHAPTER VII

## What followed the Murder

NOWHERE did the assassination of Andrew rouse more interest and cause more sensation than at Avignon, whose magnificent Papal palace stood in Joanna's dominions, for as heiress and Countess of Provence she owned the whole of that province, through the Angevine line. The people of Provence never wavered in their allegiance to Joanna, whom they called "la bonne Reine Jeanne," and so long as Provence remained distinct from the French monarchy her memory was idolised there.

Immediately Clement VI. received the Queen's letter announcing the tragedy which had befallen her, he ordered Philip de Cabassole, who had been created a Cardinal with the title of St. Mark, to hold an inquiry into the crime and to punish the murderers: the Pope did this because he had assumed the government of Naples during Joanna's minority.

The Cardinal was ordered to keep the evidence secret if it implicated the Queen or any of the royal family, but he was unable to arrive at any definite conclusion.

Some of those who were suspected of being conspirators fled to their own castles and fortified themselves there; some, it is said, were put to death secretly; others, who were arrested on suspicion, were taken out of prison at night by those who dreaded that they might confess and incriminate them, and to prevent this they cut out their tongues.

The rumour that Joanna was a participator in the crime was at first only whispered, but it was fostered no doubt by Friar Robert and the Hungarians, till it grew louder and louder, and the poor young Queen found herself surrounded by treason.

Naples was in such a state of anarchy that the streets were unsafe. The young noblemen and officers went about armed, challenging the passers-by to open combat, which frequently ended in loss of life; while the great barons in their castles openly defied what government there was, and highwaymen infested the roads, robbing and murdering any travellers they happened to meet. Two or three months thus elapsed without any of the conspirators being brought to justice. Joanna is blamed most unjustly by her detractors for this delay, but it was clearly no fault of hers. The Pope having placed the reins of government in his legate's hands, she was powerless to exercise any legal authority. If she had interfered with the Cardinal's efforts, her enemies would have said that she wanted to turn aside the course of justice, and that her guilty conscience prompted her to intervene. Moreover, if she had possessed the legal power to act, her delicate state of health would have incapacitated her from exercising it, as the birth of her child was daily drawing nearer.

Shortly before Christmas the Bishop of Cavaillon, who was far too meek and gentle to cope with a situation so distasteful to him, obtained the Pope's consent to his resignation of his appointment as head of the Council of Regency, and to his return to his bishopric in Provence ; and on December 23rd he embarked from Naples for Marseilles, but a violent storm drove him ashore on the coast of Herculaneum, where he landed with difficulty. In the meanwhile a great commotion was going on at Castle Nuovo : the Queen was taken ill, doctors and ministers of State were summoned to the palace to await the interesting event, and while the storm was still raging Joanna gave birth to a son and heir.

The Pope had already promised to stand godfather to her child, and the Cardinal Bishop was required to represent His Holiness. Baptisms in Italy are celebrated within twenty-four hours of birth, so messengers were at once dispatched to Herculaneum to bring back the shipwrecked Cardinal to stand proxy for the Pope.

It was the custom to name the Neapolitan princes after the paternal grandfather, and Joanna scrupulously observed this etiquette, and named her son after Andrew's father, Canrobert, the late King of Hungary. There were great rejoicings in Naples at the birth of an heir to the throne, and these were a great consolation to Joanna, who looked upon them as proofs of the affection and loyalty of the greater part of the nation.

The day after the baptism the Bishop of Cavaillon re-embarked for Marseilles, but he was caught in a more terrific storm than before ; and as he himself relates in his autobiography, which he wrote shortly afterwards, he was saved this time miraculously by St. Mary Magdalene, the patron saint of Marseilles, whom he invoked. Petrarch was in Provence at this time ; and when the Cardinal arrived at Avignon in January, the two friends met, and having heard de Cabassole's account of the assassination of Andrew and all he had done to discover the conspirators, Petrarch wrote the letter from which we have quoted, to his friend Barbatus of Sulmone. Surely if there had been the slightest truth in the scandalous rumours about Joanna, the Cardinal would have told his intimate friend, who always believed in the Queen's innocence.

Immediately after the Cardinal left Naples the Pope sent two bishops to the Neapolitan court to take charge of the young prince, for Joanna being a minor was not allowed to bring up her own child. Perhaps Clement may have feared that there might be some foul play, as he knew the Queen was surrounded by traitors, and the murder of the King had made the Neapolitans a byword all over Europe; at any rate the Bishops of Padua and Monte Casino arrived at Castel Nuovo before the baby was a month old.

Joanna was now eighteen, and as soon as she had recovered from the birth of the child she sent for the most trusted friends of the late King Robert, and took counsel with them as to the best means to be pursued to bring the murderers of her husband to justice. She did not wait to ask the Pope's sanction, knowing he would refuse it on account of her youth; but she acted on her own initiative, and displayed that good sense and wise policy for which she was afterwards so famed.

A deputation from the nobility of Naples waited upon the Queen, and begged her to take the administration of affairs into her own hands now that the Cardinal legate, who had signally failed in his mission to discover the conspirators, had retired. The members of this deputation with remarkable frankness told the Queen of the rumours which were afloat about her complicity in the murder, saying that some boldly accused her of it, and adding that the disaffection was growing daily.

Her next move was to cause to be affixed to her palace-walls and to other public buildings a severe edict against the conspirators. She then signed a commission empowering one of the Neapolitan barons, named Hugh de Baux, to execute justice on all who were found guilty, without respect of persons. This edict was signed in February, 1846 (old style)—that is, five months after the assassination, but the reasons for the delay have, we hope, been made sufficiently clear to exonerate the Queen.

Joanna now wrote a second letter to Louis of Hungary, from which we shall quote the most salient passages. She says:

"I hear that many wonder that I have suffered the parricides [sic] who have slain my husband and your brother to go so long unpunished. What is this, then? Why do the people accuse me of this great iniquity, when I have always dearly loved King Andrew, my excellent husband, and he as long as his life lasted always lived in peace with me? But whatever the rest of men may suspect, I earnestly desire that you should believe that it has not been possible for me to avenge this great injury done to me, from my ignorance of the assassins, and from the difficulties of the times, and that I have suffered so much anguish of mind from the murder of my beloved husband that, stunned by grief, I had well-nigh died of the same wounds." The last sentence has been quoted before in this book, but it is as well to repeat it with the context in which it so naturally occurs and seems to give such unconscious evidence of her innocence. For if she had found Andrew a peaceable, excellent husband whom she loved tenderly, why should she have consented to his murder?

Hugh de Baux's methods of getting at the truth, or attempting to do so, were barbarous in the extreme, but they were the constant practice of the age in which he lived. He seized some of Andrew's chamberlains and proceeded to torture them, to extract so-called confessions, in which no sort of confidence could be placed, for the victims would say anything when on the rack.

The Duke of Durazzo opposed the original plan of holding these ghastly inquisitions in the halls of the public courts of justice, where all the people would have heard them, and instead examined the prisoners in his own palace. This on the face of it looks very suspicious, and as if the Duke had only too good reason to fear that he might be accused himself; whereas if the examination was held under his roof, the victims would say anything and accuse any one but the Duke, in the hope of cutting short their sufferings.

The chamberlains, Nicholas di Mirazzano and Jacobo de Pace, made many accusations. Among others they accused Charles Artus and his son—no doubt justly; and then it was that these two fled to the Empress of Constantinople. Others who were accused of being in the plot fortified themselves in their castles, while Philippa and her son the Count d'Evoli, her son-in-law, her granddaughter Sancha and her husband, who were also denounced, were all living either in the Castel Nuovo or in Naples, and daily frequenting the court.

Now it is very remarkable that none of those who were tortured, either now or later, ever accused Joanna of being in any way connected with the crime, and apparently she had never for one moment suspected Philippa—her father's foster-mother, the old tried friend of her grandfather and Queen Sancha, and her own faithful nurse and governess and friend, who had been all but a mother to her —of having had any part in the conspiracy.

Philippa and her granddaughter Sancha had continued to live at Castel Nuovo with Joanna, and we can fancy Philippa, who had nursed Joanna and her father, now idolising the infant prince. She had evidently been with the young Queen all through the terrible trials which had befallen her, and there is no doubt that Joanna was greatly attached to her; and therefore it can be imagined how great was her horror when the messengers of Hugh de Baux, to whom she had given such absolute power over the murderers when he had discovered them, arrived at the palace to arrest Philippa and Sancha. They are said to have been sitting with the Queen, either at their spinning-wheels or embroidery-frames, when the guards entered the room and dragged them forcibly from Joanna's presence, in spite of her protestations, which were in vain. Philippa, who must have been nearer seventy than sixty at this time, is described by some writers as a decrepit old woman, while others say she was still handsome, though it is true that Sicilian and Neapolitan women age much sooner than their Northern sisters, so it is possible the Catanese may have been old in appearance as well as in years.

Sancha was only about twenty, a young wife in the prime of her beauty; but neither her youth nor Philippa's age availed them anything. They were dragged down to the sea-shore, and there, in the presence of crowds of people, were tortured in a manner too horrible to describe. The mob was not allowed to come near enough to hear what the sufferers said under torture, but they were able to witness the horrible proceedings.

A place was prepared for the execution of these two unfortunate women, who, whether guilty or not, evoke our sympathy for the brutal manner in which this so-called justice was administered. To the scaffold they were dragged on a sledge, but, happily for her, Philippa died on the way thither, exhausted by the torments to which she had been submitted; while Sancha, whose tortures were even more horrible than her grandmother's, was burnt alive. Philippa was disembowelled, and her head affixed to one of the gates of the city. Her son, the Count d'Evoli, and her son-in-law, the Count of Trelice, were not executed until August 2nd, and a few days later some of the other barons who were arrested were put to death. The mob was so demoralised that after these executions they mangled the bodies of the executed conspirators with their teeth and nails out of sheer vicious ferocity. It is said that the Count d'Evoli was much favoured by Joanna in the beginning of her reign, but she was as powerless to save him from execution as she had been in the case of Philippa and Sancha.

Joanna's whole life was, to some extent, saddened by these events, for she was tenderly and deeply attached to Philippa, and Sancha had been the companion of her childhood and youth, for they had been brought up together; while Philippa had never been separated from her for a single day ever since her birth until the day she was dragged from her to torture and death.

From that day the young Queen, taught by this most bitter experience, never wholly trusted any one again; from henceforth she bore alone the cares of royalty, and the solitude of those whose high rank places them above their fellow men.

Before these trials befell the young Queen she

is said to have been of a most joyous disposition, full of mirth and high spirits, loving gaiety and all the pleasures of the court; but from henceforth dignity and majesty are the first characteristics mentioned in every description of her. In private life she was from this time kind and affable rather than gay and lively, while in public life she was noted for her masculine energy and firmness.

Boccaccio says of her that "from the time that she began to govern not in name only, but in fact, she conducted herself with so much prudence that she daily transacted the affairs of State with barons, warriors, counsellors, and other ministers, with such unblemished fame that neither the eyes nor ears of envy ever perceived anything with which to calumniate her. She was modest in her manner of living, and the very character of her beauty was rather that of majesty than of softness or voluptuousness." Yet she ever retained a charm of manner, which together with her beauty made her the centre of admiration of her brilliant court and the idol of the courtiers who surrounded her, while the fame of her majestic, or, as some writers say, angelic loveliness was a theme of conversation in all the courts of Europe.

It is not certain what became of Charles Artus and his son. It is said by some authors that they were imprisoned at Benevento, and put to death privately there, out of respect to King Robert, of

*From an engraving after the painting by Titian.*

GIOVANNI BOCCACCIO.

whom Charles Artus the elder is believed to have been the natural son. Other writers deny this, and say that he was the husband of Robert's natural daughter, the Princess Maria of Sicily.

The Empress of Constantinople, who had sheltered them, died in the October following the execution of Philippa and Sancha. Her death took place at Naples. She was the last of the Queen's relatives of the elder generation, except Maria of Sicily; and as now the Duke of Durazzo had rebelled against her, she was deprived of the society of her sister, and, the friends of her youth having fallen on the scaffold, she was more than ever alone.

The Princess of Taranto died without living to see the marriage of Joanna and her second son Louis accomplished, for which she had certainly planned and plotted—if she had not actually, as many believe, arranged the assassination of Andrew to make way for Louis.

The next trial that befell Joanna was civil war, brought about by the rebellion of the Duke of Durazzo, who now openly accused the Queen of the murder of her husband, and hoisted his standard against her. He was joined by his own brothers and by his cousin Philip, the youngest of the sons of the Empress of Constantinople, whose youth made him a prey to the flattery of Durazzo.

Robert, the eldest of the Princes of Taranto, had just returned from Greece, and he and his second brother Louis took Joanna's part, and commanded her troops and went out to meet the Duke of Durazzo's forces. But while these princes were fighting against each other, both were dreading that the King of Hungary would invade the kingdom to avenge his brother's death.

Joanna, foreseeing this event, had sent an embassy, with the Bishop of Tropea at its head, to Louis of Hungary, after the birth of her son, to deliver the letter we quoted above, and the Bishop did not return until early in the following year, 1347 (old style).

Friar Robert and Nicholas the Hungarian had already gone back to Hungary, fearing the power of their adversaries after the death of Andrew; and they had of course given their version of what had happened to their master, and had succeeded in so misrepresenting Joanna that they had convinced him of her guilt, and Louis, burning with rage and the desire of revenge, was now making alliances with other powers, and preparing a large army to invade Joanna's dominions.

The Bishop of Tropea reported all these things to Joanna on his return, and the threatening letter he brought with him from the King of Hungary to Joanna fully confirmed his observations.

Louis, King of Hungary, surnamed the Great, who had succeeded his father Canrobert, or Charobert, in 1342, was one of the most powerful European monarchs of his time. His father had left the kingdom to him after it had acquired under his government a high degree of splendour, for it embraced Bosnia, Servia, Croatia, Wallachia, Moldavia, Dalmatia, and Transylvania, besides Hungary proper. Louis was most warlike and ambitious he fought successfully the Transylvanians, the Croatians, Wallachians, and Venetians, and, as we shall see, twice during Joanna's reign he invaded Naples and made himself a terror to the inhabitants.

His father, we know, had considered he had a claim on the kingdom ; and when Joanna's sister, Maria of Sicily, whom Friar Robert had advised Louis to marry, eloped with Charles of Durazzo, Louis was intensely annoyed, for this, as the wily friar foresaw, would have been a stepping-stone to the coveted crown of Naples, which probably Louis would in any case have endeavoured to wrest from Joanna. The murder of Andrew gave him some pretext for attempting this, and when it was announced to him his wrath and desire of revenge as well as of conquest knew no bounds, and are apparent in the following letter to Joanna.

"Joanna! your former irregular life, your continuing to retain the power of the kingdom, your neglected vengeance, and your subsequent excuses prove you to have been a participator in the death of your husband. Remember, that none may escape the Divine and human vengeance due to such enormous iniquity."

This threatening and historic letter is supposed to contain the strongest arguments against Joanna that can be urged; but happily the four so-called proofs of her guilt can be refuted. The first accusation of leading an irregular life is an absolute calumny for which there is no evidence, and is dismissed by de Sade as insupportable. As Hallam points out, "The name of Joanna of Naples has suffered by the lax repetition of calumnies." He adds that "the charge of dissolute manners so frequently made is not warranted by any specific proof or contemporary testimony."

The second accusation that she continued to retain the power of her kingdom only shows what Louis was aiming at. What else should the Queen have done? It was her kingdom, and Andrew's death in no way detracted from her claims. While her husband was alive the poor young Queen had no power in her own kingdom, as we have seen, for Friar Robert and his Hungarian followers had supplanted her and her interests.

The third accusation, of "neglecting vengeance," we have been endeavouring to show was unavoidable under the circumstances in which Joanna was placed.

The fourth, of her "subsequent excuses," is more difficult to refute, if we endorse the French proverb "qui s'excuse s'accuse"; but if Joanna had taken the more dignified course of behaving as if she were like Cæsar's wife, "above suspicion," and had scorned to defend herself, they would have said that her silence gave consent to the assertions of her guilt.

The poor young Queen found herself in most difficult circumstances. It was most perplexing to know how to act, surrounded as she was on all sides by treason and treachery, her every action cruelly criticised, and the worst interpretation put upon all her deeds: she did the best she could, and if venomous tongues aspersed her fair fame it was no fault of hers. Directly she received Louis's cruel letter she called together her councillors and laid it before them, who recommended immediate preparations for defending the kingdom from the impending invasion which it was clear Louis was bent upon attempting, and, as a most necessary preliminary step, they counselled their sovereign to marry again.

## CHAPTER VIII

## Joanna Marries a Second Time

THE consort chosen by the councillors for the Queen was Louis of Taranto, the prince who is accused by Joanna's enemies of having been her paramour. The very fact that her ministers suggested him as the most suitable husband for her should be the answer to this calumnious report; for unless they desired that all future historians should write them down asses, would they have been so sublimely foolish as to choose for her protector and the partner of her throne her supposed lover? They must have known that there was not a particle of truth in this scandal or they would never have dared to set all Europe talking by marrying Joanna to the man her enemies and detractors said was criminally intimate with her.

Louis was at this time twenty-five; he is described as both handsome and charming, renowned for his valour and also for his talents. He was proposed to the Council as a suitable husband for the Queen by his eldest brother, Robert of Taranto, who had lately married a daughter of the Duke of Bourbon. The other councillors, feeling the necessity of conciliating the princes of Taranto, lest if this offer were rejected they should join their younger brother Philip and the Duke of Durazzo, immediately agreed to the proposal. They were hampered in their choice, which was confined to the Neapolitan princes, for it would not have done at this juncture to propose a foreign prince ; neither the royal family nor the great barons would have agreed to that.

There was no difficulty with either of the parties most interested in the marriage. Louis was known to be madly in love with his beautiful cousin and Queen, and Joanna is believed to have favoured his suit: she had known him from childhood, and he was from all accounts a very attractive man. Nevertheless it was some months before the marriage was arranged. Louis, although a brave man in war, was very diffident in love, and finally it was his friend and tutor, Nicholas Acciajuoli, who did his wooing for him and made all the preliminary arrangements.

The Duke of Durazzo opposed the marriage vehemently, for it was a death-blow to his hopes of securing the throne for his wife, Maria, which he and the Durazzos were labouring to do by calumniating Joanna, so as if possible to deprive her of the allegiance of her people.

The marriage took place on August 20th, 1347 (old style), two years after the murder of Andrew; but in spite of this fact Joanna's detractors have accused her of marrying before the year of her widowhood had expired, whereas two years all but a month had elapsed since Andrew's death. According to many writers, this second marriage was disapproved of by the other European courts, who had apparently heard the scandalous reports of the intimacy between Joanna and Louis and were only too ready to put the worst interpretation upon them. Of course it is quite possible that if Joanna had been consulted about her first marriage, she might have preferred the handsome, talented Louis of Taranto to the half-imbecile, boorish Hungarian prince to whom from motives of policy the late King Robert had wedded her. But even if this were so, it does not follow that there was anything wrong in her relations with Louis, although vicious tongues asserted that there was.

As Louis was her cousin, a Papal dispensation was necessary to enable them to marry, and there is a difference of opinion among historians as to whether Joanna waited till this arrived, many asserting that she did not do so; but Villani says that the Pope granted the dispensation, and at the same time made Louis Regent of the kingdom, but that the marriage caused " scandal to all zealous Christians "—whose zeal, we venture to think, would

## Joanna Marries a Second Time

have been much better employed in saving their own souls than in criticising Joanna's conduct, which in no way concerned them.

While the preparations were going on for the marriage Louis of Hungary sent ambassadors to the Papal court at Avignon, to demand the investiture of the kingdom of Naples for himself, thus excluding not only the reigning Queen, but also her little son Canrobert, or Charobert, for the name is spelt in both ways. Clement VI., however, refused to receive his ambassadors because he was an ally of the excommunicated Emperor Louis of Bavaria, who had brought this punishment upon himself, in the time of Pope Benedict XII., for denying the Papal authority in Germany.

The Pope sent a message to the King of Hungary to say that nothing criminal had been proved against Joanna, and that even had she forfeited her throne the claims of Andrew's son could not be set aside. This was a great blow to Louis of Hungary, who had believed that the Pope would favour his cause at the expense of Joanna.

His next move made about the same time was to lodge an accusation against Joanna and all the Neapolitan princes of the murder of his brother Andrew, at the court of Rienzi, now Tribune of Rome. He had a twofold object in appealing to Rienzi—first to enlist his sympathy and secure if possible his help, and secondly to justify himself for the attack upon the Queen of Naples and her allies by casting a public slur upon their characters.

The royal family of Naples did not disdain to send advocates to Rome to plead their cause and clear themselves from the odious stigma this accusation had cast upon them, and Rienzi listened to them, seated upon his throne in great pomp; but he put off from day to day passing any judgment in the matter, and left it undecided. His own downfall, precipitated by the Count of Minervino, who accompanied the Hungarian ambassadors to Rome, followed soon after, and the great Tribune was sent a prisoner to the Pope at Avignon, where he was cast into a dungeon.

In the month of May preceding the marriage of Joanna and Louis, Nicholas the Hungarian, the former tutor of Andrew, had returned to Aquila, near Naples, with large sums of money in his possession, with which he proceeded to bribe the Neapolitans whom he had won to his side on his previous residence in the kingdom, to forsake the cause of their lawful Queen and join that of the usurping King of Hungary, and unfortunately he succeeded in corrupting many of Joanna's subjects. He was joined by a rebel baron who had previously established himself at Aquila.

It was these traitors within the camp which made the cause of Joanna and Louis of Taranto so desperate: if all their subjects had been faithful, it is believed that, notwithstanding the large army the Hungarian King was bringing against the Neapolitans, they would have been able to repel the invasion.

The Duke of Durazzo joined the Queen's party for a short time, because he had discovered that he himself was a greater object of vengeance to Louis of Hungary—who imputed Andrew's murder to his hand—than even Joanna herself. He nevertheless contrived to injure her cause by his malice, even when nominally fighting for her, and soon after her marriage he raised the siege of Aquila and retired to his own dominions.

The first division of the Hungarian army which entered Naples in October was commanded by the Bishop of the Five Churches, a natural brother of the Hungarian King: he is described by Villani as a wise and good soldier. It was the custom in the Middle Ages for bishops to go to battle, and even for popes to do so: our English Pope Adrian IV. led his troops against his arch-enemy, Frederick Barbarossa, so there was nothing unusual in this proceeding.

Such was the disaffection in the country, and so great was the terror Louis's threats of vengeance had kindled among the people, that many castles and towns surrendered to the Hungarian troops without resistance, and some of the nobles went over to the side of the enemy. One of the causes of this treachery against Joanna was the unpopularity of the princes. The people themselves were indifferent to the royal cause partly because of the rumours that the Queen was concerned in the assassination of the late King, partly because of the ambition and haughty demeanour of the royal princes. Louis of Taranto, in spite of all these discouragements, collected an army at Capua large enough to stop the force of Louis of Hungary when he entered the kingdom in December.

On reaching the frontier the King of Hungary was met by the Papal legate, who commanded him to retire in the name of the Pope, to whom the suzerainty of Naples belonged. Furthermore, the legate bade him cease from attempting any further vengeance against the innocent Queen, saying that two persons alone had been guilty of the murder, and those two had already been executed. It is most tantalising that the legate should not have mentioned the names of these two guilty people, and thus have solved the mystery of the murder of Andrew, which must remain now undisclosed until the day of judgment.

Louis had the insolence to reply to this remonstrance by saying that he had come to take possession of a kingdom which by right belonged to him through his father Charles Martel (who, by the way, must not be confused with his illustrious namesake, the King of France who lived in the seventh century).

## Joanna Marries a Second Time 119

The haughty Louis went on to say that he should not trouble himself about his excommunication, which he considered undeserved; and as for the murderers of his brother, a dozen rather than two had been guilty of that crime. Having thus disrespectfully delivered his soul, his army continued to march to Naples viâ Benevento, an ancient city standing upon a hill and surrounded by mediæval walls, with a celebrated gate upon the north side erected in the year A.D. 114, in memory of the Roman Emperor Trajan, and called the Golden Gate.

There were no standing armies in those days: the cavalry were the mounted nobles and knights, whose men-at-arms, bound under the feudal system to fight for their feudal lord, were the infantry. The mounted soldiers wore plate-armour and chain-mail, but gunpowder was now coming into use, and with it the wearing of armour decreased. We doubt very much whether the Hungarians and Neapolitans used gunpowder in this war, though the English did at Crecy in the previous year for the first time. More likely the half-civilised Hungarians were armed with cross-bows, swords, pikes, javelins, battle-axes, and sabres, while the foot soldiers were furnished with any weapon which came handy—very often with their flails; but in spite of the indifferent equipment they fought with the greatest ferocity, and the Hungarians were more noted than the more civilised

Neapolitans for their fierce, barbarous methods of war.

The Duke of Durazzo now basely betrayed Joanna to the Hungarians. Though he was still fighting nominally upon the Queen's side, he kept up a secret correspondence with the Hungarian camp, hoping ultimately to establish his wife, Maria, upon her sister's throne. Durazzo knew that even if the Hungarians should be victorious, which was still doubtful, the Neapolitans would never submit for long to their yoke. So he was playing a double game; and sad to say many of the Neapolitan nobles followed his bad example, and courted the favour of the Hungarian King.

Louis, desiring to strike terror into the Neapolitan people, had had a banner made of black silk or velvet, upon which was painted in most realistic style and colours a sensational picture of the assassination of Andrew. This ghastly standard was borne by a band of mourners robed in black to heighten its effect.

Finding herself deserted by so many of her subjects, and believing her cause to be hopeless, Joanna, disheartened by the vile reports current about her, determined to leave Naples and retire to Provence, where she as Countess of that country was idolised and certain of a welcome. Accordingly she called a general council of all the principal and wisest men of her kingdom, and with that eloquence for which she was so famed made a speech in which she declared to them the resolution at which she had arrived. She began by telling her audience of the danger which threatened the capital from the approach of the King of Hungary, who was now close at its gates, and of her powerlessness to resist him because of the calumnies which had been spread abroad by her enemies, who without any crime of hers had accused her of the most atrocious iniquity, insensible of the pity which they should have felt for their Queen, who in the earliest bloom of youth had been the victim of misfortune.

She then went on to say that in order to make known her innocence to the Vicar of Christ on earth, as it was known to God in heaven, and to force the whole world to acknowledge it also, she intended to go to Avignon and plead her cause before the Holy Father, whose absolution she would beg.

She continued : " Only against me is the anger of the King of Hungary directed, me whom he holds as the murderess of his brother Andrew. You I know will take my part ; you will not refuse to defend me and my rights—if not for my own merits, at least for the love you bore my grandfather, the late King Robert. I know this ; but innocent blood shall not flow in a fruitless struggle. I yield my rights for the public good. I absolve you all, both nobles and people, from your oath of allegiance to me. I command you to make no resistance to the King of Hungary. Submit yourselves to him and disarm his anger by obedience. Deliver to him the keys of all the towns and castles in my kingdom, without waiting for the summons of herald or trumpet.

"I leave you behind me my most precious pledge, my little son Charobert. May his innocent smile be your advocate, and soften the angry monarch. To me, the persecuted Queen, shall distant France give a place of refuge until the solemn judgment of God's viceregent on earth shall absolve me from this shameful reproach, and then full of honour I will return to my country as Queen, which I now leave with a broken heart, but a pure conscience."

This touching speech, delivered with all the grace not only of the most lovely woman of her day, but also of one of the most accomplished orators, moved the assembly to tears. But the majestic young Queen had sufficient self-control to command her own emotion, and sat there sad but dignified while both burghers and warriors were weeping at her feet; and the solemn silence with which they had at first listened was now broken by cheers and exclamations, imploring her to remain and dare every risk, the nobles vowing to lay down their lives for her and her children.

The age in which Joanna lived was the age of chivalry, so it is not surprising that this speech of one of the most fascinating woman that the world

## Joanna Marries a Second Time 123

has seen should have won the hearts of her hearers, for devotion to beauty at this time of day was carried to a degree of enthusiasm bordering on madness.

It was not only the younger barons and knights and citizens who were moved by Joanna's beauty and eloquence; the old sage councillors were also touched. They not only applauded her resolution and approved of her plans, but they too vowed not to rest until she was able to return, and they placed their lives and fortunes at her service.

The journey from Naples to Avignon, in days before the use of steam had been discovered, was slow and by no means sure, for as the greater part of the way was a sea-voyage the travellers were at the mercy of wind and waves.

On January 15th, 1347 (old style), the Queen embarked for Provence, taking with her her household, a few most faithful friends, among them Nicholas Acciajuoli, and the Princess of Taranto, her sister-in-law, wife of Robert, Prince of Taranto, Louis's elder brother, and her celebrated diamonds and other jewels.

Three galleys were the means of transport. A galley was usually a three-masted vessel with one deck, supplied with oars, the number of which varied; a Venetian galley had sixty-four, and probably Joanna's had not less. They were rowed generally by criminals: hence the expression, "sent to the galleys." When Joanna reached the sea it is said that every man and woman in the city was at the harbour, to catch a glimpse of the young Queen. As many as could get near enough to do so kissed her hand before she embarked, and both men and women wept bitterly as she left the shore, and stood on the beach watching as long as there was a sign of the disappearing galleys.

The voyage, owing to the ignorance of nautical science of the times, was a dangerous one, and as it was performed in mid-winter the Mediterranean was quite capable of giving them a very rough time; and as soon as the vessels were out of sight the crowd besieged the churches, and, kneeling round the altars, invoked every saint—especially Our Lady and St. Januarius, the patron saint of Naples—to protect their beloved sovereign and grant her a safe voyage and a speedy return to her country.

As Joanna sailed past the isolated rock in the bay, crowned with the gloomy Castel del Ovo, her mother's heart must have been pierced with grief and fear, for there she had left her little son Charobert—now at the interesting age of two, just beginning to prattle—with his guardians chosen by the Pope, who had selected this castle as the safest place for the heir to the crown. The poor young mother was destined never to see her child again; but she could not know this when she left him, although she must under the circumstances have felt very anxious.

## Joanna Marries a Second Time 125

Her husband, Louis of Taranto, was with her for three days, and on the 18th he landed on the Italian shore, which was neutral ground.

The Princess of Taranto, whom her husband had sent to her father, the Duke of Bourbon, as Naples was in such a disturbed state, also landed here with Nicholas Acciajuoli, who, bent himself on an important mission to Florence, was to escort the Princess thither ; and now Joanna was left almost alone to proceed to Nice, where she landed two days later, intending to travel the rest of the way to Avignon by land. But on reaching Achisi she met Raymond de Baux, Prince of Orange, who was her second cousin, the Count de Soult, and some other Provençal barons, who were evidently on the look out for her, having heard from the Hungarians that she was coming to Avignon. To her amazement, they seized her suite and sent them all back as prisoners to Nice, and led Joanna herself, with great respect and courtesy, but as a State prisoner, to Aix, the capital of Provence, where they lodged her in the now deserted palace of her ancestors, the ancient counts of Aix.

Orange, we must explain, was a tiny principality, the chief town of which was about thirteen miles north of Avignon, and called Orange ; it was at this time an independent State, and remained so until the sixteenth century. The Barons de Baux had been the reigning princes of Orange since the eleventh century; they were constantly fighting for the titles of Count of Provence and King of Arles.

The reason for this extraordinary reception of Joanna from these Provençal barons, who were so loyal to the Angevine family, and supposed to idolise their beautiful Countess, the Queen of the Two Sicilies, was the reports spread by her enemy, the King of Hungary, to the effect that she intended to dispose of her Provençal dominions in order to obtain the means to carry on the war against Louis of Hungary.

For this purpose, the emissaries of Louis had declared, she was travelling to Avignon in order to meet there her cousin John, Duke of Normandy, who in 1358 succeeded his father, Philip de Valois, as John I. of France, and sell her Provençal possessions to him. The Provençals, who were a proud race and, as we have said, devoted to the Angevine line, were determined to stop this sale at all costs, and so seized Joanna and confined her as a state prisoner at Aix, whither they conducted her with all courtesy and respect.

She was treated as a Queen in this gloomy, fortress-like castle, but she was not allowed to see any one unless her attendants were present. This was in order to prevent her from making any attempt to negotiate the sale of Provence. In this desolate building, formerly the scene of revelry and magnificence, whose now silent walls once rang with the songs of the Troubadours, we must now leave the unfortunate Queen while we relate what happened in her absence from Naples.

Little did Joanna think when she set out for Provence, where she as Countess was so revered and loved, that this would be the reception she would meet with on stepping on to Provençal soil.

## CHAPTER IX

## The King of Hungary's Vengeance

BEFORE leaving her kingdom Joanna had commanded that the same governors should continue to hold their offices in all the towns and fortresses during her absence, so that on her return she might find her country in no worse state than when she left it. She had confidence in those to whom she had entrusted the government to safeguard her interests, and she trusted that by ordering the gates of every town to be thrown open to the King of Hungary, and no resistance offered to his army, his anger would be pacified, and that he would not carry his threats of vengeance any further into execution.

Aversa was the place to which the special vengeance of Louis was directed, and thither his troops were advancing with threatening steps. Fear went before; all trembled at the report of his approach. One town, Sulmone, in the north of the kingdom, refused to obey Joanna's command to surrender, and opposed him, but he took it and sacked it, and continued his march.

The Neapolitan princes of the blood, hearing of the resistance of Sulmone, sent an embassy to Louis begging him to grant them a safe-conduct, and a written declaration that he considered them innocent of the murder of Andrew. The Hungarian King granted both these requests, and the princes, trusting in his honour and chivalry, advanced in a body to meet him at Aversa, that scene of one tragedy destined to be the scene of another scarcely less terrible drama.

Louis had assumed the title of King of Jerusalem and Sicily already, though both belonged to Joanna; but the princes, to appease his wrath, recognised these titles by performing their homage according to the etiquette of the times, by kissing him on the mouth, and then they all sat down to a meal. By virtue of these two acts, either of which was considered sufficient to ensure their safety, they had declared themselves his vassals, and he had virtually pledged himself to protect them; and by all the laws of chivalry, then held in the most sacred esteem, their lives and persons were inviolable.

The King of Hungary received them apparently as friends, but after the banquet he and the other Hungarians all armed themselves, while the Neapolitans were defenceless. In the courtyard of the castle where they were all assembled, both Neapolitans and Hungarians mounted their horses, and Louis announced his intention of proceeding with them to Naples ; but as they started, with the Duke of Durazzo riding by the side of the Hungarian monarch, the latter turned to Charles and said in an ominous tone, which struck terror into Durazzo's heart :

" Lead us to where my brother Andrew was killed."

Durazzo, noting the ferocity which shone in the King's eyes, answered :

" Don't trouble yourself about that. I was not there."

The accounts of what followed vary. One says that Louis, on reaching Aversa, at once took prisoners the Duke of Durazzo and all the princes who had remained in Naples, including the little Charobert, whom this writer says the Neapolitans had brought with them in his cradle—which, seeing he was two years old, seems improbable. Carraccioli, the author in question, says that Louis then ordered the Duke of Durazzo to be beheaded on the same spot on which Andrew was murdered, and then kept the others whom he had arrested chained in irons most strictly until he could send them to Hungary.

We prefer to follow Villani's version, which tells us that Louis, persisting in his demand to be shown the spot where Andrew was murdered, was led to the Celestine monastery, where they all dismounted and proceeded to the castle, going up to the gallery in which Andrew was first seized, and then on to the balcony from which he was hanged and thrown over into the garden.

When they reached this spot the fury of the King knew no bounds. He turned to Durazzo in a transport of rage, and said :

"You have been a false traitor, and compassed the death of your lord my brother, and intrigued in the Papal court together with your uncle, the Cardinal of Périgord, who, at your request, delayed and endeavoured to prevent his coronation, which should, as was becoming, have been performed by the sanction of the Pope, and this delay was the cause of his death.

"With fraud and deceit you obtained a dispensation from the Pope to take your cousin, his sister-in law, to wife, in order that, by the death of him and the Queen Joanna, his wife, you might become King in their stead.

"Moreover, you have been in arms with that traitor Louis, Prince of Taranto, our rebel, who has done as you have done, and with fraud and sacrilege has married that iniquitous and adulterous woman, traitorous to her King and husband, who was Andrew, our brother, and therefore it is fitting that you should die where you caused him to die."

Durazzo vehemently protested his innocence, and

implored the King's mercy, but in vain. Louis now produced the letters to Charles Artus, written in Durazzo's name and sealed with his seal, concocting the assassination of Andrew, and then demanded how he could excuse himself.

Without giving the unhappy Durazzo time to examine the documents in question, which are considered to be of very doubtful authenticity—for Charles Artus was not yet taken, so it is not easy to see how they could have come into Louis's possession, and Durazzo's seal was easily imitated, as it was well known all over Europe—the angry King called forward one of his suite, who stabbed the unarmed Duke in the breast, while another Hungarian seized him by the hair. A second stab in the throat, which partially severed his head from his body, killed him.

Nothing can justify the conduct and treachery of Louis in this murder. It was a gross breach of faith and trust, it was a dastardly action, cowardly in the extreme; and whether Durazzo was guilty of Andrew's death or not it was unjust, because he was murdered without any trial or examination, or witness against him except these very doubtful letters.

Under pretence of zeal to punish his brother's murderers, Louis was bent on obtaining the crown of the Two Sicilies for himself; and as Durazzo was certainly aiming at the same object, he was a special object of hatred to Louis, who had not forgiven him for stealing his bride, Maria of Sicily, from him. But, fortunately for Joanna, his zeal outran his discretion, for this foul murder, coupled with his treachery, revolted the feelings of all classes, rich and poor, against him, and a reaction set in in favour of the Queen.

Not content with murdering Durazzo, he threw the body over the fatal balcony and forbade any one to bury it till he gave permission, thus denying his victim, whom he had already deprived of the last Sacraments, Christian burial.

He seized all the other princes who had been his guests an hour before, and threw them into the Castle of Aversa as prisoners for the present, until he could make other arrangements for taking them to Hungary. He then set out for Naples, but he was met at Melita, which is half-way between the city and Aversa, by a deputation of the citizens, who saluted him with the greatest reverence—of which he scorned to take the least notice, but rode into Naples as a conqueror, his terrible banner carried before him, his helmet on his head, refusing to pass under the canopy which the chief nobility brought out to hold over him.

He also declined to meet the governors of the city and the representatives of the nobility, but demanded the keys of the city to be given up to him, and sent them to Hungary in token of conquest. He then let loose his soldiers with orders to destroy all the palaces of the royal family, and the terrified Neapolitans feared he was going to pillage the whole city; but this he forbade his soldiers to do, his chief wrath being directed against all the royal princes.

Louis then held another inquiry—or rather inquisition, for torture was the means employed to get evidence—into Andrew's death, and many nobles were executed as the result of these mock trials; the real object of which was to obtain incriminating evidence against Joanna, and to remove all the barons who were opposed to the Hungarian cause. The first object was completely defeated, for neither death nor torture could extort a word of evidence against the Queen; another proof of her innocence.

Louis now took possession of little Canrobert, Joanna's child, whom he loaded with caresses and then sent him to Hungary with the other princes. The child did not live very long after reaching Hungary, and it was far better for Joanna that he died there; for had his death taken place in Naples, her slanderers would have said that he had been murdered to make room for the children of her second marriage. The other royal princes were sent, chained, to the Castle of Wisgrade, which is described as a roomy prison, but "where there was little to have and less to spend."

In the meanwhile Maria of Sicily, the young

# The King of Hungary's Vengeance 135

Duchess of Durazzo, was waiting in the Castel Nuovo to meet the Hungarian King, whom she expected to return with her husband, who had gone to meet him. Her two children were with her when a messenger arrived to inform her of the King of Hungary's treachery, and the horrible murder of the husband of her youth, whom she loved passionately, and who had saved her from marrying Louis of Hungary, whom she hated. On hearing the ghastly news, and knowing Louis was now on his way from Aversa—that place so fatal to her and her sister Joanna—to her place of retreat, where she dreaded he would tear her children from her arms and send them prisoners to Hungary, while what form his vengeance might take against her who had jilted him she did not know, she immediately left the Castel Nuovo and took refuge for the rest of the day in some neighbouring buildings.

Here she assumed the disguise of a beggar, laying aside all signs of her riches and high rank, and as soon as it was dark she issued forth with her two babies, and fled for protection to the neighbouring monastery of Santa Croce. We can well imagine the sensation her arrival must have caused among the monks, when the young Duchess of Durazzo, who was second in rank only to the Queen, knocked at their postern-gate disguised as a poor beggar, carrying two babies in her arms, the elder of whom could not speak, while it was plainly visible that a third child would soon be added to her family. The monks could not have denied shelter even to the beggar she was counterfeiting nor did they hesitate to take in the Duchess; though her presence was a source of the greatest danger to them, for if Louis had discovered it he would undoubtedly have sacked the monastery.

The monks kept her for a few days while Louis was making a strict search for her, and had she fallen into his hands would no doubt have imprisoned her, though for the sake of the unborn child he might have spared her life, at any rate until that was born. During these few days a plan was made for her escape by a few friends and the monks, who decided that an attempt must be made to send her to her sister in Provence. Apparently the news of the Queen's imprisonment had not reached the monastery or Naples. Maria was to learn on her arrival in Avignon, if she ever got there, of Joanna's captivity.

The disguise of a beggar was not considered sufficient for one so well known as the Duchess of Durazzo, so she put on the habit of one of the monks, and with a few faithful friends managed, after undergoing many hardships and dangers by sea and by land, to reach Aix, where we left Joanna confined.

The reason of Joanna's captivity at Aix was

partly due to the affection of her Provençal subjects, partly to the false reports which the Hungarians had circulated about her among the nobility of Provence, to the effect that she was going to Avignon to endeavour to sell her Provençal dominions in order to get money to continue the war against the King of Hungary. To prevent this sale, which neither their pride nor their affection for the ancient Angevine rulers could brook, they subjected Joanna to a captivity which they had the grace to make as pleasant as possible under the circumstances, and in which she was treated with all the respect due to her as Queen and Countess of Provence, and we are told also with the utmost courtesy.

Maria, the widowed Duchess of Durazzo, was only eighteen when with her two little baby girls, Joanna and Agnes, she reached her sister, the captive Queen, who was separated from her own little son. The meeting between the two sisters was no doubt very touching, when after so many perils Maria at last found herself in a place of safety, although that place was a prison.

Both these young widows had lost their husbands by a violent death, and, strange to say, Andrew and Charles of Durazzo had been murdered on the same spot, and the same cruel enemy was pursuing them. Joanna, generously forgetting that Charles of Durazzo had been a traitor to her, took upon herself the care and education of his children, and when the third child was born adopted her as her daughter. No doubt the two little babies of Maria were a source of amusement and consolation to both sisters in their captivity, and to some extent atoned to Joanna for the loss of her boy, of whose fate she was so uncertain.

We must now see what had become of Joanna's husband and Nicholas Acciajuoli, who, when they left Joanna, had intended to proceed by different ways to Florence, where Angelo Acciajuoli, the brother of Nicholas, was bishop, in order to enlist his services on Joanna's behalf, for he was a man of great influence in the Papal Court.

The fate of Louis and Joanna was, it may be said, in the Pope's hands. If he judged them guilty of the murder of Andrew, he had the power to send them not only to prison, but to the scaffold; while, on the other hand, if he pronounced them innocent, and took them under his fatherly protection, Joanna might recover her fair fame and her kingdom.

It was therefore of vital importance to both Joanna and Louis to leave no stone unturned to procure a favourable verdict at the Court of Avignon, and they were most fortunate in being able to approach such a powerful advocate as the Bishop of Florence with such an influential friend as his brother Nicholas to plead for them.

Angelo Acciajuoli once proposed to pay Petrarch

a visit in his hermitage at Vaucluse, to see him and the celebrated fountain, said never to have been fathomed, which is the source of the River Sorgia, and rises in the midst of a gloomy cavern at the foot of a huge rock. Petrarch, highly delighted at the prospect of receiving so honourable a guest, scoured the neighbourhood to obtain delicacies to set before him when he should arrive.

The Bishop, who was on his way from Avignon to Florence, was expected to the midday *déjeuner* at twelve o'clock. Everything was ready at the appointed time; twelve o'clock struck, but no Bishop appeared, and the poet, who wanted his luncheon, grew impatient, and while waiting wrote some lines to the Prior of the neighbouring monastery to the following effect:

"There is no more faith in the world. We can depend on no one; the more I see the more I feel this. Even your Bishop, upon whom I thought I could rely, he deceives me. He promised to dine with me to-day. I have done for him what I never did for any one. I have upset my house to treat him well. He fears, no doubt, that he will meet with the repast of a poet, and deigns not to visit the place where the great King Robert, where cardinals and princes have been: some to see the fountain, others to visit me. But if I am unworthy to receive such a guest, it seems to me that he is still more unworthy for breaking his word."

By the time these lines were written a great commotion was heard outside the hermitage, and the good Bishop arrived, having been delayed on the way.

But to return to Louis of Taranto and his tutor. When they reached the Florentine frontier they were met by an embassy from the chief magistrates, forbidding them to enter Florence, lest by so doing the inhabitants should suffer from the vengeance of Louis of Hungary. The Guelph party in Florence took no part in this protest, and were highly indignant at it, for they owed much both to the relations of Joanna and to the uncle and brother of Louis, who had laid down their lives for them in battle.

But though the Florentines had received so many favours from Joanna's father and King Robert, as well as from Louis's relations, the chief citizens decided it would not do to run the risk of incurring the anger of the Hungarian King, so Louis was obliged to take refuge for ten days in the Castle of Valdepeso, which belonged to a chief of the Acciajuoli family.

This was all the more galling to the Guelphs because a month before, when Philip Gonzago of Mantua, who had been fighting on the side of the Hungarians, passed through Florence on his way from Naples he was received with the honours they wished to show to Prince Louis of Taranto.

## The King of Hungary's Vengeance

Nicholas Acciajuoli was, however, too faithful and too clever a friend to his pupil, Louis, and to his sovereign, Joanna, not to find a way to help her; so he chartered two armed galleys from Genoa, and on board them he and Louis sailed for Provence. But on nearing the shore they found they could not land with safety either at Marseilles or Nice, and they heard the bad news that Joanna was in captivity, the Barons in open rebellion, and Louis's Hungarian agents very busy doing all the mischief they could. Neither Louis of Taranto nor Acciajuoli were men to be easily baffled; they were determined to reach Avignon by hook or by crook, so they sailed past the Provençal shore to Aigues Morte, which is on French soil, and landed there, and, following the course of the Rhône, arrived at Villeneuve, on the opposite bank of the river to Avignon. Arrived here, all they had to do was to cross the celebrated Bridge of St. Bénézet at Avignon. Louis, however, thought it more prudent to remain at Villeneuve until he knew what kind of a reception he would meet with at the Papal court, while Acciajuoli and his brother, the Bishop of Florence, who had joined them at Valdepeso, went to see Clement VI. and consult with him as to what was to be done to reinstate Joanna on her throne.

# CHAPTER X

## Joanna Pleads before the Pope and Cardinals

THE city of Avignon has many claims to celebrity. The fact that it was the chosen place of residence of the seven French Popes, from 1309 to 1378, would in itself be sufficient to invest it with an interest second only to Rome itself, but it has other claims to fame. It was, as we have already said, the home of Petrarch's Laura, and in one of its churches he first met her. Its streets and gardens were traversed by the poet and his beloved lady, and in another of its churches is her tomb. During the residence of the Popes it was visited by most of the various European sovereigns, by their ambassadors, and, especially during the reign of Clement VI., it was resorted to by the most learned men in Europe.

In the seventeenth century the celebrated Crillon died there and was buried there. He was one of the most renowned soldiers of the sixteenth century, and distinguished himself during the reigns of five French kings, and was the first officer to receive the title of Colonel-General of the French infantry. Henry IV. of France always spoke of him as "le brave Crillon," and after the battle of Arques wrote on the battlefield this pregnant dispatch to him:

"Hang thyself, brave Crillon. We have fought at Arques and thou wast not there."

Another very celebrated man was a native of Avignon, the Chevalier Folard, who was born there in 1669, and died there in 1752. He was one of the greatest tacticians the world has seen. He took part in all the wars at the end of the reign of Louis XIV., and supplied the generals under whom he served with plans of defence; he wrote several works on war-tactics and defence, all of course now hopelessly obsolete, but most valuable at the time they were published.

At the close of his life he joined a Jansenist sect of fanatics known in France as the "Convulsionnaires," whose vagaries gave rise to a celebrated witty couplet. They used to visit the tomb of the deacon François de Paris, one of their members, who had died in the odour of sanctity, and there they fell into all sorts of convulsions, and pretended that miracles took place in this churchyard of St. Médard. At last they became such a nuisance that the authorities were obliged to order the cemetery to be closed. Whereupon some wag wrote upon the gate:

> "De par le Roi défense à Dieu,
> De faire miracle en ce lieu."

Another of these sects which sprang up some years later, about 1373, was the Dancers; they were the offspring of the Flagellants, and originated in Aix-la-Chapelle. They spread throughout Liége, Hainault, and Flanders. These fanatics fell suddenly into fits of dancing. Men and women joined hands, and danced violently till they were almost suffocated, when they fell to the ground and then said they were favoured with visions. The priests declared they were possessed, and exorcised them.[1]

In the year 1226 the town of Avignon was nearly destroyed by order of the Papal legate, sent there to oppose the Count of Toulouse, who had favoured the cause of the Albigeois, and at the time of Joanna's visit it had not recovered from the punishment inflicted upon it, so that like Rome it presented a striking mixture of great luxury side by side with the direst poverty. Among the low, ill-built houses of the natives stood the magnificent palaces of the Cardinals, and perched upon a grand rock above the glorious river Rhône was the fortress-like but most splendid of all these mansions, the majestic palace of the Popes, which still survives, though now used as a prison.

[1] Mosheim, vol. i.

Petrarch, who was most indignant at the luxury of the Papal Court, thus comments upon these buildings. "What a shame to see these people raising magnificent palaces, resplendent with gold and superb towers which threaten the skies in this new Babylon, whilst the capital of the world lies in ruins!"

The poet as an Italian could not tolerate with patience the removal of the Holy See from Rome to Avignon, and with his usual exaggerated but picturesque language he inveighs against it.

In one of his letters called the "Mysteries" he thus describes the licentiousness of Avignon: "All that they say of Assyrian and Egyptian Babylon, of the four Labyrinths, of the Avernean and Tartarean Lakes is nothing in comparison with this hell. We have here a Nimrod powerful on the earth, and a mighty hunter before the Lord, who attempts to scale heaven with raising his superb towers. A Semiramis with her quiver, a Cambyses more extravagant than the Cambyses of old. All that is vile and execrable is assembled in this place. There is no clue to lead you out of this labyrinth, neither that of Dedalus nor Ariadne; the only means of escaping is by the influence of gold.

"In this place reign the successors of poor fishermen, who have forgotten their origin. They march covered with gold and purple, proud of the spoils of princes and of the people. Instead of those little boats in which they gained their living on the Lake of Gennesareth, they inhabit superb palaces. To the most simple repasts have succeeded the most sumptuous feasts; and where the apostles went on foot covered only with sandals are now seen insolent satraps mounted on horses ornamented with gold, and champing golden bits. Poor old fishermen! For whom have you laboured? O times! O manners!"

It was under the pontificate of Clement VI., to whom he alluded as " Nimrod," that Petrarch wrote this, and that the luxury and licentiousness of Avignon reached their highest point; for Clement VI. was a man of most gentle temper, very easily led, most generous, and very fond, it must be confessed, of luxury. He liked the society of ladies, and they were admitted to his palace and formed a court there, at the head of which was Cicely, Duchess of Turenne—Petrarch's "Semiramis with her quiver." She married the son of Alphonsus IV., King of Aragon, and became Duchess of Turenne in her own right by the death of her brother, the Viscount, in 1340.

This woman was excessively proud and imperious, and very cunning also, and managed to obtain a very strong influence over the Pope, and amassed great riches from all hands. She was the special object of Petrarch's hatred. She lived in the greatest splendour, and completely dominated the Court of Avignon, and disposed of a great deal of the patronage attached to the Papal Court by virtue of her friendship with Clement, who allowed himself to be influenced by her; but there is not the slightest ground for the suggestions of some unscrupulous writers, who have calumniated the Holy Father by suggesting there was more than friendship existing between them.

The scenery round Avignon is most varied; the deep blue waters of the Rhône rush past the lordly palaces, and receive the Durance, which winds about on the other side of the city. Just below it wide avenues of elms surround the town. The land is very rich: vines crown the hills, olive-trees cover the meadows, while islands in the great river, magnificent trees, and rich fields all combine to make a fairylike prospect.

The walls round the city were built in 1358, but they are more ornamental than suitable for purposes of defence, and are flanked with square towers. The mystic number seven regulated everything in Avignon: there were seven gates in these walls, seven churches, seven monasteries, seven nunneries, seven colleges, seven parishes, seven hospitals, and seven Popes lived there in succession—though this last was by accident or coincidence, not by design. We must not forget to mention the celebrated Bridge of St Bénézet[1] which spans the Rhône at Avignon, on the opposite side of which stands the town of Villeneuve, where on their arrival Louis of Taranto remained, while Nicholas Acciajuoli and his brother, the Bishop of Florence, went to Avignon to obtain an audience of the Pope. Clement is said to have received them with his usual courtesy and affability, and no doubt entertained them at one of his regal banquets, for he was famed for the delicacy of his table as well as for the sumptuousness of his furniture and table appointments.

His first step upon hearing their errand, and learning of the imprisonment of Joanna, was to send for the Duke of Normandy and prevail upon him to leave Provence, and return immediately to his own dominions, to show the Provençals that Joanna was not about to sell Provence to him ; this quieted their fears, and paved the way for Joanna's release.

There was living at Avignon at this time a relation of Joanna's, namely, the Duc de Berri, who on hearing of her captivity also exerted himself to obtain her release, working most zealously on her behalf. He went round to all the principal

---

[1] St. Bénézet was originally a shepherd living in the second half of the twelfth century. He built this bridge, and was the founder of an order called "les Frères Pontifes," or the Makers of Bridges; he was also the patron saint of engineers, and of the city of Avignon. He died in 1184.

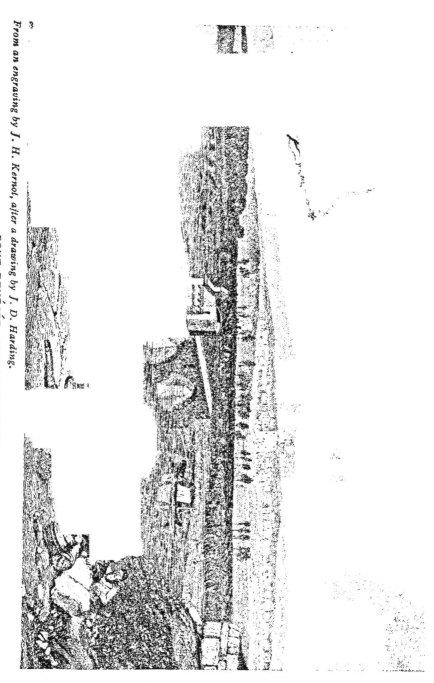

From an engraving by J. H. Kernot, after a drawing by J. D. Harding.
PONT BENEZÉT, AND VILLENEUVE
From Avignon.

nobles in turn, and assured them on his word as a prince that there was no truth in the report spread by the Hungarians, that Joanna was about to sell her Provençal dominions.

These measures prevailed. The Barons, at last convinced that they had been deceived by the malice of the Hungarian emissaries of Louis of Hungary, went to Aix and assured the captive Queen of their fidelity, removed all the restrictions under which she had been placed, and renewed their oaths of allegiance to her. Joanna then selected a new court from the nobles of Provence, and prepared to leave Aix for Avignon to plead there her cause before the Pope. She knew no rest until this object had been fulfilled and her character cleared in the eyes of all Christendom from the odious charges brought against her.

Her captivity had lasted nearly two months: she was taken prisoner on January 20th, and on the 15th of the following March she made her triumphant and most magnificent entry into Avignon, the streets of which were hung with silk and cloth-of-gold and of silver, and decorated with garlands of flowers for the occasion. The balconies of the splendid palaces and houses of the rich were filled with ladies dressed in ceremonial robes of such costliness that they were handed down from generation to generation.

Here we may mention a sumptuary law in existence in Provence and France at this time, by which it was prohibited to all women below a certain fixed rank to wear silk, gold, furs, pearls, or other precious jewels, and in the thirteenth and fourteenth centuries not even the relations of Popes, or the wives and daughters of marshals and barons were exempt from it. These laws were made to repress the luxury and extravagance of the age, especially among the lower classes primarily : but they afterwards, in England and Scotland, became protective in character. Edward III. in 1336 passed a most arbitrary sumptuary law in England, limiting the number of courses his subjects might take at one meal ; but this law was never enforced from the very beginning, and yet it remained on the Statute Book until 1856.

Laura's nobility is said to be proved, if proof were needed, by the fact that she possessed some silk gloves embroidered in gold—one of which she once dropped and Petrarch picked it up, but was not permitted to retain it even for a minute. Unless Laura had been of the requisite high rank, she would not have been allowed to possess these gloves, nor to have worn the other magnificent clothing for which she was famed.

Of course the Queen of the Two Sicilies and Countess of Provence was exempt from all sumptuary laws, and entered Avignon with all the pomp and insignia of royalty. It must be confessed that

## Joanna Pleads before the Pope

Joanna was very fond of purple and fine clothing; and if it be considered a fault in a woman of her exalted rank to be clad in magnificent robes on grand State occasions, then Joanna was guilty of that fault, of which much has been made by her adverse critics.

She entered Avignon, seated on a milk-white palfrey caparisoned with purple and gold, wearing a robe of crimson velvet, and over it a mantle of purple velvet, embroidered all over with the *fleur-de-lis* in gold thread, and bordered with the regal ermine; on her shoulders glittered the crosses of the kingdom of Jerusalem—one of her titles being, it will be remembered, Empress of Jerusalem—and in her hands she bore her orb and sceptre. Over her head was carried the canopy of State, ornamented with gold fringes, and its four gilt poles borne in turns by the highest noblemen in her kingdom. These canopy-bearers wore coronets upon their heads and splendid attire.

The Queen, who was the admiration of all beholders, her beauty calling forth shouts of delight, was accompanied by her husband, Louis of Taranto, who must have felt intensely proud of his young wife and sovereign, and also by Nicholas Acciajuoli and his brother the Bishop of Florence, and by a large escort of her Ultramontane knights, with their ladies all dressed in great splendour. Some of these ladies were carried in litters; others sat on side-saddles made in the shape of a chair, which could not have had a very equestrian appearance. Joanna was an excellent horsewoman, and may have dispensed with this arrangement; her palfrey was led by two knights of princely birth.

As the procession passed along the narrow crooked streets it was delayed by the most cosmopolitan of crowds which thronged the city, attracted thither from all parts of Christendom by the presence of the Pope, and it is not likely that in those days crowds were regulated as they are in twentieth-century London.

The convent of the Ursulines had long been the usual place of residence of the sovereigns of Naples when they visited Avignon, and here they stopped for the Queen to alight to take the customary refreshment of wine and confectionery, and also to give the Cardinals time to meet in the Consistory Court at the Papal palace, before which she was now about to appear and plead her cause.

This court was held in one of the magnificently proportioned halls in the Pope's palace. It was arranged with a throne of crimson and gold for the Pope, raised above all the other seats, at one end, and round this, arranged in a semicircle, were seated the Cardinals, on a lower level; they were all vested in their robes of scarlet silk, with their gold crosses upon their breasts and their jewelled episcopal rings on their right| hands. The Pope is said by one author, from whom we are now quoting, to have worn the triple tiara. This is a mistake. The Papal tiara at this time was only a double crown; the third crown was not added until the pontificate of Urban V

The same writer says Clement was attired in dazzling white robes of silver tissue. This may have been the case; but white was not adopted by the Popes as the colour of their robes until the time of the Dominican Pope St. Pius V., who introduced it because it was then the custom for a Pope to wear robes of the same colour as his habit if he had been a member of a religious order before his election, and Pius V. was a Dominican, whose habit is white. Clement VI. was not a member of any religious order, so he was at liberty to wear what coloured robes he chose. He was of high rank, belonging to the ancient family of Roger, and loved refinement and splendour, and is described as having more of the chivalry of the knight than the austerity of the priest about him. He was very fond of hunting, and his stud was celebrated all over Europe, while his stables were most luxurious.

Popes at that time wore white linen slippers, with a cross embroidered in gold upon them, which it has ever, until the present pontificate, been the custom of the faithful to kiss on being presented to the Pope. In mediæval days the cross was often used in dress to procure marks of homage, which would have been denied without it.

A story is told of one of the Doges of Venice in this connection. In 1363 the father of the reigning Doge chose to go bareheaded rather than uncover his head to his son, whereupon the Doge had a cross placed in front of his hat, and his father then took to his headgear again, and when he met his son took it off saying, " It is not him I salute, but the cross."

The same idea, only more forcibly expressed, is present in an anecdote relating to the late Tsar of Russia. It is the custom on Easter Day in Russia for all the congregation to kiss the hand of the priest on leaving the church after Mass. On one occasion the Tsar was staying at one of his country palaces at Easter, and went to Mass in a small village church. The priest, who was a peasant, was terrified when the Tsar was about to kiss his hand as he left the church, and drew back, saying he was unworthy of such an honour. The Tsar gave him a most scathing rebuke, saying, as he insisted upon obeying the ritual of his Church, " It is not you I kiss, but Jesus Christ."

Joanna was led into this consistory between two cardinals, and followed by a crowd of friends and vassals, all anxious to hear the verdict of the Papal Court upon their Queen.

CLEMENT THE SIXTH.

## Joanna Pleads before the Pope

As the Queen in her splendid robes entered the doors of the Consistory Hall she knelt for the first time, then in the middle of it she genuflected a second time on both knees, and finally, when she reached the foot of the throne covered with crimson and gold, upon which the Pope sat, she knelt the third time, and stooping her head kissed his foot and then his hand—a privilege granted to her on account of her high rank. The Pope raised her and kissed her on the lips, and after a few words had passed between them he placed her on a seat prepared for her on his right, rather lower than his own, with a crimson and gold cushion for her feet.

The hall in which the Consistory was held was filled from end to end with prelates of high rank, princes, nobles, and ambassadors from every court in Europe.

Conspicuous among them were two ambassadors from Louis of Hungary, who had only just arrived at Avignon from Naples to represent their King, to accuse Joanna of the murder of Andrew, to justify and defend the invasion by Louis of her kingdom, and to demand not only the throne but the life of Queen Joanna, the cynosure of all eyes as she sat there in all the pride of her youth and beauty.

The Hungarians felt confident of winning their cause, for their King was on very good terms with Clement VI., and it was believed that the Pope would favour Hungary, for there were reports that he had a personal dislike of the Queen concerning whom such sinister reports had reached him. The fact that Joanna was an exile, driven out of her country by the avenger of her murdered first husband, might also militate against her, though on the other hand it might evoke pity for her tragic fate.

Immediately following upon Joanna was her second husband, Louis of Taranto, who likewise made his obeisance to the Pope, and was allowed the privilege of kissing Clement's hand and lips because of his rank as the consort of the Queen; then Nicholas Acciajuoli and a few of the most distinguished barons in her suite were duly presented to the Holy Father, while she sat by his side meditating upon what she would say to defend herself. Not only her throne, but her life also depended upon the verdict of the Consistory. She well knew the power the Pope had over her crown and her person; she knew it was popularly believed that he had been prejudiced against her, and was on very friendly terms with her arch-enemy, that he had been shocked and horrified at the murder of Andrew, and probably believed some of the tales that were afloat about her.

She must have trembled as she waited till these presentations were over, when she rose and, leaving her seat, began to address the Pope and Cardinals sitting in judgment upon her. Fortunately for

Joanna, eloquence was one of her gifts; still more fortunate perhaps, that greatest of all feminine gifts was hers in abundance—beauty; most fortunate of all, her judges were men, to whom her youth, beauty, and terrible misfortunes would appeal strongly. We can well imagine that every eye was turned upon her, from the Pope's to the youngest knight's in the hall.

We read that "her figure was tall and nobly formed, her air composed and majestic, her carriage altogether royal, her features of exquisite beauty, and, with a character of grandeur, had a certain air of natural goodness that softened their expression and won the love whilst she commanded the respect of those who beheld her."

What would the verdict be?

# CHAPTER XI

## Joanna's Acquittal and its Results

LATIN is the language of the Consistory Court of Rome, and, as no mention is made of any interpreter, we may safely conclude that Joanna pleaded her cause in that tongue, which she wrote with ease; for as her audience was so cosmopolitan and the effect of her eloquence was so immediate, she must have spoken a language understood by all or most of her hearers. Had she addressed them in either the Provençal or Italian language, both of which she spoke with great fluency, only part of her hearers would have understood. On one occasion when Sancho, Prince of Castile, who had to have an interpreter, was present at a Roman Consistory he heard loud applause, and asked his interpreter what was the meaning of it.

"They have just proclaimed your Highness King of Egypt," said the interpreter.

"Indeed! Well, it does not become us to be

wanting in gratitude; rise up and proclaim his Holiness Caliph of Bagdad," said the Prince.

Joanna's defence of herself is said to have been the most masterly piece of feminine oratory ever heard. She first of all stated the points in her defence so logically, clearly, forcibly, and briefly, that long before she had finished speaking her judges were convinced of her innocence She then went on to express the greatest horror of the foul murder of Andrew, and deplored his sad fate, cut off in the very flower of his youth, with deep pathos, and then spoke of her own great grief and horror at his untimely end, weeping so touchingly that her fierce accusers, the Hungarian ambassadors, were confounded, and attempted no reply when the Queen had finished speaking. But before she concluded she defended herself for the delay in bringing the guilty to judgment, of which she had been accused, and impressed upon her audience that no tortures had been able to force one of the conspirators to accuse her of having had any part in the plot against Andrew.

The result of her eloquence was that the court declared her not only innocent, but above the suspicion of guilt. The most ample acquittal which she and her subjects could demand to reinstate her in the good opinion of all men was unanimously pronounced, and a decree passed confirming this verdict. The Pope then publicly absolved her, for hers was a case reserved to the Holy See; and as Joanna was a devout Catholic, she had earnestly desired this grace to wash away all traces of any sin her soul might have incurred during the terrible trials she had been passing through, and she now left the Consistory Hall at peace with God and with man.

When, with the tears of joy upon her face, she rose from her knees at the Pope's feet after receiving absolution, he conducted her through the Hall of Consistory and the ante-chamber, which was as far as etiquette permitted him to go, and then parted with her, and Louis of Taranto led his innocent wife and Queen to the apartments prepared for her in the Ursuline Convent. Clement VI. was prevented by another rule of etiquette from visiting her there more than once, but he duly paid this visit; and so long as she remained in Avignon his palace was open to her and her husband, upon both of whom he bestowed every mark of honour.

Among the favours Joanna received from the hands of the Sovereign Pontiff during her residence in Avignon was the Golden Rose, which Clement had intended giving to the King of Majorca, then in Avignon. This Rose is an ornament made of gold in the shape of a rose, which is blessed by the Pope on the fourth Sunday in Lent, and then bestowed by him upon some sovereign or monastery.

## Joanna's Acquittal and its Results

It was not an annual custom until the reign of St. Urban V., who came to the throne in 1363, and it is now generally given to a sovereign. It was a rarer favour in Joanna's day, and very highly valued. It was bestowed upon her on March 27th, and that same day the Queen and Louis of Taranto were led in procession all round the walls of the city of Avignon, as Count and Countess of Provence, and afterwards received the homage of the Provençal barons assembled for that purpose.

The allegiance of this proud race was not lightly given nor lightly valued; but as they had always been faithful to the Angevine line, so were they always tenderly attached and absolutely loyal to Joanna, whom they loved to call "la bonne Reine Jeanne."

Joanna would have had a far happier life if she could have remained in Provence where she was loved and revered by her subjects, instead of having to return to Naples where so many misfortunes awaited her, but during her visit to Avignon the city was visited by one of the most terrible calamities that ever befell suffering humanity. The festivities at the Papal Court were all suspended by the Great Plague, which, having already swept away millions in other parts of Europe, now broke out in Provence.

It was during this visitation that Clement VI. showed his charity and wisdom in so marked a manner, thus rendering the fell disease less disastrous in its consequences at Avignon than it was in other places. To prevent the spread of the infection, he established a special body of police; he bought a field outside the city as a burial-ground for the dead, and spent large sums of money on the transport thither of the infected corpses, besides paying doctors to attend the poor and providing winding-sheets for them. Avignon was at the time the plague broke out full of visitors, many having come from the country to pay homage to Joanna, which may perhaps account for the enormous numbers—which were estimated in Avignon at one hundred and twenty thousand—who are said to have perished of this terrible scourge.

The disease was at its height during Lent, and during the three last days of Holy Week fourteen hundred people are said to have died of it in the city. The fact that it was worst during those days when the Lenten fast was most strict shows that to live well was one of the best means of warding off an attack; but at that time the Lenten fast was very much stricter than it is now, and dispensations not so easily granted. The greatest number of victims were among the women and children of the poorest classes.

The rich, however, were by no means exempt, and one of the Avignon victims was Laura, the beloved of Petrarch, who died on April 6th after three days' illness. She had a presentiment that she

## Joanna's Acquittal and its Results 163

would not live beyond three days after the fever set in, so she made her will and sent for a priest and received the Last Sacraments, and died with great resignation, surrounded by friends and relations, whom not even the fear of the plague could keep away from one they so loved and admired. She died about six o'clock in the morning of April 6th, and was buried that same day after vespers, in the chapel attached to the monastery of the Franciscan Friars Minor.

Petrarch, who was still madly in love with her, was at Verona at the time of her death, anxiously expecting news of her; but the plague had stopped all communication with Avignon, as the couriers who carried the letters could not pass. He did not get the news of her death until May 9th, when he was at Parma, and his grief, as may be imagined, was intense. He passed several days without eating or drinking, rendering himself, we should think, exceedingly liable to an attack of the dread disease.

He said of himself that "he dared not think of his condition, much less could he speak of it, and that the loss convinced him that there was no longer anything worth living for; and since the strongest cord of his life was now broken, he should renounce the world, where his cares had been deceitful and his hopes vain and perishing."

Before Petrarch had ceased to weep for Laura his friend Cardinal Colonna also died of the plague at

Avignon, where his loss was greatly felt; for his court was a brilliant one, attended by literary men and men of genius from all parts of Europe. But the Italians who visited him could not bear Provence after their Mæcenas, as they called him, was dead, and most of them left the city of Avignon and returned to Italy.

Villani, the historian, was another victim to this terrible pestilence, which had been predicted by astrologers. But he left an account of the beginning of it, and among other things he tells us that the mortality was greater in Pistoja and Prato than in Florence, and greater in Bologna and Avignon and Provence and the whole kingdom of France, but greatest in those countries beyond the sea among the Tartars.

The Mendicant Friars came out splendidly during this calamity. They attended the plague-stricken, and administered to their spiritual needs, when other priests neglected, and feared to go near them; they preached, heard the confessions of the dying, and buried the dead. But the fact that many of the dead had left their estates to them out of gratitude roused the jealousy of the secular clergy, who petitioned Clement VI. to suppress them. This petition was presented to the Pope in the same Consistory Court before which Joanna had pleaded, and was supported by some cardinals and bishops. The Pope refused to grant their request, and rebuked

From an engraving by J. D. Harding, after a drawing by J. T. Willmore.

AVIGNON.
The Pope's Palace in the distance.

# Joanna's Acquittal and its Results

them in the following strong terms for their envious conduct

"The Mendicants have exposed their lives by attending dying persons, and administering the sacraments to them, whilst you, consulting your own safety, fled from the danger and abandoned your flocks. You have therefore no reason to complain of what they have got, as they have got it by performing the duty which you have neglected, though incumbent upon you. They employ the little they have gained in building or repairing their churches, but you would perhaps have applied it to very different uses. They preach nothing but what they show by their example to be practicable, whereas many among you preach one thing and practise the contrary."

The credulity of the age led to a persecution of the Jews, who were accused of having caused the plague by poisoning the fountains. But Clement VI. with his usual clemency defended them in two Bulls which he published, forbidding them to be forcibly baptised, under the severest penalties, as such was the alternative given to the Hebrews if they wished to escape death.

Another outcome of the fear and panic which the plague roused was the revival of the fanatics known as the Flagellants, who first appeared in the eleventh century, and during the feuds of the Guelphs and Ghibellines they spread throughout

France, Bohemia, Austria, Italy, Russia, Poland, and Hungary, but they did not appear in England until this second outburst of their fanaticism in 1348.

They were penitents who went in procession through the various towns and cities to which they penetrated, naked to the waist, and armed with scourges, with which they lashed themselves until the blood flowed, and marked their progress on the ground. Clement suppressed them in the following year, but they have frequently made their appearance since.

It is computed that 100,000 victims perished of the plague in Venice, 60,000 in Florence, 1,200,000 in Germany, and it is said that more than 200,000 villages and small towns were left without any inhabitants. While of the good Friars who worked so nobly to help the sick and dying, no less than 124,434 died of this terrible disease.

The cardinals and rich barons at Avignon shut themselves up in their palaces, and burnt huge fires to keep away the infection; and Clement VI., who refused to go away from Avignon while it was raging, also took this precaution of burning large fires and remaining indoors.

The Great Pestilence, or the Black Death as it was also called, did not appear in England until August of this fatal year, 1348, and before it was exterminated it carried off 5,000,000 victims during the year it lasted.

Boccaccio, who had left Naples when the King of Hungary invaded it, went to Florence and there wrote his description of the ravages of this ghastly scourge, which first of all began in the Far East. He tells us that in his native city "no human wisdom, no precautions, availed to avert the calamity. In vain by the orders of the magistrates were the streets cleared of every impurity; in vain were the gates of the city closed against all infected persons, and the counsels of the most prudent put in practice for the preservation of health. And equally unavailing were the humble supplications, not once but often made to God by devout persons, in solemn processions and other forms."

His account is much too long to quote in full, but he describes some of the attendant horrors with great pathos, as when he says that in the panic " brother abandoned brother, the uncle his nephew, the sister her brother, the wife her husband, and, what is more surprising still and scarcely credible, fathers and mothers deserted their children as if they were children (*sic*) and feared to visit or serve them." Another horror he mentions was the sick being thus deserted by neighbours, by friends, by relatives, so that no woman, however delicate or beautiful or noble, made any scruple to be served by a man, let him be who he might, old or young, from which cause many who survived lost much of the modesty of their manners.

The plague had one good effect as far as Joanna was concerned: it frightened Louis of Hungary out of Naples, although it was not so bad there as in other parts of Italy, or as at Avignon and Provence. He, however, thought it better to remove the great body of his men to Apulia, to avoid the infection in Naples, where its ravages were sufficiently serious. His retreat paved the way for Joanna's return, and about this time the news of her acquittal by the Roman Consistory reached Naples, and a revulsion of feeling towards their exiled Queen set in amongst the Neapolitans.

With the exception of a few important men, who had gone too far in encouraging the Hungarians to hope for forgiveness from Joanna, all classes now united in earnestly desiring her return and restoration to the throne of her grandfather. The nobility, who hated the haughty Hungarians and their insupportable yoke, resolved to throw it off; but knowing this would be impossible without the help and support of their Queen, they sent secret messengers to Avignon, begging her to return and take up the reins of government again, and promising if she would supply them with a few men and some money they would fight for her and do all in their power to reinstate her in her kingdom.

At first Joanna was not inclined to agree to this proposal, knowing that it would be no easy task to

## Joanna's Acquittal and its Results 169

get rid of the Hungarians; but she laid the letters brought by the Neapolitan ambassadors before the Pope and the Cardinals, who were only more certain of her innocence when they read them than they had been before. They counselled her to grant the petition of her subjects as quickly as possible, and Clement, anxious if possible to prevent more bloodshed, tried to restore her to her throne by diplomatic measures. To which end he sent an apostolic legate to Louis, Cardinal Guy of Boulogne, who was a relation of the Queen of Hungary, and was remarkable for his gentle manners and persuasive powers of speech, by which the Pope hoped the King of Hungary might be persuaded to retire and leave the throne to Joanna.

While the Cardinal was treating with Louis of Hungary in Naples, Joanna's staunch friend Nicholas Acciajuoli was engaged in trying to raise men and money in order to wrest the kingdom from the invader by force, if diplomacy failed to accomplish the reinstatement of Joanna. The States of Provence and Piedmont vied with each other in contributing to the expedition, but their combined efforts fell far short of the required sum, and the Queen was reduced not only to selling her famous diamonds, but all her other jewels, and finally to offering the city of Avignon with the surrounding country to the Pope.

Louis of Hungary, feeling sure that possession was nine points of law, refused to listen to any of the proposals of the Cardinal of Boulogne for a peaceful settlement, so there was nothing for it, if Joanna was to recover her kingdom, but to resort to arms.

The sum the Queen asked for Avignon was 80,000 golden florins. A gold florin was at that time worth about a fifth of an ounce of gold, so that the price for which she sold it was equal to about 60,000 pounds sterling of our money. The Pope immediately paid this sum, which was used to defray the cost of ten galleys fully equipped, and armed with the men Acciajuoli had enlisted to relieve Naples from the Hungarian yoke.

It is said that the Queen had succeeded in winning the friendship of Clement so completely that he would now do anything for her, and willingly agreed to pay the sum she demanded for Avignon. He knew that Joanna earnestly desired the coronation of her husband, Louis of Taranto, as King of Naples, and that she wished for this almost as much as she wished for the restoration of her kingdom; and when he gave her and Louis his parting blessing he bestowed the coveted title upon him.

In consequence of this sale the Emperor Charles IV. yielded to the Pope all the rights which he possessed over the town of Avignon, in the month of November, 1348, at Gorpiet. The Latin contract, still in existence, states among other things that Joanna sold Avignon with the consent of her husband, Louis of Taranto. By this sale she sacrificed the lesser possessions of Avignon to regain the throne of the Two Sicilies. The contract of sale was signed on June 19th, 1348, in the house at which Joanna was residing in Avignon at the time.

Joanna remained about three weeks longer in the plague-stricken city of Avignon after the signing of the contract for its sale, and then, all their preparations being complete, she and Louis went to Marseilles and embarked there for Naples, full of hope and elated with the knowledge that at any rate the campaign would not be crippled for want of means.

They were returning under very different circumstances from those under which they had left Naples. Then Joanna was suspected and openly accused of the murder of her first husband; now she was returning with her character not only cleared, but with the assurance of the Pope and Cardinals that she was above suspicion, and was now under the special favour and protection of the Holy See—a valued friend of Clement VI., the idol of the gallant Provençal barons. Moreover, she was going back at the earnest invitation of her Neapolitan subjects, who were now only too ready to lay down their lives, if need be, to restore her to her throne.

## CHAPTER XII

## Peace is Proclaimed

ALL the Neapolitan castles were occupied by the Hungarians, so it was not possible for Joanna to land in the harbour. Accordingly, when her galleys reached Naples, they stopped short at the little river of Sebeto, on the Vesuvian side of the city, by the Ponte della Maddalena, to which the inhabitants flocked in crowds to welcome them with every demonstration of joy, so that the whole of that part of the city rang with the shouts with which the people acclaimed their returning Queen.

Foremost among the barons who hastened to offer their congratulations and allegiance were the Count of Minervino and his brothers, who had originally been on the Hungarian side, and now hurried to proffer all the help they could to expel the enemy.

One of the former enemies of Joanna did not return to his allegiance. This was Francis de Baux,

## Peace is Proclaimed

Count of Montecagiuso, a nephew of the late King Robert, whose mother Beatrice was a nun, but was taken out of her convent to marry Francis's father, Bertrand de Baux. This was sometimes allowed in the Middle Ages, from reasons of State or policy, when a dispensation was obtained from the religious vows to enable the person to marry.

During the absence of Louis of Taranto this Francis de Baux had married one of Louis's sisters, without first getting his or Joanna's consent. The poor young Princess of Taranto had found herself alone and unprotected in Naples on the day when the Hungarians had pillaged and destroyed the palaces of the Neapolitan royal family, on that occasion when Joanna's sister Maria had fled in disguise. Francis de Baux had taken pity on the Princess, who was his cousin; and she, knowing her brothers were, with the exception of Louis, all in captivity, consented to marry Francis without waiting to obtain the sanction of her family. The young couple, not knowing what kind of reception they might meet with from Joanna and Louis, were afraid to appear before them; but the Queen, well aware that the de Baux were some of the richest and most powerful of her subjects, with her usual prudence and tact resolved to conciliate them and overlook the breach of royal etiquette of which they had been guilty.

Accordingly she sent the Count letters-patent

conferring upon him the Dukedom of Andria, an honour which none but a prince of the royal line had hitherto enjoyed. Upon receiving this signal mark of royal favour, de Baux and his bride went to court and throwing themselves at Joanna's feet, he vowed allegiance and devotion to her cause, and from that time became one of her most zealous supporters.

Nicholas Acciajuoli was now made Grand Seneschal of the kingdom, in reward for all his services in Provence, for to some extent Joanna owed the successful issue of her cause in the Papal Court to his exertions and those of his brother the Bishop of Florence. Joanna also rewarded with presents of land and money, and with various honours and privileges, all those who had been faithful to her, and all the young knights who had fought for her. Joanna's cause had been recommended to all the knights of Europe, by the Papal Court, as one which in those days of chivalry they were peculiarly bound to defend, and they were not slow to become the champions of the beautiful young Queen. As soon as Joanna returned to Naples she gave a series of entertainments to signalise her return, and these festivities and rejoicings greatly increased her popularity, and made her court a striking contrast to that of the barbarian Hungarian invader, whose courtiers treated the Neapolitans with haughty disdain, which they naturally resented deeply.

Louis of Taranto was of great help to Joanna in winning popularity, for he was said to be " as beautiful as the day," being gifted, like his royal spouse, with extraordinary personal beauty; he also possessed the charming manners for which all the Angevine family were famed. He was a fine soldier, and highly distinguished in all the accomplishments of a mediæval knight, such as jousts, tournaments, and field-sports. In fact, he had all the qualities calculated to win the hearts of the pleasure-loving Neapolitans, but he did not possess the more solid virtues of a faithful husband, at any rate in his later years.

Joanna is greatly blamed by her enemies for the gaiety of her court, the lavish entertainments in which she indulged, the luxury of her table, the brilliancy of her attire, and the constant round of balls, banquets, pageants, tournaments, and other festivities on which she spent so much money; but she was eminently a wise woman, and probably she knew that this was the best way to retain her husband's affections, which she succeeded in doing during the first years of her married life. Later, as we shall see, Louis led so wild and profligate a life that he shortened his days by his excesses.

So long as he was engaged in fighting Joanna's battles for her Louis was a good husband. The excitement of war kept him out of mischief, and satisfied his energetic temperament and craving for excitement, without which he could not live even in the fourteenth century. What he would have done in the twentieth century, when the craze for something new possesses old and young, rich and poor, all classes of men and women, we do not know. On first returning to Naples, with the Hungarians still in occupation, Louis had plenty of scope for his martial energy: he at once undertook an expedition against the Count of Apici—a powerful baron who obstinately adhered to the Hungarian cause, but was soon reduced to obedience and heavily fined for his rebellion.

One of the most audacious of the captains of mercenaries, after our own Hawkwood, in these days was a German who went by the name of Duke Warner. This ruffian went about with the following legend embroidered in silver letters on his surcoat: "I am Duke Warner, the Chief of the Great Company, the Enemy of God, of Pity, and of Mercy."

This blasphemous creature, who spread terror wherever he went with his band of pillaging, murdering, merciless adherents, was serving under the Hungarian King's lieutenant, Conrad Wolf, when Louis defeated the Count of Apici. As he had three thousand horsemen under him, it was very important to enlist his services in Joanna's interest if possible, and Louis took the money exacted from the Apici as a fine to buy Warner over to the Queen's side. Louis now gained a succession of small victories. With Warner's help he captured some of the castles and garrisoned towns which were in the Hungarians' hands, but he was not strong enough to risk a great battle, into which Wolf tried to draw him. "Duke Warner" counselled him to avoid this, though the Hungarians passed close to the Neapolitan trenches, taunting and insulting the nobles and endeavouring to induce them to accept their challenges.

Foiled in these tactics, Wolf now encamped himself in Foggia, whose inhabitants he induced, under conditions which he violated immediately, to yield their city to him, hoping that Louis would try to relieve Foggia. Again foiled—for Louis resisted this temptation, and has been severely blamed for so doing—Wolf now advanced upon Naples, and endeavoured to persuade Warner to rejoin him. Warner played into his hand by encamping without sentinels and suffering himself to be taken, and then asked Louis to ransom him and pay thirty thousand florins to the Hungarians. Louis very wisely refused to do anything of the kind, and Warner attached himself to Wolf, who was further reinforced by troops from Hungary and another band of mercenaries commanded by the Count of Lando.

The Neapolitans of all classes now put forth their whole strength to repel their cruel foes. The peasants thronged into Naples armed with reaping hooks, scythes, spades—anything they could lay hands on for want of proper arms — to try to deliver their country from the hated Hungarians. The nobles, including the Count of Minervino, who had originally been on the Hungarian side, now collected all the armed men they could muster, and poured them into the city; but unfortunately Wolf cut off the supplies of provisions from the Terra di Lavoro, so that the city was reduced to what it could obtain by sea from Calabria and other places.

The Neapolitans, impatient at having their rations reduced, and quite against the advice of Louis, who knew they were not strong enough to give battle to the Hungarians, allowed themselves to be tricked into an engagement, in which many perished, for they were surrounded on all sides by the enemy. The mercenaries whom the Hungarians had engaged now became dissatisfied with their wretched payment, and threatened to leave their employers in the lurch, so the Transylvanian General, Prince Stephen, delivered into their hands in the place of money all the prisoners of war whom they had taken. The unfortunate prisoners were subjected to the most horrible tortures by these cruel bands, who were guilty of rapine, murder, and every vice. The prisoners paid large sums of money to ransom themselves; but the mercenaries, when they found they could not extort sufficient to satisfy their greed, resolved to take Stephen himself prisoner and torture him in the hope of getting a larger sum of money. Fortunately the Transylvanian prince was warned of these intentions, and one night managed to effect his escape with some of his officers.

Duke Warner had formerly been employed in the service of the Church, so he was known to the Cardinal Legate Ceccano, as were also other of the German officers; and on his offering them 120,000 florins, they agreed to deliver up the two towns of Aversa and Capua, and to go back to Germany. Louis of Taranto then fortified these two towns very strongly, so that the following year Aversa was able to resist when besieged by the Hungarian King.

Another celebrated character fighting on the side of the Hungarians was Fra Moriale, a knight of Jerusalem, whose real name was Montreal D'Albano. He was a Provençal by birth, and had formerly been in the service of Joanna's brother-in-law, the Duke of Durazzo. He now retired to Apulia with Conrad Wolf, and sent word to Louis of Hungary that the Germans had forsaken him and gone back to their own country.

Fra Moriale's end was a tragic one, though it is rather anticipating events to mention it. After the Hungarians had left Naples, Fra Moriale remained behind; and collecting together a large band of adventurers, he ravaged Italy, finally making war against the Viscontis. He was taken prisoner in Rome, and, being brought before the tribunal of Rienzi, then in power, he was sentenced to death, and beheaded in 1354.

On hearing that the Germans had left Naples, Louis of Hungary soon after entered Apulia with a large force of 10,000 horsemen, besides a number of foot-soldiers. No sooner was Louis of Taranto aware that his enemy was so near, than he sent him a challenge to decide the matter by single combat with him, and gave him the choice of Naples, Avignon, Paris, or Perugia, as the scene of the encounter.

Louis of Hungary agreed to accept the challenge, but objected to all the places named, as being too favourably inclined to his adversary, and suggested that the duel should be fought in the presence of the Bishop of Aquila, or of the Emperor of Germany, or else in that of their common friend, the King of England, or in that of their respective armies, in which latter case there is every reason to suppose the Hungarians would have been guilty of some treachery.

For some reason or other this duel never came off, and soon after the King of Hungary, while besieging the city of Canoza in Apulia, was dangerously wounded and picked up apparently dead before the walls, and carried back to his own camp,

# Peace is Proclaimed

where he recovered and soon after captured Salerno. The citadel of Lucera was given up treacherously to him by the governor, and he then advanced to Aversa, thinking to take that easily.

He was, however, mistaken, and the siege of Aversa lasted three months before Pignatello, the governor, was forced by starvation to capitulate on honourable terms.

It was while the Hungarians were still invading her kingdom that Joanna heard of the death of her little son by Andrew, Canrobert, the heir to her throne, who it will be remembered had been sent to Hungary by Louis of Hungary soon after he first came to Naples. Some few months after Joanna returned to Naples from Avignon she gave birth to a daughter, who was baptized Francesca. The child was idolised by both her parents, and before she was three years old a marriage had been arranged for her with the heir of the kingdom of Aragon.

A year after the birth of the Princess Francesca Joanna gave birth to another daughter, who was named Catherine. She, however, died in infancy, and thenceforth all Joanna's hopes were concentrated upon Francesca, her only son having perished in a foreign land.

After the capitulation of Aversa the Queen and her husband and child, with some faithful friends, went to Gaeta by sea, fearing that Louis of Hungary, now on his way to Naples, might take them prisoners, and hoping in case of necessity to be able to retreat to Provence, in ten galleys which were in waiting for them at Gaeta.

These ten galleys were not considered sufficient, so the High Admiral of the kingdom, Rinaldo de Baux, was ordered to bring eight more from Naples. Once more was Joanna threatened with treason; for while she was waiting at Gaeta for the reinforcements her Admiral was commanded to bring, there arrived one day a messenger who desired a secret audience of the Queen, in the course of which he informed her that de Baux, who was supposed to be laying in provisions before he left Naples, had concluded a bargain with Louis of Hungary by which he pledged himself to deliver Joanna and her husband and the little Princess Francesca, together with Joanna's sister, Maria of Sicily, the Duchess of Durazzo, and her children, into the hands of the King of Hungary. The reward he asked for this act of treachery was the hand of Maria's eldest daughter, the heiress of the principality of Durazzo, for his son.

As soon as the Admiral and his fleet reached Gaeta, Joanna sent a message to him to come at once to the palace to see her. De Baux refused on various pretexts, and even declined to enter the harbour; and as, so long as he remained outside with his fleet, the flight of the Queen to Provence, if it should become necessary was prevented, Louis of Taranto decided upon very summary measures. He took three or four faithful friends with him, and embarking on board a small boat managed to get on board the Admiral's ship before he was aware of his approach; and making his way into the traitor's presence, Louis attacked him and slew him there and then with his sword. It was a bold move, quite in keeping with the rough times and with the character of Louis, and perhaps justified by the circumstances. Indeed, it seemed the quickest way out of the dilemma in which de Baux's treachery had placed the Queen, who was fated so often in the course of her adventurous life to suffer from treason.

While these things were happening at Gaeta Louis of Hungary had entered Naples with his ragged, half-starved army, and had encamped on the spot where now stands the Church of the Incoronata, afterwards built by Joanna.

Naples was then divided into twelve sections called Piazze, and from each of these twelve divisions a proclamation was issued in which Louis of Hungary offered to save the city from destruction on condition of the people contributing a heavy fine, to compensate his soldiers for the plunder they would gain if he allowed them to pillage it.

He called a meeting of the nobility and principal citizens at Castel Nuovo, and made the same proposal to them, and rebuked them for the affection they had shown their Queen and all they had done for her. The sight of the miserable horses and soldiers of the Hungarian army, however, excited the ridicule of the Neapolitans, who collected together from every quarter of the city, and threatened to give battle to their enemies if they attempted the least violence, and absolutely refused to give a penny to buy them off.

Louis, thinking that his enfeebled troops would not have much chance against the Neapolitans, who were determined to strain every nerve to save their beautiful city, thought it prudent to retire to Apulia, and if possible join his forces to those of Conrad Wolf there.

The Pope, hearing of this move, thought a favourable time had arrived for him to try to conclude peace, as both sides were getting exhausted; and, according to one account, he commanded Louis, under pain of excommunication, to leave Naples—or rather Joanna's dominions—at once, and allow Joanna and her husband to take possession of her kingdom.

Louis proposed a truce for a year, and demanded another trial before the Pope and Cardinals of Joanna, promising, if she were declared innocent again, to give up her kingdom to her, and Joanna promised to resign it if she were pronounced guilty.

Of course Joanna was pronounced innocent a second time—no one ever had any misgivings on

## Peace is Proclaimed

that score; and the Pope then drew up a treaty with the Hungarian ambassadors, in which it was stipulated that Louis of Taranto should not bear the title of King, and that if Joanna had no children to survive her, her rights were to pass to Louis of Hungary or his successors, to the exclusion of her sister, the widowed Duchess of Durazzo.

The Hungarians signed this treaty, but when it was put before Joanna she refused absolutely to exclude her husband from the throne, or to sign away her sister's right of succession, or to submit her people to the danger of the hated Hungarian yoke. As Joanna was firm, and it was evident that she would never yield, and would refuse to sign any treaty except one of whose terms she approved, the Pope gave way to her eloquence, and drew up another treaty, in which the title of King was granted to Louis of Taranto, and all the conditions as to the succession contained in the will of the late King Robert were agreed to; the Pope stipulating that Joanna should pay Louis a sum of 300,000 florins for delivering up all the castles and fortresses he had captured in Naples.

At this juncture Louis's haughtiness stood Joanna in good stead, for with the pride of his race he refused to accept the money.

" No ! " he cried : " not for the sake of lands and gold, but only out of revenge of the murder of my brother have I fought. My work is finished.

The angry shadows are reconciled. I desire nothing more."

Would not this conduct be sufficient to prove the innocence of Joanna if more proof were wanting? for if she had been guilty of the murder of Andrew, Louis of Hungary had received no satisfaction for it.

The Pope and the Cardinals were much pleased at this magnanimity on the part of the Hungarian King, and thanked him cordially for it; and Joanna, as soon as the treaty was signed, sent an embassy to Clement to thank him on her part for all the trouble he had taken on her behalf, and at the same time to beg him to issue a Bull for her own coronation and for that of her husband. The Pope granted her request, issued the desired Bull, and sent the Bishop of Bragança to perform the ceremony of coronation on Whit-Sunday, which that year fell on May 25th.

# CHAPTER XIII

## The Coronation of Joanna

ONE of the conditions of the treaty of peace between Joanna and Louis of Hungary was the liberation of all the princes of the blood royal, who had been sent to Hungary after the murder of the Duke of Durazzo, and had been imprisoned now for four years in the castle of Visgrade. Their imprisonment had been for Joanna the soul of good in the evil of the invasion of her kingdom, for if they had been at liberty, their quarrels with each other and their ambition would have weakened her cause by creating divisions in her realm, and it would have been better for Joanna if they had never been liberated, as it turned out, for they were a turbulent set.

Preparations were now made for the coronation, and people began to flock into Naples from all parts of the kingdom to witness what promised to be a magnificent spectacle, for it was well known that Joanna loved pomp and grand functions. But not even Joanna's coronation was allowed to take place peacefully; a serious disturbance took place just before it came off, and a great sorrow befell her immediately after it was over.

One of those mercenary bands which were one of the terrors of the Middle Ages, commanded by a German named Beltram della Molta, waylaid a number of the barons and their wives, who were proceeding to the coronation, near Aversa, and robbed them of the splendid dresses they were about to wear at it, and of all the jewels and other valuables which they had brought with them. This band of robbers was a thousand strong, all mounted men, and the barons were powerless against them; but Louis of Taranto, hearing of the outrage, went in pursuit with five hundred knights, and succeeded in dispersing all the band, except Beltram and twenty of his followers, who alone escaped, for those who were not slain by the swords of Louis and his knights were killed by the peasants.

The coronation took place on the Feast of Pentecost in the chapel of the old Palais de Justice, which was afterwards included in the Church of the Incoronata, which Joanna built in 1352 to commemorate her coronation and her marriage with Louis of Taranto. Pentecost was ever a favourite feast with the Angevine family.

After the High Mass, which was celebrated with

## The Coronation of Joanna

all the grand ritual of the Catholic Church, the beautiful and majestic young Queen and her handsome husband, clad in violet velvet robes (violet being the colour of the Neapolitan royal family), knelt before the Bishop of Bragança to receive the crown from his hands, Louis being crowned as King-consort. The splendid robes of the King and Queen and their courtiers and the handsome vestments of the Bishop and clergy made a magnificent blaze of colour in the chapel on this day, which is said to have been the happiest of Joanna's life, although it was destined to end in sorrow.

After the ceremony was over Joanna and Louis went in procession round the city, to give the populace an opportunity of seeing them: they rode on horseback, with their crowns on their heads, their horses led by two noblemen. Just as they passed the church of San Giorgio Maggiore, after coming through the Porta Nolana, where the hospital of San Giovanni now stands, some ladies threw some flowers from a balcony to greet them. Unfortunately this so startled the King's horse that it reared and broke the bridle-reins held by two barons, and Louis threw himself off its back; he escaped unhurt, but his crown fell from his head and broke in three pieces.

The attendants and bystanders all cried out with the vehemence of their nationality that this was a dreadful sign portending all sorts of evil; but the King only laughed and called for another horse, and, fastening the broken crown together as well as he could, set it on his head again and continued his progress round the city. It was late in the evening when Joanna and her royal consort returned to the Castel Nuovo, to find these unhappy prognostications realised sufficiently to justify the superstition of their subjects, at least in their opinion.

The little Princess had been left in charge of her attendants in the Castel Nuovo, which was that day deserted by every one else, as all had gone to see the coronation and the procession, and during her mother's absence she had been taken ill, probably with convulsions, as she died before Joanna returned, and this was the sad news which greeted her parents when they got home from the grand ceremonies in which they had been engaged. Joanna was now dashed from the happiness she had that day enjoyed in such fulness, and was plunged into the grief which only a mother's heart can know. This was the third child she had lost within a year or two, and it was the idol of her and Louis, on whom all their hopes were fixed. Her little son had recently died in a foreign land, after being taken from her when only a baby, then the infant daughter of Louis had died, and now the little Princess Francesca was cut off.

So far as the child was concerned, it was a

merciful dispensation of Providence, for had she lived she would probably have fallen a victim to some of her mother's enemies in that age of violence, but it is not to be imagined that her mother saw it in that light. Joanna never had another child of her own; she adopted one of her sister Maria's little girls, and later on she adopted Charles of Durazzo as her heir, and nourished a viper in her bosom when she did so.

That same year, not long after peace had been proclaimed, another sorrow met Joanna in the death of her friend Pope Clement VI., who had been a second father to her, in not only pronouncing her innocent of the crime of which her enemies had accused her, but in also restoring her to her throne. The memory of this Pope, who was one of the most profound scholars of the age, and a most mild and benevolent sovereign, has suffered much at the hands of Italian historians, because of his persistence in residing at Avignon instead of at Rome. On the other hand, the French historian de Sade says he was one of the greatest men who ever filled the Chair of Peter, and that if he had some faults, they were atoned for by great virtues and amiable qualities, and that he accomplished a great undertaking in which his predecessors had failed—namely, he deposed the troublesome Louis of Bavaria and elected Charles of Luxembourg in his place. This Louis of Bavaria was the great enemy of the

Pope John XXII., and had presumed to set up an antipope in his place after the Pope had excommunicated him, and the Prince Colonna had the courage to affix the sentence to the walls of the Vatican. By the deposition of this Emperor the great struggle, which had troubled the Church so long, between the Papacy and the Empire was ended.

Petrarch says of Clement VI. that none merited better the name of Clement, which was well deserved by his actions. An example of his clemency is given by his biographers which well illustrates this trait in his character. A person who had grievously offended him once ventured to ask a favour of him; the Pope was tempted to seize the opportunity of revenging himself by refusing to listen to his request, but he resisted the temptation and granted the favour.

He was very eloquent, and spoke with great fluency and dignity. He succeeded in the difficult task of reconciling Joanna and the King of Hungary, and in obtaining a truce between the Kings of France and England, whose wars disturbed his reign. He just failed to reconcile the Greek and Latin Churches, for which he laboured with great wisdom and prudence. His conduct during the Great Plague, when his charity and generosity were so conspicuous, may well atone for faults of worldliness and love of luxury, which made him refuse to transfer the Papal See back to Rome, even at the bidding of the great Swedish saint and mystic, St. Bridget, Princess of Nericia.

Another of Clement's good actions was that he ordered Casimir, King of Poland, who was leading a most immoral life, to send away his mistresses and to be faithful to his wife. The King refused at first to do this, but he afterwards submitted, and performed the penance the Pope imposed upon him. Petrarch never liked Clement, and often satirised him because his luxurious life was so unlike that of the Apostles, so his remark quoted above about his clemency is the more valuable.

Upon the death of Clement, the Cardinals, seeing the need for reform in the Church, and thinking that the new Pope should be a man of austere life, turned their eyes upon a very holy Carthusian monk named John Birel, who was at that time General of his Order, the strictest in the Church. He was a native of Limousin, and was famed for his sanctity of life, and his zeal in preaching repentance, and his courage in exhorting kings and princes with the utmost frankness and severity.

One of the Cardinals, named Talleyrand, an ancestor of the diplomatist, took alarm at the prospect of so strict a successor to Clement, and said to the other Cardinals :

" What are you going to do ? Don't you see that this monk, accustomed to govern anchorites, frequently declined. Nearly the whole of the poetry of Zanobi has been lost; all that remains of his works are some prose translations of the works of Gregory the Great. Not long after his appointment as Apostolical Secretary he died of the plague at Avignon, to which court his post attached him. The Florentines held him in such high estimation that they proposed in 1396 to erect monuments worthy of Dante, Boccaccio, Petrarch, and Zanobi de Strada.

The island of Sicily had revolted from the Angevine rule in the latter part of the thirteenth century, the first outbreak taking place at the Sicilian Vespers, when the French were murdered at Palermo, the signal being the bell for Vespers. The islanders then placed themselves under the government of the Aragonese dynasty; but at the time of Joanna's coronation, the King Frederick being a minor, the Sicilians were governed by a regency, who so oppressed the people that a party arose in rebellion against it, headed by Simon, Count of Chiaramonte, who was in fact, though not in name, the ruler of the whole of the most fertile part of the island. This party, three years after the coronation of Joanna and Louis, appealed to them to send them provisions to ward off an impending famine, and troops to help them to resist their oppressors.

Naples being now prosperous, the Queen sent

them an abundance of provisions, but as the rivalry of the Princes of Taranto and Durazzo constantly led to fighting between them, Joanna could only send them a hundred men-at-arms under Nicholas Acciajuoli, and four hundred horsemen under Raymond de Baux, while Louis remained at home to defend his rights there.

The following year, Naples being quieter, Louis was able to take a small army into Sicily, and there he fought so valiantly that he soon made himself master of nearly all the island, except Catania and its neighbourhood. Frederick, the young King, was in Catania, and for three months the Neapolitans besieged the city under Raymond de Baux, whom both Joanna and Louis loved as a father.

In the meanwhile Joanna, on Christmas Eve, 1356, came across from Naples and made a solemn entry into Messina with Louis. Here they were crowned King and Queen of Sicily, and afterwards received the allegiance of the Messinese and of the chief barons of the island.

Here we will make a brief digression to tell the romantic story of a lady of Messina, who was one of the Illustrious Women of Boccaccio and lived in Joanna's time, though she was many years older than the Queen. Her name was Camiola Turinga, she was very rich and was as good as she was beautiful, and when she was young and unmarried, a young and handsome Prince of Aragon, named

Orlando, excited her compassion. During the reign of his brother Peter, King of Sicily, Orlando had, against his brother's express command, given battle to the Neapolitan fleet, and had lost all his own ships and was taken prisoner and cast into a Neapolitan dungeon in one of their castles, from which Peter refused to ransom him, and, but for the compassion of Camiola, he would probably have been doomed to pass his life in this durance vile. She, wishing to procure his liberty, sent a messenger to his prison in Naples to offer to pay his ransom if, in return, he would promise to marry her on his release.

Orlando, delighted at the prospect of regaining his freedom, willingly signed a contract of marriage, and Camiola paid his ransom; but no sooner was the prince set free than he absolutely refused to marry her, and treated her with scorn and haughty contempt.

Camiola now appealed to the King Peter, who decided that Orlando belonged to Camiola, as by the law of the land he was now her slave, whom she had bought with her money, and a day was fixed for the marriage to take place. Orlando arrived on the day fixed with a splendid, princely retinue, and went to Camiola's house, where he found her dressed as a bride in magnificent attire, and wearing costly jewels; but instead of receiving him with signs of affection, she told him she would scorn to ally herself with a man who had broken his knightly word and disgraced his royal birth and violated the sacred laws of chivalry, and that all that she could do for him was to make him a present of the ransom she had already paid, seeing that all he cared for was money; she would henceforth dedicate herself and her fortune to Heaven and enter a convent.

Orlando pleaded for forgiveness, but she refused to listen or to change her mind, and the prince, who was shunned by all honourable men, his equals, fell into a state of depression and died not long after, friendless and forlorn.

But to return to Messina in 1356. When Joanna arrived at the Castle she found the two sisters of the King of Sicily, the Princesses Bianca and Violante, were imprisoned there : she at once had them liberated and treated them as her own sisters. The King Frederick was very delicate, and in case of his death Bianca was the heiress of Sicily. The Count de Chiramonte asked for her hand in marriage as soon as she was liberated, as a reward for his services; but Joanna and Louis dared not consent to this, in case the young King should die, so they refused their consent, but offered Chiramonte the Duchess of Durazzo instead. This would have been a splendid match for the Count; but he died a few days after the Queen's refusal to his proposal for the Princess Bianca, which he had deeply resented. His family also were so angry at his rejection that they all went back to their allegiance to the house of Aragon, and left Joanna in the lurch.

At the end of three months de Baux was obliged to raise the siege of Catania, as he had not sufficient means to pay the Sicilian troops who had joined him, and after some fighting, in which he was at first victorious, he was eventually defeated and taken prisoner by the Catanians, who were superior in numbers. Acciajuoli escaped by the skin of his teeth, but de Baux was confined in the Castle of Francavilla. The Queen had not sufficient money to ransom her faithful servant, so she sold her jewels and offered the proceeds, which were a large sum of money, for his release. The Regency, however, refused to accept the money, and asked instead that the two Princesses Bianca and Violante, who were very happy with Joanna, should be exchanged for de Baux.

This exchange was agreed to by the Queen, and the two Princesses were set at liberty ; but the governor of the castle in which the High Admiral was confined declined to release him, notwithstanding the orders of the Regency, and demanded an additional ransom of two thousand ducats, which the Queen paid.

Unfortunately, during the absence of the Queen and Louis war had broken out between Louis of Durazzo

*From an early woodcut portrait, by kind permission of Mr. St. Clair Baddeley.*
JOANNA THE FIRST, QUEEN OF NAPLES.

on one side, and Louis's eldest brother, the Prince of Taranto, on the other. The Count of Minervino (who, it will be remembered, had been released from the perpetual imprisonment to which he had been condemned in the reign of King Robert) now joined Louis of Durazzo; and as this civil war was ravaging the kingdom, Joanna and Louis of Taranto were obliged to leave the conquest of Sicily, which they would otherwise have completed, and return to Naples to restore peace there.

On their arrival they summoned the Prince of Taranto, Louis of Durazzo, and the Count of Minervino to appear before them. The Prince of Taranto at once obeyed, and submitted to the Queen's authority; but Louis of Durazzo absolutely refused to come into the presence of either the King or the Queen, or to yield them any obedience. The Count of Minervino appeared at court, but behaved in so haughty a manner and made such unreasonable demands that the sovereigns had no choice but to oppose him on the battlefield. He was very rich, for he and his brothers, the other Pipini, had acquired great wealth by their former ravages, and they were assisted by the barbarian mercenaries they hired.

The throne was now in great danger, and a civil war ensued which disturbed the country; but in the end the Queen's forces were happily victorious, and the Pipini destroyed root and branch. The Count of Minervino was taken prisoner, and condemned to the ignominious death of hanging. One of his brothers was thrown down from a high tower by one of his own soldiers, and the third of the Pipini managed to escape from Naples, but was never afterwards heard of, and is believed to have perished. Thus this family, which had given so much trouble to the late King as well as to Joanna, was at last exterminated.

The Queen, with her usual generosity, granted Louis of Durazzo a free pardon, on account of his royal birth and relationship to her. A great banquet was given in the Bishop's Palace by Louis and Joanna to celebrate the reconciliation. All the members of the royal family were invited to be present, and after the banquet the whole of the Neapolitan nobility attended the King in a royal progress round the city.

For several days tournaments and jousts were held to amuse the people, and in the evenings what were called "solemn balls" were given at court, at which the majestic Queen was the most striking figure and the object of universal admiration. This took place in 1359.

In the following year the haughty Louis of Durazzo died, and Joanna undertook the education of his eldest son, Charles, whom she afterwards unfortunately adopted as her heir, for he turned out a traitor and the worst of her enemies, in spite of all the affection she lavished upon him. He was a child of twelve at the time of his father's death.

About this time Joanna adopted her sister Maria's youngest daughter, Margaret, whom Charles of Durazzo afterwards married, and brought her up as her own daughter. Maria resigned her to Joanna the more readily because, soon after the peace celebrations were concluded, she married a second time, her second husband being Philip of Taranto, the younger brother of Joanna's husband Louis. Thus the two sisters were now married to two brothers. The little Princess Margaret was only a few months younger than the child Joanna had lost on the day of her coronation, and no doubt helped to console her for that loss. The unhappy Queen needed consolation, for Louis of Taranto, now there was no more fighting to be done, seems to have grown tired of Joanna, and to have been unfaithful to her, and given himself up to intemperance and other vices while Acciajuoli was continuing the war in Sicily.

It was at this time that the Neapolitan court was at its gayest. Pageants, balls, tournaments and banquets, and all kinds of gaiety were the order of the day, into all of which Louis entered with such extravagance that he ruined his constitution, and, about three years after the defeat of the Pipini, he died at Castel Nuovo of a fever in May, 1362, and Joanna was left a widow for the second time.

# CHAPTER XIV

## Joanna's Second Widowhood

LOUIS of Taranto had the misfortune to live too long for his reputation, but he has also suffered at the hands of the historian Villani, who has exaggerated his vices. For the first years of his married life he was a good husband. Twice by his gallant fighting he saved Joanna's crown for her, and he had shared her troubles with her at the beginning of their joint reign, but prosperity did not suit him. He fell into the hands of dissolute companions and shared in their vicious lives, ruined his constitution by his excesses, and died at the early age of forty-two.

A royal widow in the Middle Ages was almost as much to be pitied as a Hindoo widow is now. She was condemned to lie on a bed covered with white linen for a certain number of days, which varied in different countries. In France the Queen was not supposed to leave her room for a whole year after the death of the King, but Joanna certainly did not follow this example. She had to wear mourning for a year, but white, not black, was the colour worn by Queens for widow's mourning then. She was forbidden by the fashion then prevalent to wear any jewels, gloves (at that time a great luxury), rings, ribbons, or costly furs, and her apartments certainly during the first three months of widowhood were hung with deepest black—and horribly depressing they must have been. Her dress had to be made in fashion like that of a nun, her glorious hair was hidden under a hood and veil, her face shrouded in a white linen binder. Some of the restrictions imposed upon her were removed at the expiration of each three months during the year of mourning, but all that time she was condemned to live in the greatest seclusion.

It is believed that Joanna was deeply attached to this her second husband, who had shared so many troubles with her, and his handsome presence and bravery and skill in all active sports were calculated to win her affections. One of his good acts was the founding of the first Order of knighthood in Italy, on the first anniversary of his coronation. This was the Order of the Knot, and was dedicated to the Holy Spirit. The members wore a blue mantle embroidered with golden *fleur-de-lis*, and jewelled and fastened on the breast with a knot of gold and silver. When a knight performed any feat of arms, or achieved any knightly success, a fresh knot was added to his mantle, and this was repeated at every fresh victory. The two mottoes of the Order were "Si Dieu plaît" and "Au droit désir."

The same day that Louis instituted his Order of the Knot, Joanna laid the foundation-stone of the Incoronata Church and the hospital attached to it. This was built on the site of the court in which the Duke of Calabria sat when he administered the justice for which he was so famed. During her second widowhood she also enlarged and decorated the then unfinished monastery of San Martino, which her father had begun, and she also richly endowed the monastery of the Poor Clares, in whose church the late King and Queen, Robert and Sancha, and Joanna's father, the Duke of Calabria, were buried.

Joanna was most generous and charitable, and during her reign she founded and endowed many other churches and institutions, among others the church and hospital of St. Anthony of Padua; so that one of her biographers says, "The various monuments we have of her show how great must have been her piety and religion."

There is an unfinished building in the Piazza Mergellina, called to this day by the Neapolitans "the palace of Queen Joanna," which is now a beautiful ruin; this she also began to build. She enriched the city with many secular buildings notable for their magnificence and good art. There were at least five first-rate Italian architects in the thirteenth and fourteenth centuries. To begin with there were Giovanni and Nicholas of Pisa, Brunelleschi, and the two Masuccios, the second of whom designed the monastery belfry at St. Clare.

Giotto di Bondone, who painted the frescoes in the Church of St. Clare—begun, as we have just said, by the late King Robert—died when Joanna was about eleven years old, but his glorious art had been epoch-making, and there were many of his disciples whom she could employ to beautify the churches she built. A rather amusing story is told of Giotto, who, as all the world knows, was taken by Cimabue from tending his father's sheep into his own house, and trained by him because he in passing had seen the boy's talent displayed in drawings of his sheep with a piece of chalk.

Giotto is said to have been remarkably ugly, and very small, and on one occasion he was riding near Florence with a friend, who was equally ugly, and as celebrated as a doctor-of-law as Giotto was as an artist, when they were overtaken by a thunderstorm and were obliged to take shelter in a peasant's cottage; and as they were wet to the skin, they had to borrow clothing of their host. Giotto looked so sublimely ridiculous in his borrowed garments, which were much too big for his little body, that his friend burst out laughing and said, " Who to see you, Giotto, would ever think you were the greatest painter in the world?" "And who to see you, could ever think you knew your alphabet?" replied the artist.

Giotto's frescoes in the Church of St. Clare at Naples were destroyed later by a Spanish viceroy, who had them whitewashed to make the church lighter—the "dim religious light" and Giotto's delightful art not appealing to this Philistine.

Giotto was succeeded by Simon Martini, who is mentioned by Boccaccio; but though Giotto's influence was undoubtedly felt at Naples, there has never been a great Neapolitan school of art, either in painting or architecture. The two Masuccios are usually regarded as the founders of Neapolitan sculpture, but little that is reliable is known of them.

It was during this second widowhood that Joanna showed her capabilities as a ruler. Her character had now developed, and she began with both prudence and vigour to try to restore tranquillity to her kingdom, which was torn asunder by so many broils and dissensions. She endeavoured to suppress the brigands who were such a pest, and to bring to justice the malefactors who infested the country; and she succeeded in accomplishing this great and glorious task, which would have taxed the powers of her illustrious predecessor—the wise King Robert.

She showed great clemency and even munificence to those who had rebelled against her, or who had been partisans of her enemies, and forgave injuries

## Joanna's Second Widowhood

freely; so that Caracciola says that no prince before her had ever acted so generously and benignly towards the Neapolitans, that she forgot injuries and remembered benefits, and most richly rewarded all those who followed her adverse fortunes. He also says that "if there exist other rulers who have enriched individuals more richly, there are none who equalled her in the multiplicity of her benefits."

"Never," says this same writer, "shall we see this city more populous than under this same Queen; never was the arrival of mercantile ships more frequent than under her government and protection. This was all due to the love she had for her people, and the care she lavished upon them. The people increased so fast that they almost turned the churches into houses for them to live in. Everywhere there was abundance of food and plenty of commerce, and the nation enjoyed great ease and security."

This was perhaps the most prosperous part of Joanna's reign, but the period of peace did not last long. Her calumniators attributed every misfortune, including the death of Louis, to the vengeance of Heaven for the murder of her first husband, Andrew; and fearing that as a widow she might on account of her great beauty be exposed to slander and evil report, at the conclusion of the term of her mourning for Louis, she was advised by her friends to marry again in order to have a protector. More over, the nation earnestly desired that she should have a son to inherit her crown, otherwise it was to be feared that civil war would break out again among the turbulent Neapolitan princes.

Soon after the death of Louis of Taranto the Pope Innocent VI. died—indeed, one of his last public acts was to celebrate Mass for the repose of the soul of the late King of Naples. In the conclave which followed his death the Cardinals were almost as puzzled whom to choose for his successor as they had been when his predecessor died. Their first choice fell upon Cardinal Hugh Roger, the brother of Clement VI., but he refused to accept the honour. The result of the next ballot, which is piously believed to have been the work of the Holy Spirit, was the election of the Abbé William de Grimoard, a most holy man, then Abbot of the Monastery of St. Victor, Marseilles, who was celebrated for his great wisdom and virtue.

Although a Frenchman, he sympathised with the claims of Rome as the seat of the Papacy, and considered Avignon as a temporary place of residence only, and desired to move the Chair of Peter back to the Eternal City. At the time of his election de Grimoard was at Naples, where he had been sent by the Avignon Court, ostensibly to convey messages of condolence on the death of Louis to Joanna, but in reality to watch her conduct and to report upon it. For five months he resided at

## Joanna's Second Widowhood

the Neapolitan Court as the Abbot of St. Victor, and during that time formed so high an opinion of the Queen that he became one of her great friends, and after he was raised to the Papal throne he treated her with even greater respect and honour that Clement VI. had done, and, as will appear, bestowed honours upon her such as have never before or since been conferred upon a woman.

Joanna's appearance when the future Pope was residing at her court must have been very striking. Her majestic figure was robed in pure white, and the absence of all ornaments and artificial aids to beauty must have given a kind of angelic severity to her classic features. Her devotion and charity made a great impression upon the holy Abbot, and completely won his esteem and affection. The fact that when he was called to the highest dignity upon earth he found himself in a very difficult position—as he soon saw many reforms were necessary—must have been another link between him and the widowed Queen, who was beset with difficulties on all sides.

One of Joanna's first actions when she took up the reins of government after Louis's death was to send her trusty servant Acciajuoli to Messina to conclude the war there by making a truce with Frederick, after which he was counselled to return to Naples with as many troops as he could muster to oppose Louis's eldest brother, the Prince of

Taranto, who was intriguing to obtain her throne for himself. He hoped that he could persuade Joanna to allow him to administer her government for her; but she was much too wise to do this, foreseeing clearly enough that if she did so she would be a Queen in name only, while her ambitious brother-in-law would be to all intents and purposes the ruling monarch; so she promptly determined to nip this project in the bud.

She called together a council of all her wisest men, and absolutely refused to allow the Prince of Taranto to have anything whatever to do with the government of her kingdom, and the Prince, finding his efforts were useless, retired in high dudgeon to his own estates. This and other similar circumstances made it imperative that Joanna should marry a third time, and there was no lack of suitors. The King of France was very anxious that she should choose his son Philip, the Duke of Tours, for whom such a marriage would have been most advantageous; but he was ten or twelve years younger than Joanna, and she very wisely considered that a barrier which could not have been got over had there been no other objections to such a match. John, the French King, endeavoured to get the new Pope Urban V. to support this proposal; but Joanna, dreading the difficulties and quarrels in which the inexperience and youth of the boyish Duke of Tours and the haughtiness of his courtiers would probably involve her, most wisely declined the offer.

One of the handsomest princes at this time about the Neapolitan Court was James III. of Majorca, a king without a kingdom. Majorca, the largest of the Balearic Isles, had been taken from the Saracens about the year 1230 by James I., King of Aragon, and by him erected into a kingdom; the other Balearic Isles, together with the two counties of Roussillon and Montpellier being dependent upon it.

James II. of Aragon in 1295 married an Angevine princess, the daughter of Charles II. of Anjou, by whom he had two sons, Pedro and James. The elder succeeded him as King of Aragon under the title of Pedro III., and the younger as King of Aragon under the title of James I. of Majorca; they were always at war with each other, and left the quarrel as an inheritance to their sons, Pedro IV. of Aragon and James II. of Majorca.

In 1349 Pedro IV., surnamed the Ceremonious, succeeded in despoiling his brother of the kingdom of Majorca, in a battle in which James II., as some assert, was killed, and his son James III. was taken prisoner. He was in captivity for many years, but at last succeeded in effecting his escape, and went to Naples, where he was one of the most attractive members of that gay court. It was upon him that the choice of Joanna and her council fell as the most suitable candidate for her hand.

The conditions imposed upon the nominal King of Majorca were that he should possess of Joanna's dominions the Dukedom of Calabria only, and that he was not to expect to have any share in the government, nor to assume the title of King, but to wait the Queen's pleasure to bestow either of these privileges upon him, in case their marriage should be blessed with children or even one child to inherit the throne. The fact that Montpellier and Roussillon were adjacent to Joanna's Provençal possessions made James more acceptable to the Queen's advisers, as they were valuable adjuncts to her French dominions.

James raised no objections to the conditions—indeed, notwithstanding them, Joanna was the most brilliant match he could have found in all Europe—and the marriage was duly celebrated with all the pomp and magnificence which had graced the Queen's former weddings.

Some writers say that James's father was not slain on the battlefield, but was kept a prisoner by Pedro, and that three months after his marriage James heard his father had been treacherously murdered in prison, and that he at once left Naples for Spain with all the troops he could muster to avenge his father's death.

However this may be, whether the King was

slain in battle or in prison, it is certain that James III. set out very shortly after his marriage with Joanna to try to recover his kingdom. Joanna was not able to render him much assistance in this expedition, for she was obliged to send a force to defend her Provençal dominions from the inroads of the Dukes of Milan and Savoy, who were in league together to deprive her of them. The prompt measures which Joanna took, and the fidelity of her Provençal subjects, soon succeeded in defeating the two Dukes, but her husband was less successful in his campaign against the King of Aragon.

After three months' wedded happiness Joanna was, to all intents and purposes, again a widow, at least a grass widow, for her husband was absent almost the whole of their married life, and frequently she did not know whether he was alive or dead. The means of communication were slow and by no means sure, and the life of James was fraught with so many adventures on the battlefield and in captivity that it was exceedingly difficult for the Queen to obtain reliable information as to his movements.

There is a long account of James III. and his exploits in Froissart's Chronicles, but his account of Joanna has been proved to be so inaccurate that it will not do to place too much reliance upon his tales of the adventures of her third husband.

Of certain facts, however, there seems to be little doubt—at any rate, most historians repeat them as true.

He appears to have fought for three or four years against the King of Aragon quite unsuccessfully, and then to have fled to Bordeaux, where the Prince of Wales was then residing, and to have joined him. According to Froissart, this was in 1367, and he says that while James was with the Black Prince in Bordeaux the Princess of Wales gave birth to a son, who afterwards succeeded to the English throne as Richard II. The little Prince was baptized in the church of St. Andrew, in Bordeaux, and the King of Majorca was one of his god-fathers. Froissart says the Prince of Wales received James well and treated him handsomely, "for he was a stranger, and far from his own country, and his finances were low." Edward then joined Peter the Cruel, King of Castile, in an expedition in Spain, and he promised to restore James to his kingdom if he would accompany him on this campaign, which turned out to be a brilliant success. In this splendid expedition, in which the Black Prince won such great honour, James of Majorca fought side by side with him.

At the end of the campaign the Prince of Wales went to Valladolid, or, as Froissart calls it, the Vale of Olives, translating the Spanish word; and there the heat was so great that they were all more or less affected by it, and James was so ill that when the Prince of Wales moved on he was confined to his bed, and had to be left behind. The Black Prince sent some of his English knights to the King of Majorca to tell him his troops were suffering so much from the heat that he was obliged to leave Spain, and to ask if he wished to go with them.

James replied that he was so ill that he could not lift his foot to the stirrup; and on being asked if he would like some men-at-arms left behind as a guard, he declined, saying it was uncertain how long he might be forced to remain there. Peter the Cruel turned out a perfidious ally, failing to keep all his engagements, and proving himself a most ungrateful friend; for as soon as the English army had left all the towns they had reconquered, he went back to his brother, Henry of Transtamare, who marched to Valladolid, where he heard the King of Majorca, his bitter enemy, was lying confined to his bed, to take advantage of his weakness and make him a prisoner. James at once asked whether Henry would make him his own prisoner or whether he intended to send him to the King of Aragon, as he would rather die than fall into his hands.

Henry replied that on no account would he act so disloyally as to send him to his greatest enemy, but would retain him as his own prisoner until he was either ransomed or it pleased him to set him at liberty. James now found means of communicating his plight to Joanna, who, as soon as she heard of it, set about raising the money for his ransom and finding trusty messengers to negotiate the business. She succeeded in procuring his ransom at an immense cost, which, Froissart says, was paid so graciously that the King of Castile thanked her for it.

Directly he was released from his captivity James returned to Naples, but he was so bent on revenge against the King of Aragon that he only remained with Joanna long enough to collect men and arms and money sufficient to carry out another campaign, which he set out upon much against Joanna's wish—if we are to credit Froissart, who says Joanna wished and counselled her husband to join his forces with her cousin, the King of France, instead of with the English under the Prince of Wales. He resisted all her arguments and entreaties to remain with her in Naples and abandon the hope of recovering his own very small kingdom; but James was obstinate, and would not be persuaded, so the Queen yielded to his wishes, and gave orders that as he passed through Provence the highest honours should be paid him, and a sum of 10,000 golden florins given him for his expenses, which, seeing that he was disregarding her wishes, seems very handsome treatment.

Before we record the end of his somewhat mythical, or at least very uncertain, fortunes, we must make mention of a characteristically mediæval incident which occurred to Joanna about this time. At a large and, as it was called, "solemn ball," which Joanna held at Gaeta, at which she was the admired of all eyes, there was present Galeazzo of Mantua, one of the most accomplished Italian princes of the time, and Joanna chose him as her partner in one of the dances.

Joanna was a beautiful dancer, and Galeazzo also excelled in this art; and at the conclusion of the dance he knelt before the majestic Joanna, who was now about forty and a magnificent creature, and thanked her humbly for the honour she had so graciously bestowed upon him in allowing him to be her partner, and then and there he made a solemn vow that he would not rest until he had found and challenged and defeated two valiant knights, to give to her as a present.

Joanna replied, "that in good time, and by the grace of God, he should accomplish his vow, since such was his pleasure and the custom of knighthood."

Galeazzo then travelled half over Europe, going to France, Spain, Germany, Hungary, and other countries where the flower of knighthood was to be met—we do not hear that he went to England—and having found two knights worthy of his prowess, he challenged, fought, and defeated them, and brought them captive to Naples at the end of the year following the solemn ball at Gaeta.

Arrived at Naples he sought an audience, and genuflecting before the Queen, he presented the two captive knights to her. Joanna thanked him cordially, congratulating him upon having accomplished his vow so gallantly, and then thus addressed the knights:

"Sirs, you are, as you see, my prisoners. By the laws of chivalry, I may cause such as are in your captive condition to serve me in any ignoble office I may best please; but I think you will judge by my countenance that cruelty does not dwell in my heart, to dispose of the unfortunate in such a manner. Of my clemency then, and humanity, I give you from this hour entire liberty and franchise to act as you please, whether to return free to your own country, or, before you depart, to solace yourselves in my kingdom, and view the curiosities of it, which are sufficiently admirable. After having visited them return to me, and when you choose to depart I shall be well pleased to commend you to God."

We of the twentieth century, whose ideas are so different, can hardly imagine such a scene as this ever taking place; but in mediæval days redeemed slaves and prisoners and the vanquished became so much the property of their purchasers and conquerors that they were frequently disposed of by will. A few years later Joanna redeemed a Tartar princess from slavery, and sent her as a present to her friend, St. Bridget of Sweden, the widowed Princess of Nericia, who was then dying in Rome. This extraordinary present arrived just after the death of the saint had taken place; but the captive was adopted by Bridget's daughter, St. Catherine, who took her to Sweden, where she became a nun in the convent of Wadstena, in the Order founded by St. Bridget, and died herself in the odour of sanctity.

Many of these captives and conquered knights were less fortunate, and did not meet with such clemency as Joanna showed her two prisoners. Brantôme records the fate of a vanquished knight, whom his conqueror bestowed upon the canons of St. Peter's Church in Rome, with his arms, his horse, his armour and trappings; and says that they kept the unfortunate man a prisoner in the church for the remainder of his life, which he spent in walking to and fro, his recreation being to stand at the open door, whose threshold he never passed, and watch the traffic outside. The laws of chivalry were so binding on the honour of all knights that this one could not break his parole, but was obliged to submit to his sad fate.

Prisoners of war were treated more or less as the personal property of their conquerors, even in Christian Europe, until the institution of standing armies, when they passed under the care of the State to which they belonged.

## CHAPTER XV

## The Death of Acciajuoli

THE shadows in Joanna's life were beginning to deepen again; the prolonged absence of the man she had married to guard her fair name and be a helpmeet to her was a source of grave anxiety and trouble, for she did not know whether he was alive or dead, in prison or at large.

About this time—that is, in the summer of 1367—there arrived in Naples the celebrated prophetess and mystic, the afterwards canonised Saint Bridget of Sweden, with her beautiful young daughter Catherine, also a widow, her friend Nicholas Orsini, and a small band of Swedish pilgrims in her train. The Neapolitan nobility vied with each other in their eagerness to show hospitality to the Swedish Princess, the fame of whose sanctity and of her visions and her prophesies and revelations had already reached them, for they were the talk of Europe.

The honour of entertaining so distinguished a

visitor fell upon Jacqueline *née* Acciajuoli, sister to Nicholas Acciajuoli, the Grand Seneschal of Naples, and wife to the Count Buondelmonte. The Countess was a very devout woman, and the simple austerity of her *ménage*, together with her high rank and the important place she occupied at the Neapolitan Court, made her house peculiarly agreeable to the Princess of Nericia. From the Countess the saint learnt the story of Joanna's life, the murder of Andrew and its consequences, her second marriage with Louis of Taranto, and her third nuptials with the handsome King of Majorca; she heard too of the brilliancy of Joanna's court, of the splendour of her banquets, "solemn balls," "Court of Love," tournaments, and other entertainments, renowned all over Europe for their magnificence; she heard of the envies and jealousies, of the quarrels and constant warfare of the royal princes of the houses of Durazzo and Taranto, of the feuds between the nobles: and, as she had already admonished and threatened with divine vengeance Magnus II., King of Sweden, and his Queen Blanche, of whose gay court she had once been Grand Mistress, she now determined to try to reform Joanna's court, and preach repentance to the Queen herself and to all her gay courtiers.

St. Bridget was a great reformer, not only of monasteries and convents, of monks and nuns, of bishops and clergy, but she had not scrupled to remonstrate with the Popes for their residence at Avignon, and was at this moment on the verge of inducing Urban V. by her counsels to return to Rome.

Joanna, who if she liked gaiety was nevertheless a devout and faithful Catholic, was anxious to see the mystic, of whom she had heard so much, and with whom she had corresponded. The Queen had probably read some of St. Bridget's Revelations, and soon after the arrival of the Swedish pilgrims an audience was arranged.

The saint, who was of very small stature, and was clad in a nunlike costume of coarse serge, with a black veil on her head, which hid her still glorious golden hair—which is said to have clothed her like a mantle when unbound—was presented by the Countess Buondelmonte to the majestic Neapolitan Queen, who was dressed in her usual magnificent style, and was surrounded by a group of admiring courtiers equally magnificently attired, many of whom were in love with her and all were ready to die in her cause.

St. Bridget then presented her daughter Catherine, clad also in the nunlike widow's dress of the period, who was herself so beautiful that several Roman noblemen had attempted to carry her off by force in Rome. But Catherine and Joanna never seem to have liked each other, whereas in spite of St. Bridget's most severe admonishments, Joanna became greatly attached to her, and promised the saint to reform her court, and to lead a much stricter life in future. A sort of religious revival in Naples seems to have been the outcome of this visit of the Swedish saint to that city. She became the rage : the Neapolitan nobles willingly left their palaces to stand with the poor and infirm who besieged the Buondelmonte mansion, to wait their turn for an interview with the prophetess. They and their wives and daughters took to visiting the poor and the hospitals and tending the sick as Bridget and Catherine were wont to do in Rome ; the reported miracles wrought by St. Bridget in healing the sick created a great sensation ; the churches were crowded. In short, Naples went from one extreme to the other, from the extreme of gaiety to the opposite pole of devotion, and, as might have been expected, after the departure of the saint relapsed into its former normal condition.

But before the Swedish pilgrims quitted Naples St. Bridget established her claims to the gift of prophecy in a remarkable manner.

She was sitting with Jacqueline Acciajuoli one day, when she suddenly told her that the days of her brother Nicholas, the Grand Seneschal of the kingdom, were already numbered, and his death imminent. Greatly shocked, Jacqueline, who was devoted to her brother, at once went in search of him, and found him with the Queen, treating with her concerning the ransom of her husband the King of Majorca, then in captivity in Spain. Nicholas was apparently in excellent health; he was only about fifty-six, and a strong man, but that very night he was taken suddenly and seriously ill. St. Bridget was sent for, and watched and prayed at his bedside, where she fell into one of her ecstasies, and received one of the revelations for which she was so famous, which she afterwards wrote down and gave to her confessor to translate into Latin.

The Grand Seneschal died in her presence after receiving the Last Sacraments, her exhortations and prayers having moved him to deep repentance for the sins of his past life. His death took place on October 25th, 1367, a few days after St. Bridget had prophesied that it was imminent.

He was buried in the magnificent Carthusian monastery near Florence, which he had built, and to which he had already sent a library of very valuable manuscripts, having hoped soon to retire from office and end his days in peace and retirement there. The cause of his death is described as the bursting of an abscess in his head, but the vague and scanty medical knowledge of the times cannot be relied upon for a right diagnosis of his somewhat mysterious end. Perhaps it was an attack of meningitis. His death was a most serious loss to the Queen, for he was one of her most faithful coun-

*From an engraving by B. Holl, after an original painting.*

JOANNA THE FIRST,
Queen of Naples.

sellors and servants, and one of the most distinguished men living during her reign. He was also a very devout man, most charitable and generous to the Church.

On one occasion he quarrelled with John Barrili, also a very able man, a poet and a great favourite of the late King Robert, who chose him as his proxy on the occasion of the crowning of Petrarch with laurel in the Capitol. Petrarch heard of this quarrel from the Bishop of Florence, on the occasion already mentioned on which he dined with the poet. "I am grieved at this quarrel; you are the friend of both, and should make it up between them," said the Bishop.

Petrarch undertook the task of reconciliation, and set about it in a somewhat elaborate fashion, though one that was highly characteristic of him. He wrote three long letters—a private one for each of the offended friends, and one to both united to be opened only by the two together and read. All three letters urged the strongest reasons for their reconciliation, and he ended the private epistles by hoping that they would give a whole day to the reading of the third letter. This happened many years before the Grand Seneschal's death, for they were dated May 24th, 1352. The Bishop undertook to deliver the letters, and some months afterwards he wrote to Petrarch to tell him his letters had had the desired effect, and a reconciliation had taken place.

Acciajuoli left four sons by his wife Margareta, besides two adopted children.

Soon after Acciajuoli's death King John of France, having failed to secure Joanna's hand for his son, made an attempt to take Provence from her by force; but her wisdom and tact again stood her in good stead, and the Pope supported her so zealously and her Provençal subjects showed such fidelity to her, that the Duke of Anjou, who had based his claims on some rights which he supposed had accrued to him through the ancient Kings of Arles, was defeated at the end of six months, although during this time he had offered the largest bribes to the Provençal barons to tempt them and corrupt their allegiance to Joanna. One of these barons, Rainier of Grimaldis, Prince of Morguez, behaved with great loyalty to Joanna; she had given him a present of 4,000 florins for recapturing Tarascon for her. The Duke of Anjou offered to give Grimaldis the same sum annually if he would go over to the French side, but he refused with scorn to consider such treachery to his Queen.

Even at Avignon the influence of the Anglo-French war was felt, and the policy of John of France was galling to the French Pope. Urban V. now made a league with the King of Hungary, Joanna, and others against the Viscontis, who had for years been in rebellion against the Holy See. Barnabas Visconti, who was renowned for his cruelty

## The Death of Acciajuoli

and the exorbitant demands he made upon the Pope, when he heard of this league, said, " They are all children ; I will have them all whipped."

Ambrose Visconti this same year entered Naples with what was then considered an enormous force of 1,200 lancers, each of whom had a number of followers who were not counted in estimating the size of Visconti's army. They seized on a portion of the Abruzzi, and robbed and plundered the inhabitants without mercy.

Joanna sent only a small force at first against Ambrose (who was called the Bastard of Milan), under Giovanni Malateca ; but finding this was insufficient, she summoned all the veterans who had formerly served under her late husband, Louis of Taranto, and riding out to meet them addressed an eloquent speech to them, exhorting them to do their utmost to deliver their country as speedily as possible from these cruel barbarians who were killing their countrymen and ruining the land by their rapine.

She then wrote to the chief barons in her kingdom to the same effect, and so successfully that in a few months the Milanese army was cut up, only between two and three thousand of Visconti's men escaping from the country ; while Ambrose Visconti himself was taken prisoner, and confined in one of the Neapolitan castles, Castel Nuovo, for ten years. Some writers have blamed Joanna for treating this enemy with too great severity, but he was such a dangerous, turbulent man that he was better in captivity than free.

Urban V. now issued a Bull of Excommunication against the Visconti, and sent two legates with it to Galeazzo Visconti; but he not only paid no attention to this sentence, but forced the two legates to eat in his presence the parchment on which the Bull was written, and also the seals, which are said to have been leaden, and the cords.

It seems that about this same year, 1367, Joanna heard of the death of her husband, James of Majorca; but according to Mr. Baddeley, who has written a most scholarly essay on the Life and Times of Joanna,[1] his death occurred much later than this. This writer says that James's death took place at Soria, in a Franciscan monastery there, in the year 1375.

Caraccioli puts his death at 1368, and Froissart says it took place at sea on his voyage home from Spain to Naples about 1376. Whether alive or dead he was dead to Joanna from the time he left her after she had ransomed him, and for many years she was unaware of his fate, which was a cause of great anxiety to her. From 1367 reports were coming constantly to Naples that he was dead, and they did Joanna much harm in many ways.

[1] "Queen Joanna I., An Essay on her Times," by St. Clair Baddeley. London, 1893.

Those pests the freebooters no sooner heard that she was again a widow than some of their companies, of which Ambrose Visconti's was one, laid plans for the invasion of Naples; but after he was taken prisoner Joanna enjoyed a period of comparative rest and peace, during a reign which has been described as one long effort to keep her throne.

Her wisdom and prudence, however, succeeded in suppressing brigandage and robbery till the caves of Calabria were as safe, we are told, as her own palace. To accomplish this she had to exercise severity, and a royal edict was passed ordering that when a band of brigands or marauders was taken, who had been strong enough to fortify themselves in any castle, they were to be publicly executed as criminals, and this had a salutary effect, which Boccaccio thus describes·

"The rich man as well as the poor could traverse by night or day with perfect security not only towns and villages, but also the wildest forests, mountains, or caverns, and this the predecessors of Joanna were either not willing or not able to accomplish. And what is not less salutary, by the modesty of her own manners she has reformed the licentiousness of her nobility, and so curbed their pride that those who formerly paid little regard to their kings, to-day dread the frown of an offended woman."

Robbery was the most prominent vice of Europe

at this time, and it existed in greater excess in many parts of Italy than elsewhere; even in the time of the good King Robert, Naples was notorious for its thieves. So little was then thought of it that what was called "living by the saddle" was quite a gentlemanly profession in most European countries. Joanna did completely away with this reproach as far as Naples was concerned, and did all she could to help and civilise her people by encouraging commerce. To this end she built four streets to accommodate the inhabitants of the four nations who traded most with the capital, namely, the Provençals, the Spaniards, the Venetians, and the Genoese.

Naples under Joanna's rule became the favourite port of traders, partly for the security of the roads, partly for the exemption from all taxation and from any forced loans, which in no emergencies would she ever suffer to be levied. The city was supplied not only with all the necessaries of life, but also with luxuries from foreign countries, for Joanna was a liberal patroness of every kind of art. In a catalogue of the furniture, etcetera, of Fonthill Abbey there is mentioned a magnificent Oriental china vase, the earliest specimen of its kind known in Europe, which once belonged to Joanna, whose arms are engraved upon it.

She took pride in making her court as celebrated as King Robert's had been for learned and scientific men, whom she freely admitted to her society in private life as well as at court. Boccaccio, who after Petrarch was the most celebrated of her contemporaries in literature, says, " She was so gracious, gentle, compassionate, and kind that she seemed rather the companion than the Queen of those around her."

In those days theology ranked first of all studies, but after that law was the most esteemed in Joanna's court, for her first care was to protect the poor against the rich, the weak against the strong; and for this purpose she consulted the most eminent barristers and lawyers the University of Naples could supply. There were three most famous jurisconsults whom Joanna commanded in an edict, using the language of her period, should be revered in her dominions " as a human Trinity when interpreting the laws." These three were Luke of Penna, Andrew of Isernia, and Nicholas of Naples, all very famous men. After the death of Andrew of Isernia, Joanna in all difficult questions used to apply to the most celebrated foreign legal authorities for advice. Baldus of Perugia and Angelus of the same city, on whom the most extravagant terms of praise were lavished, were two of these, and both were enthusiastic admirers of the Queen of Sicily, not only as a wise sovereign and legislatrix, but also as a beautiful woman and a most charming companion.

Astrology was in the Middle Ages studied with astronomy, and at Naples there was a chair of astrology at the University, as well as for other sciences. Much faith was placed in casting of horoscopes and the observation of the stars, which were supposed to foretell the destinies of men and women. Diseases were also believed to be influenced by the celestial bodies, and in consequence physicians were generally astrologers, but the mass of the medical profession in those days were what we a century ago should have called quacks. Petrarch had very little faith in the prescriptions of the doctors of his time. He says, "The moment I see a physician I know beforehand what he will say to me, 'Eat young poultry, drink warm water, use the remedy the stork has taught us.'"

They might and did give worse advice than to eat young poultry and to drink warm water, but what the cryptic allusion to the teaching of the stork may mean we do not know, and perhaps we had better not inquire. Two lessons taught by the stork certainly might be followed with advantage—to be good mothers, and to take care of our parents in their old age. Fruit was a prohibited article of diet in sickness in the Middle Ages, but Petrarch struck at this medical advice, and laments that physicians seemed to regard it as equally poisonous with henbane and aconite.

Watches and clocks were in use at this period,

but the pendulum was not invented until the time of Galileo; until then it was the dial which revolved. Spectacles were also in common use. One of the most celebrated inventions of Joanna's reign is said to have been the mariner's compass; the first that was constructed in Europe was made by Gioja Flavio, a mathematician of Amalfi, near Naples; but the idea is believed to have been brought from China by Marco Polo in the thirteenth century, and the Chinese had probably understood the use of it for two thousand years before. Flavio's compass had eight points only, and the arms of the district in which he was born bear a compass with eight points in memory of him.

The most celebrated theologian in Joanna's kingdom was Paris of Pozzuoli, who has left a most enthusiastic panegyric upon Joanna behind him; but perhaps if the Queen of Naples had been consulted she would have desired no higher compliment than to be called, as she so emphatically is, " the friend of Petrarch and Boccaccio," and equally the friend of two Popes, Clement VI. and Urban V.

## CHAPTER XVI

## Urban V. returns to Rome

WE now come to the most important contemporary event of Joanna's reign, for it affected all Christendom—the return of the Pope to Rome. Urban V. had always regarded his residence at Avignon as only a temporary measure; the interests of the Church, the exhortations of St. Bridget, the terrible state of Rome during the absence of the Supreme Pontiff, the prayers and wishes of all his Italian subjects, all combined to induce him to make up his mind in the beginning of the year 1367 to leave Avignon for Rome.

He was vehemently opposed in this way by all the French Cardinals, who formed the majority of the Sacred College, for they were unwilling to leave their magnificent residences on the banks of the Rhône, and the luxurious and brilliant life at the

It is said that Urban's mother, who lived with him at Avignon was so concerned at his determination to depart from thence that she threw herself on the ground at his feet, and declared that he should not leave the Papal palace unless he trod over her body. But Urban, when once he felt it his duty to return to Rome, suffered no obstacle to stand in his way, not even his mother's dramatic opposition; and quoting the text, "he shall tread on the asp and the basilisk," he passed on, leaving the asp or the basilisk to rise from her lowly attitude.

The first stage of his journey was Marseilles. Here the galleys which he had commanded Joanna, and the Genoese, and the Venetians to provide for him met him; and the French Cardinals are said to have vented their grief at leaving France in loud cries and lamentations, and their anger in opprobrious language to the venerable Pontiff, who paid no attention, but calmly ordered the sailors to set sail for Genoa, where they met with a splendid reception from all the princes and ambassadors, who were assembled on the shore and knelt to receive the Papal benediction.

Here under the blue Italian sky, on an improvised altar, Urban celebrated his first Mass in Italy, in the presence of an enormous crowd of people. At its Papal Court at Avignon, for the unhealthy palace in the squalid and disorderly streets of Rome.

conclusion he proceeded on his journey to Rome, and, after some opposition at Viterbo, he reached the Eternal City on October 16th.

At his entry into Rome, more than two thousand bishops, abbots, and priors accompanied him; his white courser was led by Italian princes, while eleven French cardinals followed, resigned and melancholy, in his train. The bells of the city rang joyously, the great doors of St. Peter's were thrown open, cries of "Evviva il Papa!" rent the air, and then the Holy Father gave the blessing "Urbi et Orbi" from the balcony over the Golden Door.

For over a year Urban resided in Rome, the object of the greatest veneration in his spiritual capacity, for which his personal sanctity so well fitted him; but in his temporal office as Sovereign of the city of Rome and of the Papal States he met with obstinate and insolent disobedience. During his residence in Rome, at the beginning of Lent, 1368, Joanna went to Rome to visit the Pope. She went partly from a pious desire to pay her homage to the Holy Father in his capital, partly to confer with him as her best friend and most competent adviser, on the subject of her successor. Her sister Maria, who, although now the wife of Philip of Taranto, retained, as she was entitled to do, her higher title of Duchess of Durazzo, died about this time; and, as Joanna had no children, Maria, according to the will of their grandfather, the late King Robert, was the heiress to her sister's throne. It is true that the Duchess of Durazzo had three daughters; but by the custom and law of the age, they had no right to a throne which their mother had never actually possessed.

There now remained no descendants in the main line of Charles of Anjou except Louis of Hungary and Charles of Durazzo, son of Louis, Count of Gravina, of whose education, as we have said before, Joanna had taken charge. She had been a mother to this young Prince, who turned out so ungrateful, and as soon as he attained his majority he accepted an invitation from Joanna's greatest enemy, Louis, King of Hungary, to fight with him against the Venetians, with whom he was now at war. Joanna disapproved of this most strongly; but Charles disregarded her wishes, and this fact made her hesitate to adopt him as her heir, for she knew Louis hated her, and would probably poison her nephew's mind against her.

We can imagine how deeply this conduct of Charles must have wounded Joanna, for there are few things more galling than when those we have believed to be our friends become intimate with our enemies; and Joanna had been far more than a friend to Charles of Durazzo. She had been his benefactress and a foster-mother to him who now behaved in this mean and ungrateful way to her—which, indeed, was but a prelude to the lower depths of treachery and baseness to which he afterwards sank.

Joanna made the journey as far as Ostia by sea, and the remainder of the way by land, sometimes riding on horseback, sometimes being carried in a litter, but with great pomp and attended by a magnificent train of knights and followers. This visit, which brought her so much honour, was perhaps the happiest period of her life; she had left her kingdom at peace and in a prosperous condition, owing to her wise government, so she had no anxiety about that in the background to mar her delight in the spiritual and artistic treasures of Rome.

Peter of Lusignan, King of Cyprus, met her at a little distance from the gates of the city, and conducted her under a rich canopy of state to the Porta S. Pietro. Here she was met by the cardinals, clergy, and principal nobles of Rome, who were waiting to receive her and attend her to the steps of St. Peter's Church. Urban V. in full pontificals was waiting here, and as she approached, he, wishing to confer a very great mark of honour upon her, descended some of the steps to meet this majestic Queen and woman.

Joanna dismounted from her horse, and made the three customary genuflections to the Holy Father, who raised her from her knees and led her into the church, up the nave to the tombs of the holy apostles Peter and Paul, to pay her devotions at their shrine. An enormous crowd had been assembled outside the church in the Piazza to watch her arrival, and some of the people followed the procession into the church on this unique occasion.

Urban V. was a greater friend to Joanna than his predecessor Clement VI. had been; and since he became a canonised saint of the church, and during his lifetime was noted for his holiness, this friendship and respect, this affection and esteem of the Sovereign Pontiff, should have silenced the lips of all her detractors; for we may be sure that had there been truth in their vile reports, Urban V. would never have countenanced her, far less would he have demonstrated his regard for her in the public way he did. During her stay in Rome he showed her every public mark of honour it was in his power to bestow.

For the second time in her life Joanna, on Letare Sunday, received the Golden Rose—this time from Urban V. after he had blessed it and worn it during Mass. To the surprise of all present, the Pope, at the conclusion of High Mass, turned to the Queen of Naples, who was near him, and presented her with this coveted honour. It is said that the Cardinals afterwards remonstrated with him because he had preferred Joanna to the King of Cyprus, who was also present, and objected that she was the first woman who had ever received this favour.

Urban is reported to have replied in a severe tone, which did not encourage any more remonstrance on the part of the Cardinals : " There were exceptions to all rules, and who had ever before heard of a poor Abbot of St. Victor at Marseilles being Pope ? "

On Easter Sunday Urban lavished yet a greater favour upon Joanna. He presented her with the blessed hat and sword, but she, with her customary tact and grace, noticing the deep mortification of the King of Cyprus, asked the Pope to bestow the sword upon him, and Urban consenting, she gave it to Peter of Lusignan with her own fair hands, thus enhancing the gift, and retained for herself the pearl-embroidered hat.

Joanna remained in Rome until after the Easter ceremonies were over, and in the meantime, in the course of her interviews with Urban, had come to the decision that the best way out of the difficult question of the succession to her throne would be to arrange a marriage between her adopted daughter Margaret, her sister Maria's youngest child, and Charles Durazzo, and then, if she found on his return from Louis of Hungary that he was still loyal to her, to leave the crown to him and Margaret.

The two elder daughters of Maria were already married—Joanna, the Duchess of Durazzo, to Robert of Artois, and Agnes to Can della Scala,

## Urban V. returns to Rome 243

Prince of Verona; and the Queen knew that to leave her crown to either of them so long as Charles Durazzo lived would be to leave them and her kingdom an inheritance of civil war, so she asked Urban for a dispensation to enable her adopted daughter, Margaret, to marry her cousin, Charles Durazzo.

On leaving Rome she did not return to Naples at once, but went to Provence and worked there on reforming the laws of that country and Piedmont, and as soon as this was accomplished went back to her capital and celebrated with befitting pomp the marriage of her adopted daughter and Charles Durazzo. Joanna was strongly attached to her nephew, who was, externally at least, a very attractive man, with winning manners which effectually concealed his falseness and cruelty. He was a fine soldier, brave to rashness, and though of small stature he had defeated in single combat soon after he went to Hungary a gigantic Hungarian knight whom no other man had dared to challenge, and from that time he bore the head of an elephant as his crest, because that had formerly belonged to his vanquished foe.

Charles was very generous, especially to men of letters whom he patronised, and his conduct at this time was so irreproachable that Joanna unfortunately was deceived by it; and after his marriage with Margaret she issued a proclamation of her intention of bequeathing her crown to the newly married Prince and Princess, and to their issue. What must have been her feelings when very soon after this Charles returned to the service of the King of Hungary, on whose support he calculated should Joanna change her intentions with regard to her heirs?

Meanwhile Urban V. was finding the turbulent state of Rome and the deleterious effect of the unhealthy climate upon his health so unbearable that he resolved to return to Avignon, a measure which the Italian Cardinals opposed as strongly as the French had objected to his leaving it. The Pope again applied to the Queen of Naples to furnish him with galleys for the voyage, which she willingly supplied.

St. Bridget of Sweden, hearing of the Pope's intention of returning to France, demanded an audience, and informed the venerable Pontiff that it had been revealed to her by Our Lady that if he returned to Avignon he would die very shortly after.

Urban paid no attention to this prophecy; having made up his mind that he was acting for the best in removing the Papal Court back to Avignon, he was not to be deterred from carrying out his intention by what he considered might possibly be a delusion on the Swedish mystic's part. However that may be, it is certain that

URBAN THE FIFTH.

he lived only a few months after his return to France.

When he felt his end approaching he ordered the doors of his palace to be thrown open that all might see him die as he lay, in his Benedictine habit which he always wore, stretched on a wretched low bed with his crucifix in his feeble hands, making acts of humble contrition for all the sins of his past life. His death took place on December 19th, 1370. He was very infirm when St. Bridget uttered her prophecy, but he died of some unknown malady. He was deeply regretted by the Italians as well as by the French.

No less than eight hundred princes and nobles attended the Requiem sung at Bologna for his soul, and he was invoked as a saint immediately after it was celebrated, before his cause of canonisation began.

All the sovereigns of Europe, from Magnus II. of Sweden and Waldemar of Denmark in the north to Joanna in the south, demanded his canonisation, and his cause was greatly helped by the numerous miracles attributed to him, in an age when more faith was placed in miracles than in our sceptical time, and by his great sanctity, for he is said even by Protestant historians to have been a model of virtue. He made several greatly needed reforms in the Church, among them a very wise and important one forbidding the Cardinals to use their houses as sanctuaries for criminals.

By the death of Urban Joanna lost her best and most powerful friend, although the consequences to her of this irreparable loss were not felt immediately. The conclave to elect his successor was held at Avignon, and the choice fell upon Pierre Roger de Beaufort, the last of the French Popes, a nephew of Clement VI. He took the title of Gregory XI.

Shortly after his accession Joanna succeeded in putting an end to the strife which had disturbed the Two Sicilies ever since the fatal day of the massacre known as the Sicilian Vespers. A treaty was entered into between her confessor the Bishop of Gravina on the one hand, and the first chaplain of Frederick of Aragon, then King of Sicily, on the other side, by which the latter consented to acknowledge Joanna as Queen of the Two Sicilies, and to pay her a yearly tribute of three thousand ounces of gold, on condition that she left him in peaceable possession of the island. Frederick was also bound to furnish Joanna whenever she required them with ten galleys and a hundred men-at-arms. He was also required to resign the title of King of Sicily, and to take that of King of Trinacria instead. A marriage was also arranged between him and Maria, daughter of the Duke of Andria and of Joanna's sister-in-law, Margaret of Taranto.

Thus ended the long struggle for independence of the Island of Sicily, which now again acknowledged an Angevine sovereign, Queen Joanna.

## CHAPTER XVII

## Joanna and Charles of Sweden

JOANNA had now reached the summit of her greatness; from henceforth her history grows more and more sad and troubled, culminating in the final tragedy at Mora. But before we treat of a romantic episode which intervened before these shadows deepened, it may be as well to pause here to relate some incidents in the lives of Petrarch and Boccaccio, who were such conspicuous members of her court, and such enthusiastic admirers and champions of the " Jewel of Italy " as to fall naturally into the tale of her life. Boccaccio's relations with Joanna's aunt, the Princess Maria of Sicily, have already been mentioned. To her influence the world owes the immortal work, " The Decameron." It was at her command that he wrote the hundred short novels or tales it contains. For the most part they are most licentious; and the strongest evidence of the kind of intimacy which existed between the author and this beautiful princess is afforded by the loose and immoral character of a book of which Boccaccio was himself in later years so ashamed that he wrote to a friend to beg him not to permit his wife and daughter to read it.

He began to write this masterpiece of Italian prose at Naples, and finished it at Florence during the visitation of the Great Plague in 1348. Its publication was an epoch-making era in the history of Italian prose, whose standard it fixed from that day to this. The French critic Guinguène (1748–1816) says that "The Decameron," though less serious than the "Divina Commedia" of Dante, and less polished than the verses of Petrarch, has done much more to fix the Italian language. The writers of the sixteenth century speak of it with an enthusiasm which is almost religious. It is also a mirror of the manners and customs of the author's age. It opens with a most vivid description of the Plague, and the plan adopted is a hundred tales related by seven ladies and three gentlemen who make a *villeggiatura* from Florence to escape that dread scourge.

It is thought that the author owed, in a great measure, the beauty of his style to his association with Joanna for so many years, for her eloquence and the ease with which she spoke both Italian and the Provençal language were a liberal education, and the Princess Maria was also famed for her manners and conversation as well as for her wit.

In 1361, when Boccaccio was living at Florence, he was visited one day by a Carthusian friar, who asked to see him in private, and then told him he had a message for him from a member of his Order lately dead in the odour of sanctity, named Father Petroni, who had died in May, 1361, in a rapture. The name of Boccaccio's visitor was Father Joachim Ciani, and he informed him that Father Petroni had begged him on his deathbed to seek the author of "The Decameron," and warn him that unless he reformed his life and his licentious writings, of which he ought to be ashamed, he would die very shortly, and suffer eternal punishment for his sins.

Father Petroni also made several prophecies concerning other persons, among whom was Petrarch. Boccaccio asked Ciani how Father Petroni, who had never seen him or Petrarch, could know anything about them, and Ciani replied that not long before his death he had had a vision, in which many things had been revealed to him; and to prove the truth of what he said, he communicated to Boccaccio something concerning himself, a secret which he believed no one knew but himself. This made such an impression upon Boccaccio, who was terrified by the prospect of an early death and a life of eternal misery, that he was converted there and then, resolved to reform his manner of life, to renounce love and poetry, and even to part with his library, which at that time contained little but profane literature—which expression then meant the classic Greek and Latin writers. Not content with this change of life, which he faithfully carried out, he gave himself up to the study of theology, and was ordained priest after receiving the minor orders.

He then wrote to Petrarch and told him of the visit he had received, and of his resolutions, and asked him to accept his library in discharge of some debts he owed the poet. Petrarch was not so persuaded of the truth of Father Petroni's warnings as Boccaccio had been, and endeavoured to dissuade his friend from abandoning literature and parting with his library, and concluded by offering Boccaccio a home in exchange for his books, which he declared he would not except on any other terms.

Petrarch also urged that to deprive a man of Boccaccio's age of his books entirely, when he had cultivated letters so successfully hitherto, was to deprive him of what would be a great solace in his old age, and he asked him how St. Jerome would have been able to combat heresy as he did if he had had no books to help him.

Boccaccio declined Petrarch's offer to live with him, but he kept his books, and added the study of theology to his other knowledge, and soon became a noted priest, and was entrusted with an important mission by the Bishop of Florence.

Soon after he became a priest, Nicholas Acciajuoli invited him to Naples, and for a time they lived together in a palace at Amalfi; but they did not get on very well, as Acciajuoli now ranked among the highest princes, and apparently gave himself airs to one who had been his own familiar friend. He also after a while treated Boccaccio shamefully, in the hope of getting rid of him, and put him into a mean lodging, badly furnished, and sent his menials, his cooks, lackeys, and even his mule-drivers and scullions to take their meals at the same table. Boccaccio soon had enough of this kind of thing, and left Amalfi and went to the north of Italy, to stay with Petrarch in Padua for three months.

He then went to Certaldo, which was the birth place of his father, and after spending some time there returned to Naples, where he met with such a warm reception from Joanna that her courtiers all vied with each other in doing him honour. But though the Queen made him the most liberal offers to remain attached to her court at Naples for the rest of his life, he decided to return after a time to Certaldo, where he was seized with the first dangerous illness he had ever known, which ruined his strong constitution, and he never wholly recovered from the effects of it.

In October 1373, he began a course of lectures

in the Church of St. Lawrence at Certaldo, on the "Divina Commedia." The commentary he then wrote on the first seven cantos makes two thick volumes, and his enemies said he tried to display his own knowledge rather than to explain Dante's immortal poem.

In July, 1374, Petrarch died at Arqua, of a fit of apoplexy, and Boccaccio thus lost his greatest and best friend, whom he only survived for eighteen months. His lectures and the labour they involved proved too much for his enfeebled strength, and on December 21st, 1375, he died at Certaldo. By their deaths Joanna lost the two greatest ornaments of her court, and two of her staunchest friends and admirers, both of whom, as has appeared above, have left their tribute of praise to the unfortunate and beautiful Queen of the Two Sicilies.

About a year after the accession of Pope Gregory XI. there occurred one of the most romantic and dramatic incidents in Joanna's life—which was certainly not wanting in either of these elements. It was connected with the second visit of St. Bridget of Sweden to the Neapolitan court, which she made in 1371, on her way to the Holy Land, whither she, with her daughter Catherine and her two eldest sons, Charles, Prince of Nericia, and Birger, two young men of very different disposition and character.

Charles was a fine, handsome man, a brave soldier,

but of passionate, even violent nature, and yet he had great charm of manner, and was very much liked and admired. His father, who had been very proud of his eldest son and his achievements in the hunting-field as well as on the field of battle, had spoiled him, and he had given his mother a great deal of anxiety all through his life. She had great influence over him, and could to some extent curb his impetuous temper and love of the world, and by her early training had fostered the religious side of his character—which was by no means a negligible quantity, for if he had strong passions, he had also very strong faith in all the doctrines of the Catholic religion.

Birger, on the other hand, had never given his mother a moment's anxiety in his life: he was a very pious, devout man, of a studious disposition, very retiring, caring nothing for worldly pleasures; he had neither Charles's personal beauty, nor his power of attracting affection and admiration, and led a lonely life, occupying himself with works of charity and study.

These two brothers arrived in Rome in the autumn of 1371, in order to accompany their mother on her pilgrimage to the Holy Land, on which she was about to start. As the boat which was to convey the pilgrims to Naples left the harbour, St. Bridget turned to Father Peter of Alvastra, her confessor, and said, as she looked at the party, "We shall all return safely except the one I love best"—a prophecy destined to be fulfilled.

Joanna had just returned from Avignon, where she had had a most cordial reception from the new Pope Gregory XI., when St. Bridget and the other Scandinavian pilgrims reached Naples. The Neapolitan nobility again hastened to offer their princely hospitality to the Swedish mystic and her companions; but this time St. Bridget preferred a quieter residence, seeing that she was a pilgrim, so they went to the Hospice of Santa Maria dell' Avvocata, which adjoined the monastery of the Brothers Hospitaliers of St. John.

One of St. Bridget's first acts after her arrival in Naples was to ask for an audience of the Queen, her friend, and Joanna graciously accorded her one immediately.

She was apparently at the time staying in the Castel del Ovo, as it was there that the dramatic scene we are about to describe took place. She received the Swedish pilgrims at a solemn audience, with all the honours due to the high rank of the Princess of Nericia and her sons.

Joanna was now about forty-three, and her majestic beauty was by no means impaired, but had rather gained in dignity, by all the sorrows she had experienced. It was seen to the very best advantage, as she was magnificently attired; her golden hair was worn brushed back, showing her fine forehead, which was one of her best features, and was crowned on this occasion with a diadem of pearls on black velvet, which seems to have been especially becoming. There was a tender look in her great dark eyes, and the sweetest of smiles, for which she was famous, played round her lips, as she stood to receive her distinguished guests, towering over all her ladies-in-waiting, many of whom were remarkable also for their beauty, and surrounded by her courtiers and knights, among whom the chief gentleman-in-waiting was one Landolpho Crispano; some of the royal princes were also present.

St. Bridget advanced first to kiss the Queen's hand, and then turned to present her two sons. Birger knelt at the Queen's feet, according to the etiquette of the court; but Charles was so enchanted by the vision of grace Joanna presented to his gaze, that he forget everything except Joanna's beauty, and pressing impulsively forward he seized the Queen in his arms and kissed her on the lips.

The hot blood of the Neapolitan princes and gentlemen-in-waiting was raised to boiling point at this unseemly conduct to their mistress, and instinctively their hands went to their swords, and but for the restraining hand of Joanna on Crispano's shoulder Charles's days would have come to an abrupt conclusion. The Queen was not at all offended at this Scandinavian expression of admiration, and behaved most graciously to the impetuous young Swede.

St. Bridget was terribly distressed at this incident, for Charles had a wife in Sweden, with whom he was not on the best of terms; her piety did not suit his worldly taste and love of society, and it was said he would gladly be rid of her, and his subsequent conduct showed there was truth in this report. St. Bridget went back to the Hospice deeply mortified and grieved at what she foresaw would be a great trial, for the Queen was again a widow and had seemed to be by no means displeased by Charles's sudden passion for her. The saint threw herself on her knees and then prostrated herself before the altar in the chapel of the Brothers Hospitaliers on her return, and for the rest of her stay in Naples spent the greater part of her time there. Here the sick were brought to her to heal, and here she poured out her heart in prayer for her son.

Meanwhile Charles seemed to have abandoned the idea of continuing his pilgrimage to the Holy Land, and to have made up his mind to remain in Naples, where he spent his days in following the Queen, and dancing attendance upon her; and Joanna encouraged her Swedish lover, and it was said seriously contemplated asking Charles to marry her. St. Bridget, on hearing this gossip, went to the

## Joanna and Charles of Sweden 257

Queen and told her that Charles already had a wife and children in Sweden. Whether Joanna did seriously think of asking the Pope to dispense Charles from his marriage vows, which seems incredible, or whether she was unaware of his marriage till St. Bridget apprised her of it, or whether she merely intended to employ Charles to fight her battles for her (for the incursions of Ambrose Visconti into her dominions and the quarrels of the Neapolitan princes made her councillors desire her to marry a fourth time, so as to have some one to help her to defend her kingdom) we do not know. However this may be, she continued her friendship with the handsome young Scandinavian warrior, and, to the great distress of his mother, they met frequently, and not all St. Bridget's entreaties could induce Charles to leave Naples, whose Queen heaped presents upon him.

Joanna now issued invitations to one of the grand or solemn balls for which her court was celebrated, but when the evening arrived Charles did not appear. The Queen sent a messenger with a command for him to come, as she was expecting him; but on reaching the Hospice at which he was staying the messenger found he was seriously ill with a sudden attack of fever, and too weak to leave his bed or to speak above a whisper. His illness, which was fatal, lasted a fortnight, during which time St. Bridget scarcely left his bedside, watching and praying for his repentance, which, if tardy, seems to have been sincere.

When the news of his death was communicated to the Queen, Joanna commanded that Charles's funeral should be celebrated with the pomp befitting one who was of high rank and on terms of intimate friendship with her. The Archbishop of Naples sung the Requiem in the cathedral, and a very grand procession followed the remains of the handsome young Swede to the Franciscan monastery of Santa Croce, where he was buried. His death was one of the greatest sorrows of St. Bridget's life; she was seventy when it occurred, but she was present at his funeral, and almost immediately after left Naples, with the other pilgrims in her train, for the Holy Land.

The Swedish saint paid one more visit to Naples, about two years later, on her way home from Jerusalem to Rome, where she was living, and where she died soon after. On her arrival this time at Naples she found the city suffering from the Plague, and Joanna, the Archbishop of Naples, and the citizens were all assembled at the harbour to greet her when her galley was sighted. They implored her to deliver their beautiful city from this terrible scourge; for her reputation was so great that the Queen, as well as the people, believed she had the power to drive it away by her prayers, for in those days this dread disease was considered a punishment from Almighty God.

St. Bridget was not slow to take advantage of this belief, and answered that " penitence alone could turn away the divine anger from kings and peoples, and that she would pray for guidance, and tell them what Almighty God revealed to her on the subject."

The result of the saint's prayers was that she wrote a severe letter to her friend the Queen, in the course of which she admonished her as follows :

" Confess your faults with sincerity, and firmly resolve to amend them. Think on the manner in which you have fulfilled the duties of wife and Queen. Restore any wealth unjustly acquired. Be just before you are generous. Free your subjects from as many taxes as you can. Surround yourself with frank, wise, and disinterested counsellors. Do not paint your beautiful face, lest by so doing souls should be lost. Be humble. Love and solace the poor. Meditate upon the Passion of Christ, and fear the Lord, for you have led a life of ease rather than that of a Queen. You will never have any more children, therefore so rule the affairs of your kingdom that peace may reign after your death. There only remain a few years for you to live ; employ them in the service of God and in penitence : if not, at the last judgment you will be treated as an ungrateful person, odious to the Lord, to angels, and to men."

This remarkable but sensible letter was, it must be remembered, written by an ascetic who was herself leading a life of rigorous penance, treating her body with the greatest severity, to whom, therefore, Joanna's liking for society and gaiety appeared as grievous sins; moreover, St. Bridget had been greatly scandalised by her son Charles's sudden fit of passion for Joanna, and the way in which the Queen had received it.

One of the Swedish pilgrims, Magnus d'Eka by name, was entrusted to deliver this letter to the Queen, who received it with great sweetness, and did not in the least resent St. Bridget's warnings and counsels. She granted her old friend several private audiences during the two months that the saint spent in Naples.

Not content with admonishing the Queen, St. Bridget wrote several letters to the Archbishop of Naples, in which she commented most severely on the vice of the Neapolitans, and especially upon the treatment of their slaves. The Archbishop is said to have received her letters with respect, and to have had portions of them read from the pulpit in the cathedral, and also some of her revelations, which, as the saint believed, were made to her during her stay there.

The fact that the plague was raging in Naples

*From a woodcut in "Revelationes Sanctæ Birgittæ, 1500."*
ST. BRIDGET ON HORSEBACK.

p. 260]

no doubt rendered the Archbishop and clergy more disposed to listen to the teaching of the Swedish prophetess, who was already revered as a saint; but although conversions were made among the upper classes, the populace paid but little heed to the counsels and warnings given from the cathedral pulpit.

Before St. Bridget left Naples, Joanna, hearing that she was in want of money to continue her journey to Rome, with her customary generosity sent her a handsome present of money, which the saint, after some hesitation, gratefully accepted, and then, at Joanna's invitation, went to spend a few days with the Queen at Aversa, where she was then in residence, taking her daughter Catherine with her, intending to start from thence for Rome. St. Catherine did not like Joanna, and was anxious to leave as soon as possible, while St. Bridget, who was much attached to the Queen, whom she looked upon as her spiritual daughter, and saw with how many temptations the beautiful widowed Queen was beset, would fain have lingered longer with her, in the hope of persuading her to lead a stricter life. But St. Bridget was in very feeble health, and no doubt St. Catherine was anxious to get her safely back to Rome; and after a short stay at Aversa, the wind and weather being favourable, the pilgrims sailed for Rome, where St. Bridget died on July 23rd of that same year.

By her death Joanna lost another real friend, to whom she seems to have been sincerely attached, since she loved her well enough to receive her reproofs and warnings with her customary sweetness.

The very fact of St. Bridget's friendship for Joanna, in spite of the great contrast in their manner of life, speaks volumes in favour of the much maligned Queen, for we cannot suppose that if Joanna had been half as bad as some of her detractors would have us believe, that so strict and holy a woman as St. Bridget would have accepted money from her, as well as hospitality, or have visited her on three separate occasions.

## CHAPTER XVIII

## Joanna's Fourth Marriage

THE next event which disturbed Joanna's troubled reign was the rebellion of the Duke of Andria, which was coincident with the visit of St. Bridget to Naples, and resulted ultimately in the loss of Piedmont. This ambitious man had married Margaret of Taranto, by whom he had two children, a son and a daughter. The son was now, by the will of his late uncle, Philip, who made him his heir, Prince of Taranto, and he and his father now combined together to seize the lands of the barons surrounding their own dominions, with which they were not content. The first place they took was the town of Matera, which belonged to the Sanseverini, the most powerful family in the kingdom, who at once appealed to the Queen. Joanna sent a well-trusted officer to remonstrate privately with the Duke of Andria on his conduct, and to offer in her name to arbitrate for him.

The Duke treated her ambassador with great insolence, and refused to consent to any arbitration or to give up Matera. Joanna, unwilling to resort to extremes, assembled the Andria family, and sent them in turn to remonstrate with him, but all in vain. She then commanded him to appear before her in person, but this Andria refused to do.

Joanna, finding that her clemency was lost upon her contumacious subject, now called a meeting of her council, and, seated upon her throne, passed sentence upon the Duke, commanding the Sanseverini to occupy not only the lands of which the Duke had deprived them, but also his possessions in Apulia, which were held by him in fief to the crown, and now belonged to it in forfeit of his disobedience and rebellion.

The Duke had assembled all his forces in the neighbourhood of Naples, intending to invade the capital, to force the Queen to yield to his wishes. However, the Sanseverini were strong enough to defeat him and drive him back from Naples, and to lay siege to the two adjacent towns of Tiani and Sessa, which he had strongly fortified.

The Neapolitans suffered severely during the siege of Tiani, from want of provisions, and Joanna went about the city from piazza to piazza in her armour, soothing the people and exhorting them to endure privations bravely for a time, as it would be to their future advantage. The siege lasted five months, and then the Duke of Andria, seeing his cause was hopeless, fled in the night, ordering the citizens to capitulate if the enemy would set at liberty the Duchess, whom he had left behind him.

Joanna, however, insisted upon an unconditional surrender, and at the end of a fortnight the garrison yielded, and the Duchess was immediately taken to Naples. To defray the expenses of the war, Joanna sold both Tiani and Sessa, and gave the proceeds to two of the barons who had fought for her. She also gave away the forfeited duchy of Andria to one of them, but she very wisely kept Taranto for herself, as it was such an important part of her dominions. The Duke of Andria now sought the protection of the Pope at Avignon, who gave him large sums of money, with which he was able to raise a large army of thirteen thousand men, and had advanced as far as Capua, when Joanna summoned a council of war, and with the help of all her barons provided for the defence of Naples itself; but Andria advanced to Aversa, and there waited to visit his uncle, Raymond de Baux.

De Baux was a man of great weight in the kingdom, and occupied the post of Grand Chamberlain; he received his rebellious nephew with great severity, and sternly reproved him for his conduct, and told him his only course now was to throw himself at the feet of the Queen and implore her mercy, and get the Pope to intercede for him with Joanna, who was noted for her clemency.

The Duke was frightened at this attitude of his uncle, and fled secretly to Provence, where he recovered his courage, and began again to plot against Joanna, and introduced some mercenaries into her kingdom, who caused such alarm and suffering to her people that to get rid of them she agreed to pay them a large sum of money if they would leave.

At the same time a large part of her dominions in Piedmont fell into the hands of the Duke of Savoy, and she was too much hampered by the Duke of Andria's rebellion to be able to oppose him; consequently she lost for ever this principality, for Gregory XI. did not exert himself on her behalf as his predecessors had done. Close upon this misfortune came the death of one of her most cherished and able advisers, Raymond de Baux, whom she deplored deeply.

Of course the natural person to take upon himself the defence of her cause was Charles Durazzo, her adopted son and heir; but he was still fighting in the service of her enemy, the King of Hungary, and nothing would induce him to come to Naples and defend his own inheritance. Seeing herself thus lonely and unprotected from the many dangers and enemies, open and secret, which surrounded her, the only thing for her to do as it seemed to her and her advisers was to marry a fourth time.

There was then living in Naples, a frequenter of the Neapolitan Court, Otho, Prince of Brunswick, who had won a great reputation by his bravery and military exploits in Italy, where he was formerly Vicar-General of the Emperor Charles IV. of Bohemia. He was the younger son of the reigning Duke of Brunswick, and, seeing no chance of ever inheriting the duchy, he left his native land and went to Italy to try to earn distinction for himself as a condottiero or captain of one of the various companies of mercenaries, whom the Italian States employed to fight their battles for them in the thirteenth and fourteenth centuries. The condottieri had certain rules, which they observed faithfully; for instance, they spared each other, they demanded enormous sums for their services, but they always sent their prisoners back without a ransom.

Otho was about the same age as Joanna; he was very popular in Italy and was handsome as well as brave and good, and upon him Joanna's choice fell. And it was fortunate for her that it did, for he was the best of all her husbands, though unable to save her from the final tragedy which closed her life. He was generous and faithful to all his engagements, he was neither greedy nor ambitious, and agreed to the condition which Joanna imposed. This was that he should not bear the title of King, which she feared would excite the envy of Charles Durazzo, but every other honour that it was in her power to grant him she bestowed upon him. She gave him the principality of Taranto, which had been forfeited, and it is thought that one of her great reasons in marrying him was that he might undertake the government of this part of her dominions, which it would have hardly been safe to entrust to any one who was not thus closely allied to her.

She was forty-six when she married Otho, but she was so well preserved that she was still extraordinarily young-looking. In character Otho is said to have resembled her so much that the greatest harmony and affection existed between them; and at last, after three ventures which can none of them be described as ideal marriages, Joanna made experience of conjugal happiness, though it came late in life, and was destined not to be of very long duration. Still it is gratifying to know that she secured at least a lustre of real happiness from that strange mixture of joy and sorrow which we call life.

Strange to say, on the same day that Joanna and Otho were married Ambrose Visconti, who had been a State prisoner in the Castel del Ovo since his rebellion against the Queen, made his escape from prison. Whether there was some relaxation in the watch kept over him on this august occasion, or whether Joanna, so celebrated for her mercy to those who had offended her, had given orders that an opportunity for escape should be given him, we do not know.

# Joanna's Fourth Marriage

There was a celebrated astrologer living in Provence when Joanna was born, named Anselmo, who when consulted as to whether the royal infant Princess would marry answered, " Joanna maritaberis cum Alio." The superstitious Neapolitans now declared that the interpretation of this hitherto cryptic utterance was that Alio represented the initial letters of the names of her four husbands, Andrew, Louis, James, and Otho, which seems rather far-fetched.

If Joanna married a fourth time to please herself, she did not please her adopted son Charles Durazzo, nor his wife Margaret, her adopted daughter and niece, who were both very angry, fearing that if there were any issue from the Queen's marriage they would lose the crown, although Joanna took every opportunity of asserting her intention of leaving it to Charles Durazzo, her most ungrateful heir. This fourth marriage took place in 1374, according to Costanzo ; other writers, who appear to have copied each other, put the date at 1376.

At the time of Joanna's fourth marriage, and for a few years after, Naples was the only part of Italy that was at peace, for the Florentines and the Viscontis had invaded the Papal States, and the principal cities belonging to the Papacy, Bologna, Perugia, and Pavia, took this opportunity to declare their independence.

The Pope at first tried to bring back the Florentines and the revolted cities to their allegiance by fatherly persuasion; but as they disregarded all his overtures and promises of pardon if they submitted, he summoned the Florentine magistrates to appear before him at Avignon. But instead of obeying his orders, they ill-treated his messengers, and Gregory, now driven to exercise his authority if he wished for peace, issued a Bull of Excommunication against the Florentines, dated April 30th, 1376. This was a most severe punishment, for it absolved all their subjects from their allegiance, and by it they forfeited all their rights and privileges as citizens, and their estates in every part of the world became the property of any one who could seize them. Foreign princes were forbidden to receive them into their kingdoms, except as slaves, and their children to the third generation were proclaimed incapable of holding any office, either ecclesiastical or civil.

This terrible punishment destroyed the trade of Florence completely, and the citizens soon tried to make their peace with the Pope, for besides all these temporal deprivations, they were also deprived of the Sacraments, except in the case of the dying. In their distress the Florentines now appealed to the dyer's daughter afterwards known as St. Catherine of Siena, whose reputation for sanctity was even greater than that which her contemporary St. Bridget of Sweden enjoyed, and the Commune of Florence entreated her to go to Siena and intercede with Gregory for them.

St. Catherine was received with great honour at Avignon, and the Pope had such confidence in her judgment that he entrusted her with full power to make peace with the Florentines, knowing well that she would not do so at the expense of the Church. On her return to Siena the people rose against her and even threatened to kill her, but she escaped from them, and the Florentines then begged for the mediation of the neutral States of Italy.

Joanna and Otho exerted all their influence at Avignon and Florence, and were aided by the Genoese, and at length succeeded in procuring a truce. During this temporary peace the Florentines prevailed upon St. Catherine of Siena to go a second time to Avignon, and urge the Pope to return to Rome, promising to submit to the Holy See if he would remove it back to the Eternal City, but hinting plainly that if he did not they would again begin hostilities. Gregory, yielding at last against his own judgment to the remonstrances of St. Catherine, who like St. Bridget told him of the visions and revelations she had had concerning him, decided to go back to Rome, fearing that if he disregarded the letters St. Bridget had written to him, and the solemn warnings of St. Catherine and Peter of Aragon—who also claimed to have had a revelation from Heaven, commanding the Pope to return—he might be disobeying the will of Almighty God; so he set sail for Rome, whither he did not arrive until January 17th, 1377.

In the meanwhile St. Catherine of Sweden, the daughter of St. Bridget, had gone back to Rome from Wadstena (where she was now Abbess in the first convent of the Brigittines) to labour for the canonisation of St. Bridget. In 1376 Catherine arrived at Naples, bent on the same errand, namely, to collect a list of the miracles said to have been performed by St. Bridget during her visits to Naples, and to get the attestations of the Archbishop and bishops, and other witnesses of the truth of these reputed miracles.

There Catherine, who had no liking for the Queen, did not see Joanna at all, though she stayed two months at least in the city. Probably St. Catherine disapproved very strongly of Joanna's many marriages, for she herself was not only a "widow indeed," but she had never been a wife except in name, having persuaded her husband to let her live as his sister.

Perhaps there may have been some jealousy between these two women, both remarkable for their beauty. At any rate, there was no friendship between them such as had existed between Joanna and Catherine's mother.

One of St. Catherine's Neapolitan friends was the wife of Jamotti, the Seneschal of Salerno; and during

GREGORY THE ELEVENTH.

## Joanna's Fourth Marriage

the Abbess's stay in Naples, Alfarina, as she was called, confided to her that her husband's love for her had turned to hatred, because she had borne him no less than seven stillborn infants, and he believed, with the superstition then so common among all ranks, that she was accursed. Alfarina was again about to become a mother, and she dreaded that again her hopes might be disappointed, and another little coffin be required to take the place of the cradle she had prepared. Catherine comforted her and encouraged her to have hope, and gave her some relics of her mother so soon to be canonised; and not long after the joyful sound of the wail of a new-born infant was heard in the palace, which afterwards received the name of Bridget, and is said to have been the first child in Italy so called.

Gregory XI. received as enthusiastic a welcome on his entry into his capital as his predecessor St. Urban V. had done The reins of his white courser were held by Robert Orsini, one of the greatest Roman barons, and he was acclaimed with loud, joyful shouts of "Evviva il Papa!" These demonstrations were as hollow as a drum: he was beset from within by the insolence of the Roman nobility, and from without by war and rebellion; and at the end of a year he decided to return to Avignon, but before he could carry out this intention he died on March 27th, 1378.

On his deathbed he is said by some writers,

though others question it, to have warned his hearers to place no faith in visions and revelations, and to have regretted that he had been led by them to return to Rome. At the same time it must be remembered that he was on the point of adding St. Bridget's name to the Calendar of the Saints when his death occurred, and it was left to his successor to continue her cause; but the canonisation did not take place until 1391, when Boniface IX. at last rewarded all Catherine's efforts on her mother's behalf.

Although Gregory XI. had never been a great friend to Joanna, it was an unhappy day for her when he died, for his successor became her greatest enemy. Just before his death, foreseeing that there would be great difficulties in the election of the new Pope, Gregory published a Bull providing that instead of the usual number of two-thirds of the votes being necessary to secure the election of the Supreme Pontiff, when the Conclave should meet for that purpose, a majority of votes should suffice.

The Sacred College consisted at that time of only twenty-three Cardinals, eighteen of whom were French, four Italian, and one a Spaniard. There was a strong feeling among the Italians, and especially among the Romans, to force the Conclave to elect an Italian Pope instead of a French one this time, as the late Pope had foreseen. The city of Rome was now governed by a supreme magistrate called the Senator, assisted by twelve Bannerets; and during the time which elapsed between the death of Gregory and the meeting of the Conclave, these Bannerets met, and waited in a body on the Cardinals and warned them that the people of Rome were determined to have an Italian Pope, and in the event of any one of another nationality being chosen they would not undertake to protect the Cardinals from the violence of the populace.

The mode of election of a new Pope and all the arrangements for the Cardinals who form the Conclave differ very little in the twentieth century from those which prevailed in the fourteenth. Rome changes very slightly in these matters—she is "semper eadem"; but the circumstances attending the Conclave which followed the death of Gregory XI. were so unusual, and the result was of such vital consequence to Joanna especially, as well as to the whole of Christendom, that we must devote a little space to describing it, even though it be an oft-told tale.

# CHAPTER XIX

## The Beginning of the Great Schism

THE prophetic fears of Pope Gregory XI. were destined to be only too well fulfilled, and when the Conclave met to elect his successors this became apparent. Before the Cardinals assembled, deputations of Roman citizens approached many of them, to beg them to elect a Roman or at least an Italian to the Chair of Peter. They began the interview with entreaties, and ended with threats.

Later in the proceedings the Romans obtained the office of guarding the Cardinals, and proceeded to do this very thoroughly; for they took possession of the sails and rudders of all the boats on the Tiber, to prevent any of them from escaping that way until they had elected an Italian Pope. When the Conclave was sitting the noise of the mob, who blew on trumpets and played upon tambourines, and shouted and yelled, and hissed and cheered, deafened

# The Beginning of the Great Schism 277

them; but had they felt their lives were in danger, they could easily have hired some mercenaries to defend them, and the fact that they did not do so points to the validity of the election which followed, and shows that they were not intimidated into making choice of an Italian Pope, as was afterwards maintained by the adherents of the antipope.

On April 6th a terrific thunderstorm broke over the city, and a thunderbolt fell upon the cell of the Spanish Cardinal, Pierre de Luna, of Aragon, and a rumour spread that he had been elected; and so much damage was done by the storm to the Vatican that it was difficult to instal the Cardinals, and the Conclave had to be postponed for twenty-four hours.

On the 7th, when the Conclave met again at four in the afternoon, the piazza of St. Peter's was covered with a crowd of 20,000 people, who shouted at the Cardinals as they entered, "We will have an Italian Pope! Give us an Italian Pope or we shall know what to do!"

Of the four Italian Cardinals in the Conclave, Cardinal Orsini was too young to be elected—he was then only twenty-four—and Piero, Cardinal of St. Peter's, was too old, and suffered from gout so badly that he had to be carried across the square into the palace. On the night of the 7th the mob broke into the Vatican and found access to the Papal cellars, and got tipsy on Canary and Chianti, and threatened the lives of the Cardinals, demanding a Roman Pope; but the Cardinals would not be intimidated, and Orsini told them that if they were to elect any one through fear of them, the election would be *ipso facto* null and void.

Now there was an outsider, Nicholas Prignano, a Neapolitan, the Archbishop of Bari, who had been consulted by the Cardinals before they entered into the Conclave, and who had also taken part in the deliberations of the Bannerets on the same subject, and before the Conclave a good many of the Cardinals were prepared to vote for Prignano, and eventually did so on April 8th, and he, being elected by fifteen votes, took the title of Urban VI.

The new Pope belonged to a noble Neapolitan family, and was not only a very eloquent, capable, wise man, but at the time of his election he was also very good and pious, humble and mortified, and was held in high esteem by his countrymen, and especially by his Queen, Joanna, who had a very great regard for him.

While the Conclave was sitting Thomas d'Acerno, Joanna's attorney, who was in Rome, wrote to one of her chamberlains to say that the Archbishop of Bari stood a very good chance of being elected; and when the news of his exaltation to the highest earthly dignity actually came to Naples, the Queen and her people were all delighted at the honour conferred upon their countryman.

Joanna with her usual royal generosity immediately sent the new Pope a present of 40,000 crowns, a ship-load of provisions, and all kinds of things which she thought would be useful to him, and at the same time she wrote to tell him that all her kingdom had to offer was at his disposal. Later, when the Cardinals rebelled against him, Joanna sent him 200 cavalry and a large body of foot-soldiers to guard him.

We shall never know all Urban's reasons for acting as he now did; for while he accepted Joanna's presents and the service of her troops, he was plotting her downfall with her brother-in-law,[1] the Duke of Andria, who was in rebellion against her.

Joanna had now four great enemies to contend with: her life-long enemy, Louis of Hungary, was still upon the warpath; the Duke of Andria was in rebellion against her; her nephew and heir, Charles of Durazzo, was in the service of the King of Hungary, and plotting to dethrone her; and, as she was soon to discover, the new Pope was the most powerful of all her foes.

The shadows were darkening round her. The accession of Urban VI. was the first step in the downfall of the beautiful Sicilian Queen. Had she opposed Prignano's election from the first, it

---

[1] Her sister-in-law, Margaret of Taranto, was married to the Duke of Andria.

would have been easy to understand Urban's conduct towards her; but, as we have just seen, she did not do so—on the contrary she treated him with generous loyalty until the crash came.

Urban's enemies attributed his behaviour to Joanna to his nepotism, a grave fault in a Pope, of which he cannot be excused; for it is said he desired the greater part of Joanna's kingdom for his nephew, Francisco or Butillo Prignano, a most unworthy man of licentious life, and Urban determined to invest Charles Durazzo with Joanna's crown on condition that he would give up half the kingdom to his nephew, Francisco Prignano.

While the Pope and the Duke of Andria were sending secret messengers to Durazzo, to try to negotiate this business, Cardinal Orsini went to the Neapolitan Court, and in an interview with the Queen tried to induce her to refuse to acknowledge Urban, and to get the Ultramontane Cardinals to elect him as Pope in his stead.

Joanna, with her usual wisdom, refused to do anything of the kind; and so far from favouring Cardinal Orsini's proposal, she sent a splendid embassy—with her husband, Prince Otho of Brunswick, at its head, accompanied by her Chancellor, Nicholas Spinelli—to Rome to endeavour to smooth matters there, and to make peace between the Pope and the now offended Cardinals, and if possible to ward off the threatened schism.

## The Beginning of the Great Schism

This act of Joanna's should not be forgotten, as it too often is by her detractors, who, because she afterwards was unhappily led to espouse the cause of the antipope, Clement VII., and to play a prominent part in the Great Schism, heap all manner of abuse upon her, remembering all her bad acts and forgetting all her good ones, forgetting also the very great provocation she received to revolt from Urban, although nothing could excuse her from doing so. His election, though disputed, was legal, and it was the duty of all good Catholics, of whom Joanna was one, to be loyal to him in spite of his faults, which were great.

To begin with, Urban had a violent temper, and after his exaltation he became so haughty, and treated the Cardinals who had elected him with such scorn and contempt, and instituted such vigorous if necessary reforms, that they revolted against him, and thirteen out of the fifteen who had voted for him were so disgusted at the treatment they received at his hands that they withdrew from Rome and went to Anagni first, and afterwards, at the request of Onerato Cajetano, Lord of Fondi, to Fondi, where they ultimately elected the antipope Robert, Bishop of Geneva, who took the title of Clement VII.

Onerato Cajetano was a most powerful Neapolitan baron, and had lent the late Pope 20,000 florins, and when Urban came to the throne he wrote and asked him to discharge his predecessor's debt. Urban was furious, and deprived Cajetano of his title and fief, and gave them to Sanseverini, Prince Otho's Chancellor. Cajetano's daughter was engaged to be married to Otho's brother, Balthazar of Brunswick.

Unfortunately Joanna's mission to Rome was twofold. First and foremost it was to try to make peace between the Pope and Cardinals; but secondly it was to ask Urban's consent to the marriage of Maria, daughter and heiress of Frederick the Simple of Sicily, to Prince Otho's nephew, the Marquis of Montferrat.

Urban, however, desired to unite the rich Sicilian heiress with his own nephew, Francis Prignano, and he was so angry at the proposal made to him on Montferrat's behalf that he could not command his temper sufficiently to answer the ambassadors civilly. Nicholas Spinelli, Joanna's Chancellor, and Urban had been intimate friends before Joanna's favour had raised them both to the high position they afterwards occupied in her kingdom; but now Urban would not listen to his old friend, who was almost as anxious to serve him as he was to please Joanna; and when the Chancellor tried to point out that the marriage he had come to propose would be most advantageous to the Papacy, since it would unite both the Sicilies in its interests, the Pope flew into a violent passion, and said he "would soon send the Queen of Naples to spin in the monastery of St. Clare."

# The Beginning of the Great Schism

From this time matters between the Neapolitan embassy and the Pope went from bad to worse. Prince Otho and the Chancellor, Nicholas Spinelli, were naturally highly indignant at this insult to Joanna, and Urban continued to add fuel to the flame he had kindled by a succession of slights which he put upon Joanna's husband and minister.

One day, at a public banquet in Rome, Spinelli seated himself next to Otho (which indeed was his proper place as Chancellor of the kingdom he represented), whereupon the Pope ordered him to get up instantly, and not presume to occupy a place which did not belong to him, but to go lower down. The Neapolitan pride of Spinelli could little brook this insult, and it is said that he never forgave it.

Urban, not content with insulting Joanna's Chancellor and his own old friend, treated the Neapolitan Queen's husband also with marked contempt, and also with great ingratitude, for Otho had done all in his power to support the Pope and uphold his authority.

On one occasion when the Prince of Brunswick, according to custom, held a basin of water and a towel for the Holy Father to wash his hands before dinner, Urban turned away and, pretending not to see the Prince kneeling at his side, entered into conversation with some one else, till one of his friends, horrified at this behaviour to one of such high rank as Prince Otho, the Consort of the Queen of Naples, exclaimed · "Your Holiness must needs wash; Holy Father, it is high time you did so."

Otho's secretary says that Otho then repeated the remark made of an earlier Pope Urban, that he feared the Holy Father should rather be called a disturber than urbane, making a Latin pun lost in translation.[1]

It does not require much imagination to picture Joanna's just anger when Otho and her Chancellor returned to Naples and related this incident and various other insults which they had received at the hands of the Pope, whom she had originally been so anxious to help, and had treated with such generosity. Petty annoyances and slights of this kind are apt to stir up and engender more strife and bitterness than more aggressive actions. The scenes between Urban and Joanna's embassy took place at Tivoli, whither Urban had retired when the other Cardinals went to Anagni, from whence they issued encyclical letters to all the European courts, declaring the election of Urban null and void.

As a counterblast to this, Urban proceeded to create twenty-nine new Cardinals, and at the same time he offered to have his election examined by a General Council of the Church, which he proposed to call; but the Cardinals refused to consent to this,

---

[1] "Pro certo pater noster non Urbanus sed potius, timeo Turbanus dicetur."

# The Beginning of the Great Schism

and the election in September of the Bishop of Geneva by the Cardinals at Fondi, which was in the kingdom of Naples, was the beginning of the Great Schism, which disturbed the Church and the whole of Europe for forty years, from 1378 to 1418.

Robert of Geneva, the antipope, was a most blood thirsty man; he had personally led into Italy the Breton Company, the most inhuman of all the marauding bands of adventurers which molested Italy, and he had instigated them to commit atrocities. They were commanded now by Francesco de Vico, Prefect of Viterbo.

Robert of Geneva, after his election by the French Cardinals, was crowned in the Castle of Fondi, in the presence of Prince Otho and other Neapolitan nobles. Of the four Italian Cardinals who had voted for Urban, only two remained faithful, the old Cardinal Piero of St. Peter's died, and Cardinal Orsini now joined Joanna and recognised Clement VII. as Pope. When Urban returned to Rome from Tivoli he found himself deserted by the Sacred College; and it was by the advice of St. Catherine of Siena that he created the new Cardinals. She admonished him never to resign his high office, and by her admirable counsels encouraged him to persevere in his difficult career.

Very soon all Christendom was divided between the rival Popes, some countries remaining true to Urban, others joining the Clementines. The Emperor of Germany, the Kings of England, Sweden, Denmark, Hungary, Bohemia, and most of the Italian States and Flanders were loyal to Urban; whereas France and Scotland (which at that time invariably sided with France against England), Spain, Naples, Austria, Cyprus, Savoy, and some of the Italian and German States joined Clement's party.

The Papal war now began in earnest. Rival armies, each bearing the banner and Keys of St. Peter, met on the plains of the Romagna, and at first the advantage was on the side of the Clementines. Meanwhile Urban and Clement fulminated anathemas against each other, and each excommunicated the adherents of the rival Pope, so that all Europe was disturbed and unsettled by the quarrels of the Urbanists and the Clementines.

St. Catherine of Siena now proposed to Urban that she should go to Naples with St. Catherine of Sweden, St. Bridget's daughter (who was in Rome, working for her mother's canonisation, which was delayed by the schism), and endeavour to win Joanna over to his cause. But there were two obstacles to this plan. In the first place, Catherine of Sweden, who we know did not like Joanna, positively refused to go and see her; and in the second place the confessor of St. Catherine of Siena, Raymond of Capua, dissuaded her from going, and Urban reluctantly yielded to his representations, for which the saint was very indignant.

*From a woodcut in "Revelationes Sanctæ Birgittæ, 1500."*
ST. BRIDGET DELIVERING HER RULE TO THE MONKS AND NUNS.

St. Catherine of Siena, who had a high respect for the Neapolitan Queen, now wrote letters to Joanna and to some of the ladies in her court, and sent them to Naples by her devoted friend, Neri di Landuccio, entreating the Queen to be loyal to the lawful Pope. But by this time Joanna was unfortunately too closely involved in the fortunes of the antipope to draw back; moreover, she knew Urban was determined to depose her in favour of Charles Durazzo, to whom he had again offered the crown of Naples, through Joanna's enemy, the Duke of Andria, whom he sent to Charles to persuade him to accept it.

Charles, who was not so black as he has been painted, seems to have had scruples at first at treating his foster-mother in so ungrateful a way, but Andria overcame them by rousing his jealousy against Prince Otho and Robert, Count of Artois, who had married the Queen's eldest niece, Joanna, Duchess of Durazzo, daughter of Maria of Sicily, and the Duke suggested that Joanna intended to leave her crown to either one or the other of them. Joanna, however, had made different plans, and had decided to adopt Louis of Anjou as her heir.

Charles of Durazzo hesitated to obey the Pope's injunctions for another reason: his wife Margaret, the Queen's adopted daughter, and his two children lived in the palace with Joanna, and until they were removed he could not with due regard for their safety take active measures to obtain the throne.

Meanwhile Urban VI. created several Neapolitan Cardinals, and bestowed benefices upon some member of all the most important families of the kingdom, by which stroke of diplomacy he won over to his cause many of the most influential subjects of Joanna, who was now unfortunately irrevocably pledged to the antipope.

The battle of Marino between the two rival Papal armies proved victorious for Urban, thanks to the services of Sir John Hawkwood and his mercenaries, whom he had hired to fight for him; and Clement, feeling no longer safe at Fondi, determined to retire to Naples, and begged Joanna to send an escort to convey him thither.

Joanna, knowing that many of her subjects were loyal to Urban, was afraid that the antipope might meet with a hostile reception if he went to Castel Nuovo, where her court usually resided when she was in Naples; so she had the island Castel del Ovo fitted up magnificently for his reception, and went to the expense of having a temporary bridge thrown across from the rock on which the grim old castle stood to the mainland.

Clement and the Cardinals of his creation passed over this bridge in procession, making a grand display, and when they reached the great gateway of the castle met with a magnificent reception. There were assembled the brilliant Neapolitan court of barons and knights and other nobles, with their

# The Beginning of the Great Schism 289

wives and daughters in attendance on the royal princes and princesses, all attired in full court dress.

Under the great gateway, the centre of this brilliant throng of "fair women and brave men," and the fairest among them all, stood Joanna, in the royal purple velvet robes always worn by the Neapolitan sovereign, with magnificent jewels upon her head and neck and arms; a vision of majestic beauty, although no longer young. By her side stood Prince Otho, a handsome and imposing figure, and close by the three daughters of Joanna's dead sister Maria: Joanna, Duchess of Durazzo, wife of Robert of Artois; Agnes, widow of the Prince of Verona; and Margaret, wife of Charles Durazzo, the Queen's adopted daughter.

As Clement dismounted Joanna genuflected twice, and then knelt to kiss his foot and receive his blessing, and the royal princes and princesses did the same, and when this ceremony was over the antipope went into the castle to partake of a magnificent feast prepared for him and his Cardinals.

The festivities and entertainments which Joanna's superfluous generosity had prepared to welcome the disturber of the peace of Christendom lasted several days, and caused supreme discontent and disaffection in Naples, because, from the remoteness of the scene, the citizens were unable to see anything of them—and pageants are very dear to the Neapolitan heart.

19

Joanna's usual wisdom had deserted her, in the first place, when, goaded by Urban's discourtesy and plots against her, she had chosen to support Clement, and, in the second place, when through fear lest the antipope should meet with any hostile demonstration she had installed him in the Castel del Ovo, and by so doing had disappointed her people of the festivities and pageants in which they revelled. From a religious and from a political point of view, the usually wise Joanna committed a fatal mistake, one of the remoter consequences of which has been the obloquy which has ever since attached to her name, prejudicing as it has done so many loyal Catholic writers against her, so that they were unable to judge her fairly.

Nothing can excuse her conduct altogether in this matter, but at least nearly half Europe sinned with her, and no one had greater reason or stronger temptation to join Clement's party than she had. The Neapolitan people, who were too ignorant to enter into the merits and demerits of the controversy, and dared not rebel against Urban, interpreted Joanna's action in hiding the antipope in the Castel del Ovo as a sign of temerity on her part, and were in a state of ferment, when they were roused to open rebellion by an incident which occurred soon after Clement arrived.

A working-man in the Piazza of Sadlers one day spoke disrespectfully of the Queen to a group

# The Beginning of the Great Schism

of listeners in the hearing of a gentleman named Ravignano, who was riding past, and who stopped to reprove him. The man repeated his remarks, and his insolence provoked the rider to ride his horse at him with the intention of knocking him down; but in the scuffle which ensued the sadler lost his eye. His nephew raised the cry of Urban VI., and the infuriated crowd flew to arms and proceeded to pillage the houses of foreigners in the lower part of the city.

The Abbot Barruto, whom Urban had recently created Archbishop of Naples, headed this mob, and then took possession of the cathedral, driving the family of the Clementine Archbishop out of the archiepiscopal palace. This tumult was soon quelled, and reprisals followed, in the course of which the houses occupied by the Archbishop Barruto and his suite were pulled down.

These disturbances caused Clement to be seized with a fit of panic, in which he left Castel del Ovo and fled to Gaeta, and refused all Joanna's invitations and entreaties to return to Naples. From Gaeta he went to Avignon, which became the place of residence of the antipopes and their court.

# CHAPTER XX

## Joanna is Excommunicated

LOUIS of Anjou, whom Joanna had decided to adopt as her heir in the place of Charles of Durazzo, was the eldest brother of Charles V., King of France, and, after the King, the most powerful person in that kingdom; so it seemed to be an advantageous move on the Queen's part, particularly as the University of Paris had recently declared in favour of the antipope, Clement VII. Joanna hoped, by making the King's brother her heir, to enlist the services of France to defend her crown against the Pope and Charles of Durazzo. Charles had been for some time engaged in fighting for the King of Hungary, Joanna's old enemy, in the wars between the Venetians and the Genoese for maritime supremacy; and Urban now thought the time had come for him to send for his wife and children, who were living with Joanna, so he commanded him to do so prior to advancing with his Hungarian troops into Naples.

Charles obeyed the Pope, and wrote to the Queen asking that his wife and children should be sent to him; and Joanna, who must have felt this stroke acutely, with her usual generosity granted his request, although it was clearly against her own interest to do so, and sent her adopted daughter Margaret, with her little son Ladislaus, afterwards King of Naples, and his sister with a safe escort to Friuli, where Charles was then quartered. The Queen was destined never again to see Margaret of Durazzo, whom she had loved and cherished as her own daughter—a contingency she probably foresaw when with a heavy heart she parted from her.

Meanwhile Urban's unpopularity was so great in Rome that the mob had attacked the Vatican with sticks and stones; but, nothing daunted, the Pope, who with all his faults knew no fear, vested himself in his full pontificals and boldly showed himself to the people, trusting that the sight of him, whom they regarded as the Vicar of Christ, would strike terror into their hearts and terrify them into submission—as it did, and the tumult subsided.

This was in January, 1380, and in the following April St. Catherine of Siena died, and by her death the Pope lost his earthly guardian angel, who alone of all his subjects knew how to control his violent temper, and who had always urged him to be patient and merciful with Joanna and his other enemies, while at the same time she had encouraged him to defend his throne against them.

Joanna's conduct in taking so prominent a part in the election and recognition of Robert of Geneva as the antipope had naturally incensed Urban more and more with her, and a week after St. Catherine's death he issued a Bull of Excommunication against her.

In it he denounced " Joanna, formerly Queen of the Two Sicilies for her iniquities, wickedness, and enormous excesses, committed against Us and the Roman Church, and We declare her to be a schismatical, heretical, and blasphemous conspirator against Us and guilty of the crime of ' lèse-majesté,' and We deprive her of and depose her from all her dignities, honours, kingdoms, and lands, which We confiscate all and each, and We absolve from their fidelity and obedience to her all who have sworn allegiance to her, and none shall be held bound to obey her or to pay any debts due to her. And We inhibit under pain of excommunication all individual princes, dukes, barons, and nobles, and under pain of an interdict all communities and Universities, from obedience to her   Given at St. Peter's, Rome, April 29th, in the third year of Our pontificate."

At the same time Urban fulminated a sentence

of deposition against Bernard of Rhodes, the Clementine usurper of the Archbishopric of Naples, and confirmed the Abbot Barruto in the office in his place, and he excommunicated Onerato Cajetano and Rinaldo Orsini, Count of Nola, and his brother Giovanni.

The Pope now proceeded to preach a crusade against Joanna; but as this produced but little money and he was at this time nearly bankrupt, he seized the gold and silver images in the churches of Rome, and the jewels which adorned the shrines, and a great deal of the altar plate as well, and sold them or had them melted down.

About this time Charles Durazzo entered Italy at the head of 8,000 Hungarian soldiers, besides a large body of German and Italian infantry, who pillaged and destroyed the defenceless towns and villages they passed through, and would have besieged Florence if Sir John Hawkwood and his companies had not intervened and made a compromise by which the English knight and his followers entered Durazzo's service, and the Florentines agreed to lend Durazzo 40,000 florins—which he had never the smallest intention of refunding—and promised not to assist Joanna.

In the month of May Charles arrived in Rome, and was affectionately received by the Pope, but forced to agree to the conditions upon which Urban offered him the crown of Naples, which as we know were that the greater part of the kingdom should belong to his nephew, Butillo Prignano. Urban then proceeded formally to invest Durazzo with the Two Sicilies on the above conditions, to which Charles agreed, inwardly resolving that he would never fulfil them. In return Urban bestowed upon him all the treasure he had realised by the spoliation of the Roman churches, and, fortified with these sinews of war, Charles now advanced on Naples.

While Charles is thus spreading terror throughout Italy, by the excesses of his barbarian Hungarians and lawless freebooters, let us turn and see what steps the unhappy, excommunicated Queen and her husband were taking to defend her throne and life.

In a document dated July 29th, 1380, signed at Castel del Ovo, Joanna declared that she deprived Charles Durazzo of all pretensions to the inheritance of her kingdom, and that in his place she had adopted Louis, Duke of Anjou and Turenne, Count of Mans, and Lord of Montpellier, brother to Charles V., King of France, as heir to all her dominions in Naples, Provence, and Piedmont for himself and all his descendants.

This action displeased many of her Neapolitan subjects, who had known Charles from his cradle, and were proud of his military exploits, and in spite of his faults were attached to him, whereas Louis of Anjou was a stranger to them. From this time

Joanna's kingdom was torn with dissensions, political as well as religious—between not only the two parties of the Urbanists and Clementines, but the adherents of Charles of Durazzo and their opponents, the followers of Joanna and Louis of Anjou, also.

Among those who now deserted Joanna were the two Orsini, the Counts of Nola. In the midst of all this trouble, confusion was rendered " worse confounded " by a tumult in the piazzas of the city, between the nobles. Those of Capuana and Nido pretended that they had the right conceded to them by the late King Robert to precede all the other barons; whereas the barons of Portanova, Porto, and S. Arcangelo maintained, on the contrary, that they had the precedence of the most ancient nobles. This controversy led to battles in the streets and to much bloodshed, and on August 7th the whole city was in a state of alarm; but Prince Otho, at the risk of his own life, accompanied by some other barons, joined in the fray, and succeeded in quelling the disturbance.

Joanna pardoned the principal offenders, who had by their foolish ambition to precede each other placed the throne in danger; but the Queen was ever clement and merciful to a fault.

Unfortunately for Joanna, the death of the French King, Charles V., took place on September 16th in the same year, and this delayed the advent of Louis of Anjou, who was declared Regent of France, and was obliged to remain in Paris for some time; so he was unable to come at once to her aid, although it was now in his own interest to do so.

The antipope Clement confirmed Joanna's adoption of Louis, and had the insolence to bestow upon him the Papal States, which were in the possession of the true Pope, Urban VI.

As time drew on Charles approached nearer to Naples, and his forces were daily increased by deserters from Joanna's party, many of whom were terrified by the sentence of excommunication pronounced against her by Urban, and, fearing for their spiritual welfare, declared for him and Charles of Durazzo.

Nothing daunted by her falling fortunes and the perils which threatened her throne and life, Joanna took her courage in both hands, like the brave woman she was, and determined to make a bold fight for it. She placed great confidence in the valour of her husband Otho, although his adherents were few compared to those of Charles, and she trusted also in the false promises of her Neapolitan barons, many of whom ultimately deserted her. But her greatest hope was in her Provençal fleet, which she had summoned to her aid; but this took a long time in days when there were no telegraph-wires to communicate her wishes to them, and only the wind and their oars to bring them when summoned.

When matters became more desperate, and

URBAN THE SIXTH.

## Joanna is Excommunicated

Durazzo was fast approaching Naples, she sent the Count of Caserta to France, to entreat her new heir, Louis of Anjou, to hasten to her aid as quickly as possible, and he did his best to respond to her appeal. He set about collecting a large army; but the long distance from Naples and the difficulty of finding provision to feed his men, when there was no such thing as a commissariat, delayed his arrival and gave rise to the Neapolitan proverb, " The lilies of France will not take root a second time in Italy."

The key to the kingdom of Naples was San Germano, and here Otho, who was considered one of the first captains of his day, prepared to dispute Charles's advance. But many of the Neapolitan barons who had promised to join him there failed to keep their promises, and he was obliged to retire and leave the mountain passes open and fall back on Naples, where a body of mercenaries in Joanna's pay reinforced him.

Durazzo followed him so quickly that on July 17th, 1381, the two armies encamped at five in the evening under the walls of the city, so close together that the knights in the rival forces could recognise each other.

Charles had with him the traitor, the Duke of Andria, the Papal legate, Gentilis de Sangro, and Urban's nephew Francis or Butillo Prignano, now endowed with the empty title of Prince of Capua, for the title was all he ever enjoyed from that principality. Durazzo had also with him many of the prominent Neapolitan barons, a whole band of adventurers and malefactors, and some of the principal municipal officers of Naples. Otho had fewer barons in his army, as Joanna had kept most of those whom she believed to be faithful to her cause in the city to quell disturbances there if any should arise.

For three hours the two armies remained in sight of each other without attempting to fight. Charles was afraid to give battle to Otho, though his army was much the greater, lest the Neapolitans should fall on his rear while the Prince of Brunswick was engaging him in front. Otho had succeeded in getting Charles between him and the city; but this manœuvre was afterwards frustrated by the treachery of some citizens belonging to Urban's party, who managed to climb over the walls and told Durazzo the citizens were divided into two parties—one for Urban and him, and the other for Joanna and Clement; and they offered to conduct a few of his followers across the sands to the Porta del Conceria, an unguarded gate which was supposed to be sufficiently protected by the sea.

Durazzo selected a few of his soldiers who could swim, and sent them to this gate, which they reached by swimming—some accounts say by wading through the waves—and, finding it unlocked as well as unguarded, they passed through and made straight for the market-place. Here they raised the cry of "Viva il Re Carlo e il Papa Urbano!" and were immediately joined by some of Charles's old friends who were also Urbanists, and together they made their way, fighting, to the Porta del Mercato, before which Durazzo was encamped, and, before Joanna's adherents could defend it, they opened it, and Charles and a large body of his troops entered the city.

No sooner were the Hungarian soldiers under Charles inside Naples than they strongly fortified the gate by which they had entered, and marched to the Porta Capuana and placed another guard there, and then proceeded to Porta Reale, which was opposite to Otho's army, and guarded it against their entrance.

Otho soon saw what was going on, and immediately attempted to cut up the rearguard of the enemy; but he was only in time to destroy the band of Neapolitans under Cola Mostone—who had deserted Joanna—which he annihilated. The city was now in the greatest confusion. Joanna's party were vainly fighting against Charles's army and the Neapolitan people, and those of the minor nobility and gentry who could effect their escape fled to the surrounding country.

Here we must pause to tell what had become of Joanna during this siege. She who had on former occasions put on her armour, mounted her horse, and commanded her own troops—where was she now? And where was Louis of Anjou, and where was the Provençal fleet on which her chief hopes were based (for by them if necessary she might escape to Provence), and her ever faithful and loyal Provençal subjects—where were all these?

## CHAPTER XXI

## Joanna is Besieged

THE Castel Nuovo, in which the Queen usually resided when in her metropolis, had been newly fortified and strengthened in the case of eventualities, and here Joanna and her ladies-in-waiting retired when the siege of the city began, with sufficient provisions laid in to last them seven months.

With Joanna were her two nieces—her eldest niece, also named Joanna, who by virtue of her primogeniture enjoyed the title of Duchess of Durazzo, which she inherited from her mother, and her sister Agnes, the widow of Can della Scala, Prince of Verona. The Duchess of Durazzo was very rich, partly by inheriting a handsome patrimony, partly through the wealth she had accumulated by her parsimony and miserly habits.

Before the siege began the Queen had asked the Duchess to lend her some of her money, to cover part of the expenses of the war, and to provide for their defence, her own exchequer being low, and she consequently in great need of money; but the younger Joanna refused, although her own safety was at stake: her love of money was so great, that she preferred to face the danger which threatened her rather than part with it.

When the news of Charles's entrance into Naples was brought to the Queen she was besieged at the same time with appeals for help and protection from a number of noble ladies and their children, who, with many of the Clementine clergy and some of the worthiest of the old barons of her kingdom, implored her to admit them inside the castle with her and her suite.

Joanna knew that if she granted this appeal her provisions would only last one month instead of seven, but she also knew that if she refused the request of these helpless women and children and old barons, and sent them away, she would be sending them not only to death, but to endure horrors far worse than death, at the hands of Charles's barbarian Hungarians and lawless adventurers, and from the ferocity of the mob and the infuriated populace.

She could not steel her heart to abandon these delicate women and helpless children to save her own life, so, with her characteristic but in this case fatal generosity, she admitted them all to share her last refuge.

We are not told what the other less generous

Joanna, the Duchess of Durazzo, said to this action; but, judging from her character, she was, we should say, unlikely to approve it, and may have remonstrated with her royal aunt. But if so she was overruled, and all the petitioners were admitted to the castle.

Joanna's one great and only hope now was in the arrival of her Provençal fleet before her supplies were exhausted, and at the beginning of the siege this hope was very strong and well-founded. She expected it every day to arrive and bear her away to Avignon and the protection of the antipope, Clement, until her newly adopted heir, Louis of Anjou, should come with his army from France and expel Charles of Durazzo.

But day after day passed and no fleet arrived, day after day the besieged inhabitants of the castle scanned the horizon from its towers in the hope of detecting the sails of the belated galleys, on which all their hopes were based, but all in vain: the days lengthened into weeks and no sign of them rewarded the anxious watchers.

And daily the rations grew smaller and smaller, and the Queen and her nieces, the court and the garrison, and all the women and children, priests and barons she had admitted to share her fortune were beginning to feel the pangs of hunger. Presently they were reduced to feed on carrion, and were in consequence assailed with sickness, and still no sign of the Provençal fleet gladdened their aching eyes, and anxiety gave place to despair among the weaker-hearted; but Joanna was courageous as ever, and endured all these privations bravely.

Then one day her niece, Joanna, Duchess of Durazzo, when they were reduced to extreme hunger, put all her gold and jewels into a large vase, and carried it into the Queen's presence and laid it at her feet. Joanna looked mournfully at the treasure, which, had it been offered to her when she asked for the loan of it in her necessity, might have saved all their lives, but was useless now, since there was no possibility of exchanging it for food of any kind, and putting the useless offering aside, said sadly: "A sack of wheat would be more precious to me now, my niece, than all this treasure. Let that thief Charles, whom you have served so well, have it."

Meanwhile Prince Otho, who was at his wits' end to know what to do for the best to help his besieged Queen, endeavoured to entice Charles Durazzo out of Naples, to which end he returned to the walls, and destroyed the aqueduct which supplied the city with water, in the hope that Durazzo would be forced, through want of the first necessity of life, to come out and give him battle. Durazzo, however, was too wise to do anything of the kind. Moreover, the Neapolitans who had joined him showed him many springs of fresh water which were in the city, and from them he learnt that most of the houses were empty, the inhabitants having made good their escape by flight. They further counselled him not to be so rash as to make a sortie, and perhaps lose all he had already gained in one day, when it was certain that the Queen and her garrison could not hold out much longer, and must soon be forced by the pangs of hunger to surrender.

Charles took this advice and remained in the city, but he was not idle. He knew Castel Nuovo was far too strong for him to take it by storm, so he did not waste the strength of his soldiers by any vain attempts, but contented himself with addressing the people and exhorting them to submit to him and acknowledge him, whom they had known so long as the heir to the throne, as Joanna's successor; and little by little the Neapolitans, or the greater number of them, joined his party.

The fact that Charles was supported by the true Pope, Urban, and that the Queen had been excommunicated by him and had joined the cause of the antipope, Clement, had much to do with this defection of her subjects.

Prince Otho, finding that his attempt to draw Charles had failed, and that he was for the present powerless to help Joanna, retired with his forces to Aversa.

Joanna, who was now on the verge of starvation, still hoped against hope for the arrival of the long-looked-for galleys, which failed to come and rescue her; and seeing that her ladies and the women and children, and the garrison, were suffering all the horrors of a siege when the provisions are all but exhausted, began to think of surrender. She could not see all these her dependents perish, even if she were willing to die of starvation herself; so she decided to send her pronotary, Ugo de Sanseverino to Charles to try to come to some terms or arrange a truce.

This she did; and Durazzo, who was nearly related to Sanseverino, and knew him to be one of the most powerful barons in the kingdom, received him well. But the utmost concession he would grant the Queen was five more days, at the close of which, if she were not relieved, she was to surrender; but he promised that in this case she should not be removed from Castel Nuovo, but should be served there by her usual suite.

Durazzo's game now was to get Joanna to surrender willingly, and to acknowledge him once more as her heir; and with this object in view he sent a deputation of nobles to her to reassure her of his filial affection and submissive reverence for her. And to emphasise these assurances—in which he could hardly expect his adopted mother to place much faith, seeing he had so long been plotting to seize her throne— he sent her every day fruit and poultry for her table, and gave orders that she was to be supplied abundantly with all she required for her own use.

## Joanna is Besieged

If the besieged inhabitants of the castle had watched anxiously for the expected ships from Marseilles before, they now spent every hour of the five days of truce in looking anxiously from every available window and tower for some sign of their approach—but in vain.

Joanna, whose faith had always been very strong, was now a very devout woman, and spent much of her time in prayer before the altar in her private chapel in the castle. But neither did prayer seem to avail her, as far as the hoped-for fleet was concerned, for it did not make its appearance, and when the fifth day of the truce dawned there was still no sign of it.

During the truce Joanna had managed to send to Aversa to conjure her husband to make one more effort to rescue her; and on this fifth day Otho led his forces through the road of Piedigrotta, past the island of Ischia, till he reached the barriers Durazzo had erected before the Castel Nuovo, and tried to throw provisions into the castle.

This led to a pitched battle between him and Charles's soldiers, both sides fighting with such desperate valour that for a long time the result was very doubtful. The combatants were so close to the castle that the Queen was able to watch the fight from the windows. Perhaps Otho may have caught sight of her majestic figure—at any rate, her proximity and the knowledge of her captivity and sufferings so maddened him that he made a desperate attempt to seize the standard of Charles, which was surrounded by the bravest and most accomplished knights, who had fought with Durazzo in the wars of Hungary and Venice.

Otho's men, many of whom were recently recruited, were unable to cope with these well-seasoned soldiers, and he soon found himself alone in the thickest of the fight, where he received several wounds; but he still fought bravely on. The thought of his beautiful Queen and the threatened loss of her throne stimulated him, who was known as one of the bravest soldiers of his time; but fate was against him. His horse accidentally fell, and the brave and wounded Prince was thrown to the ground and taken prisoner in sight of Joanna, who is believed to have witnessed this last blow to her hopes.

With Otho were Baldassero of Brunswick, his brother; Robert, Count of Artois, the husband of the Duchess of Durazzo, who now enjoyed the title of Duke of Durazzo; the Count of Ariano, and Jacimo Zurlo, the head of the Neapolitan gentry. When Otho was taken prisoner his troops were seized with such a panic that all the efforts of Baldassero of Brunswick and Robert of Artois failed to rally them, and they ignominiously fled in all directions. Many of them dismounted and left their horses loose, and climbed up the sides of the mountain upon which the Castel St. Elmo stands, to take refuge within its thick walls.

At the time a gale was blowing and a very heavy rain was falling, which prevented Durazzo's soldiers from following them; but the horses they had left behind were seized by the Neapolitan people, who spent hours in catching them.

The battle was now completely lost. Otho's principal captains, Baldassero of Brunswick, Robert of Artois, the Count of Ariano, and Zurlo succeeded in escaping, but a good many of the nobles who had relations inside the city joined them, on receiving assurances of safety, and went over to the enemy's side, as Joanna's cause was now considered hopeless.

This contest, so disastrous to Joanna, took place on August 25th; and on the next morning she sent her surrender to Charles, as there was still no sign of the ships from Marseilles, and the time of the truce had expired.

When Charles reached the castle on the morning of the 26th he found the Queen, who—torn with anxiety for her wounded husband, now a prisoner in her enemy's hands—had passed a terrible night, walking in the garden, wishing perhaps to enjoy a little fresh air before she herself was made a prisoner.

Her majestic dignity was not without its effect on her ungrateful conqueror; and partly from long habit, partly perhaps from a sense of shame, he fell on his knees at the feet of his adopted mother, as though she were still his sovereign instead of his prisoner. Joanna looked sadly down on her former heir, whom it is said she now hated, and said ·

"Charles, I will not enumerate all the benefits I have bestowed upon you, for it would ill become a captive to humiliate her conqueror. Heaven and earth behold us and will judge between us. Remember only my regal dignity, if anything sacred can still find a place in your memory, and treat my husband with the respect due to a prince of his rank."

Charles rose from his knees, and made fervent protestations of reverence and love for Joanna, assuring her that he would never have attempted to snatch her kingdom from her if he had not been persuaded that Otho intended to dispute it with him in case of her death.

Joanna, who was the same age as Otho, and of a very good constitution, knew what value to attach to this false excuse for conduct which was inexcusable. She commanded her anger, and, with her usual royal dignity, eloquently begged him to treat Prince Otho honourably, as befitted his rank; and implored him to have mercy on all the captives in the castle, and especially on the Clementine clergy, who feared the punishment their schismatical conduct would draw on them from Urban, whose violent temper was well known, and who could not be expected to show them much mercy.

*From an early woodcut portrait, by kind permission of Mr. St. Clair Baddeley.*
CHARLES THE THIRD OF NAPLES.

# Joanna is Besieged

Charles, though now he had acquired the kingdom of Naples by force, was not content with this, but wanted also the rich inheritance of Provence, and, knowing that more was to be obtained of Joanna by kindness and consideration than by threats or attempts at frightening her into submission, trusted that he might still be able to delude her into making him once more her heir.

With this object in view he gave orders that, although his prisoner, she was to be treated with regal honours, and approached with all the customary forms, and attended by her usual officers and ladies-in-waiting.

On the fourth day after her surrender the long-looked-for Provençal fleet appeared, too late to be of any use, only adding, as it must have done, fresh bitterness to the anguish of the unhappy Queen when she saw its masts on the horizon. It was composed of twelve armed galleys, commanded by Angeluccio di Rosarno and Ludovico Antonio, Count of Caserta. Charles, as soon as he was notified of their arrival, went up to the castle to have another interview with Joanna, and endeavour, by fawning upon her, to persuade her to make him her heir.

He addressed Joanna as his Queen and beloved mother, renewed all his professions of loyalty, and saying she must now be convinced of his sincerity, he humbly begged her to nominate him heir of all her dominions in Provence, and to put all the foreign troops, which had at last so tardily arrived, under his command.

Joanna, who had no longer the least faith in the professions of Charles, and knew that the result of any document she might sign would be to lead her either to the scaffold or to lifelong captivity, could not be induced by promises or persuasions to grant this request. She knew too that her only hope—and that a very faint one—was in Louis of Anjou, whom she had already nominated her heir, and to offend him by making Charles her successor would be to cut off her only hope of release from captivity and restoration to her throne.

She inwardly resolved that she would be faithful to Louis of Anjou, and not risk alienating him for ever from her cause, but, pretending to believe Charles, she said to him:

"Give my captains a safe pass, that they may land and come to me and take my orders."

Charles, deceived by her composure, and thinking that he had at last prevailed upon her to acknowledge him again as her heir, acceded to her request, and granted a safe-conduct to the Count of Caserta and the chosen deputies from the Provençal galleys, and consented that they should have an audience of Joanna in his absence.

## CHAPTER XXII

## The Captive Queen

JOANNA was celebrated for her oratory; we have seen her pleading her own cause before Pope Clement VI. and his Cardinals in the Consistory-court at Avignon with consummate skill, and on other occasions we have heard her haranguing her councillors, but never perhaps was she more eloquent than now, when the Count of Caserta and the Provençal barons were admitted to her presence. Neither Charles nor any of his followers were present: only Joanna and her court were in the room when the French deputies were introduced.

Traces of the terrible privations and anxiety she had gone through were visible on the Queen's beautiful face, on which both mental and physical suffering had left their marks; but her customary majestic grace and dignity had not deserted her, and with them she greeted the Provençal subjects who had come too late to save her throne. If they expected reproach for their fatal delay they were not disappointed, for they were received with it.

"Why, my friends, why have you so long delayed to succour me? I have suffered what no woman and hardly any man can bear. By your negligence I have been forced to eat the vilest food, the putrid flesh of the lowest animals, and have been forced to surrender myself into the hands of a cruel enemy and become a slave. It is now too late, too late to help, but it is not too late for revenge. If you have not forgotten the good deeds of my house, and my true love for you, and the many benefits you have received from me; if you have any remembrance of your oath of fidelity to me, then I conjure you by that solemn allegiance, never in any manner or at any distance of time acknowledge as your lord that ungrateful robber who from a Queen has made me a captive slave.

"Give not yourselves up to that traitor who has pushed me from my throne. If ever it shall be told you that I have made him my heir, believe it not. If any writings are shown you to that effect, they are either false or forced from me without my consent.

"My will is that you own for your lord and master Louis of Anjou, my son and my heir, on whom I have bestowed the inheritance, not only of Provence and my Ultramontane States, but of this kingdom of Naples also. Him I have chosen to revenge this treason and violence against the person of his unhappy mother. Hasten to him, obey him truly and constantly. I do not beg this of you. I command it earnestly and solemnly, for I can still do it, since I am still your Princess, placed by God over you to rule you. Go then to Louis, Duke of Anjou, and render your obedience to him Take no more thought for me but to perform my funeral rites and to pray for my soul."

Deeply moved by these words of their fallen sovereign, the Provençal barons, with the tears streaming down their weather-beaten cheeks, excused their apparent negligence in not having arrived sooner, testified to their intense grief at her captivity, and vowing solemnly to obey her commands, they took their leave, and hastened back to their ships, to set sail at once for France to bring Louis of Anjou to avenge his adopted mother's wrongs. The Count of Caserta, who had ever been faithful to Joanna, went with them, protesting his willingness to die for her cause.

Durazzo returned to the Queen on the departure of the French barons, to hear the result of the conference, which was very different from what he had anticipated, and he learnt from Joanna's own lips that she had performed her last act of sovereignty and, as her honour demanded, urged her Provençal subjects to be true and loyal to Louis of Anjou, her present heir.

Louis of Anjou was the most accomplished of the three splendid sons of John the Good, King of France. The late King Charles V. was the eldest of these three brothers, Louis, Duke of Anjou, the second, Philip was the third. They were all three highly cultivated men, fond of splendour and great possessions, and of art, of which they were liberal patrons; but Louis was the most celebrated for his valour, and also for his magnificent collections of pictures, china, plate, jewels, books, and valuable MSS. He took great delight in all these, but he parted with many of his treasures to raise money for his expedition to Naples to secure his Sicilian throne.

Charles's wrath at finding Joanna had outwitted him, and defeated the object he had had in view when he granted her an interview with the French deputies, was very great; and when he saw the masts of the French galleys disappear below the horizon, as they were hastening to help his rival, he was furious, and determined to try the effect of harsh treatment upon his victim. With this end in view, he first of all had the Queen removed to the Castel del Ovo under a strong guard, as a prisoner, but he allowed some of her ladies-in-waiting to go with her.

Her niece Agnes, widow of the Prince of Verona, who with her elder sister, Joanna, Duchess of Durazzo, were taken prisoners with the Queen, was now married to the son of the Duke of Andria by Charles, who, to promote his own interests, bestowed her upon one of the Queen's greatest enemies like a captive slave, without consulting her.

Later on, when Charles had offended Urban, and it was rumoured that the Pope thought of deposing him in favour of this son of the Duke of Andria, who by this marriage had a double claim to the succession to the throne, Charles caused Agnes and her two innocent children, and Joanna of Durazzo, to be thrown into a dungeon, where they all died of starvation and misery, some say of poison.

The Queen had surrendered at the end of August, and on November 11th, St. Martin's day, Charles and his wife Margaret were solemnly crowned in the Cathedral of Naples, after taking the oaths of allegiance to Urban as the true Pope. When Charles was led in procession round the city after his coronation, under a canopy of state, the Duke of Andria, who had not yet deserted him, held his bridle on one side, and the Count of Conversano on the other. Before six months had passed, both these noblemen had gone back to Joanna's cause.

Great efforts were made to restore cheerfulness to Naples after the coronation by means of banquets and pageants, and all the shows in which the Neapolitans were known to delight; but so many families were in mourning for their relatives who had perished in the war, and so many houses were empty, as their owners had fled the city, that all the rejoicings did little to dispel the general gloom.

Very soon Charles found that it was very difficult for a usurper to satisfy the claims of his partisans, and impossible to content the ambition of his supporters, and the fickle Neapolitans. soon began to return to their old allegiance.

The Counts of Ariano, Fondi, and Aversa had remained in arms for Joanna, and they were now joined by that rebel, the Duke of Andria, the Sanseverini family, and the Counts of Conversano, Lece, and Montenovo. The Sanseverini and the Duke of Andria were deadly foes, nevertheless they now acted in concert, Charles having estranged Andria because he was unable to give back all his former possessions of which Joanna had deprived him, and the Sanseverini were jealous and disgusted with Charles for giving Agnes of Verona as wife to the son of the Duke of Andria.

But where, it may well be asked, was Louis of Anjou all this time? For his delay in coming to Joanna's aid was partly the cause of the final tragedy. That delay was in the first instance unavoidable, as his post of Regent, to which he was appointed on the death of Charles V., rendered his presence in Paris as necessary as it was undoubtedly agreeable to him. In June, 1381, Louis, who seems to have been enjoying himself very much at the time in his new position, received, through the Count of Caserta, Joanna's desperate appeal for help in her extremity, and, having called a Council together, he decided to leave France immediately for Naples and claim his inheritance. Then came the news of Charles's successes, and Louis realised that he had a kingdom to reconquer, as well as a frontier to defend, before he could take possession of his Sicilian inheritance. Under these difficulties his zeal to go to help Joanna seems to have cooled considerably, and after vacillating a great deal, as fresh news from Naples reached him, France decided to abandon Joanna to her fate.

This was in October, and after a while Louis, tired of doing nothing, and regretting that he had let his Sicilian crown slip through his fingers, entered into correspondence with the Neapolitan ambassador, and went to Avignon to consult with the antipope, Clement VII., and to try to get the Provençals to acknowledge him as their prince, and help him to win the Sicilian throne.

He stayed four months in Avignon, and received the encouragement of Clement to proceed to Italy, and on March 1st Clement invested him with the title of Duke of Calabria, reserved for the heir-presumptive to the throne of Naples.

He spent another three months collecting troops in Provence, and having been joined by the Duke of Savoy, at last, after all these maddening delays, he set sail for Naples at the head of a large army, amid the shouts of the Provençals of " Vive Pape Clément VII., Vive Madame la Reine Jeanne I., Vive le duc de Calabrie ! "

While he is leaving Marseilles with his splendid troops we must return to Naples to see what was going on there, and in so doing we must not forget that the Neapolitan revolution was a double revolution—it was religious as well as political. In acknowledging the usurper Charles III., so wrongly named " of Peace," the Neapolitans acknowledged the authority of the true Pope, Urban VI., and in deposing and deserting Joanna they condemned Clement VII. as antipope, and threw off their allegiance to both their temporal and spiritual sovereign, though the latter was a usurper.

There had entered into Naples with Charles, the Papal legate, Gentile de Sangro, who, if the Urbanists in Naples had suffered under Joanna, now immediately began to rule the Clementine clergy with a rod of iron. In one day, according to Urban's secretary, de Niem, he dismissed no fewer than thirty-two Clementine abbots, bishops, and archbishops ; and not content with depriving them of their benefices, he cast them into prison, and those who refused to acknowledge Urban were sent to the scaffold. Among these last was the Archbishop of Salerno.

A remarkable scene took place in the Church of St. Clare in Naples. The two Clementine cardinals who were taken prisoners with Joanna were led into this church among a vast crowd of people, and one of them, Cardinal de Giffone, intimidated by the presence of Charles of Durazzo and the Legate, di Sangro, denied the antipope, Clement, and burnt his hat, while the robes and hat of his companion, Cardinal d'Itro, were consumed in the same flames. After being thus publicly degraded, together with some other Clementine prelates, they were cast into prison, where Cardinal d'Itro died.

To strengthen his position in Naples, Urban now created a large number of Neapolitan cardinals, some of whom, later on, when Durazzo had incurred Urban's displeasure—their patience with the Pope's conduct being exhausted—conspired against Urban, with the idea of putting him under restraint as mad, or of delivering him into Durazzo's hands. In reprisal for this, Urban on discovering it put six of them into irons in the cells at Nocera, and then subjected them to torture.

Gentile de Sangro, who had himself tortured the Clementine clergy, was one of these six victims of Urban's cruelty, and, being an enormously stout man, fainted when the executioners lifted him from the ground with cords on to the rack, on which he was thrice stretched.

The old Cardinal of Venice each time that he was tortured exclaimed, "Christ suffered for us." The same authority, de Niem, says that the man chosen to apply these tortures was a Genoese pirate well known for his hatred of clerics.

Historians differ as to the date on which Durazzo caused Joanna to be removed from Castel del Ovo, for fear that her presence in Naples should cause a rebellion in her favour; but it seems most probable that it took place about March 28, 1382, and not, as Giannone says, a few days after her surrender, when, as we have said, she was taken to the Castel del Ovo.

The Castle of Muro[1] was a great, gloomy fortress, situated in Durazzo's own territory, inherited from his father, in the province of the Basilicata, to the south-east of Naples, and on this account it was from his point of view a much safer place of detention for the captive Queen. It stood in a wild, barren, mountainous district in an isolated situation, not easy of access, and as Joanna approached its gloomy towers her heart must have sunk within her.

She had been treated fairly well on the whole at Castel del Ovo, during her six or seven months' imprisonment there; but now her guard was made much more strict, and composed in part of the Hungarian soldiers, who hated her. Her nieces had

---

[1] The author of "Rulers of the South" says he knows no castle which gives so good an idea of baronial life in the fourteenth century as this fortress of Muro.

CASTELLO DELL OVO AT NAPLES.

*From an aquatint engraving after Paul Sandby*

P. 324]

been separated from her in Naples, but now she was deprived of her ladies-in-waiting also; and she especially felt the loss of Clemence di Collennucci, a young and pretty daughter of one of the Neapolitan barons, to whom she was much attached, and who was one of her maids-of-honour. Before Joanna was taken away from Castel del Ovo, Clemence was torn, weeping bitterly, from the unhappy Queen, and no entreaties would induce Charles to permit her to accompany her beloved mistress to her new prison.

It is said, however, that love found out a way to circumvent Charles; and a few days after Joanna had been removed from Naples, Clemence, with cropped hair, disguised as a Carthusian novice, and Francis de Baux, Duke of Andria, who had now returned to his allegiance to Joanna—clad in the habit of a professed monk of the same Order—set forth on foot to make a pilgrimage to Muro, and endeavour to obtain admission in this guise to the presence of the Queen, on pretence of offering her spiritual consolation.

This romantic tale does not seem to be well authenticated, and we doubt if it ever really happened; but as the Italians say, "Si non è vero è ben trovato"; and we can but hope that Joanna's last days were soothed by the presence of her favourite attendant, whose high spirit and devotion to her royal mistress may have given her courage to run the grave risk she did if she made this attempt.

It is possible, even probable, that the Duke of Andria may have earnestly desired an interview with Joanna unknown to Durazzo, to endeavour to persuade her to nominate his son (now married to her niece Agnes of Verona), as her heir, and it is quite likely he might have taken this step to attain it. He may, too, have felt remorse for his former rebellion against Joanna, which had been instrumental in bringing her to her present sad condition; he may have desired to ask her forgiveness, and consult with her as to some way of attempting her rescue; and the only way to accomplish this was to assume some disguise—and in those days that of a monk was the safest, and the most likely to obtain admission to the royal prisoner.

In this gloomy castle Joanna was kept in close imprisonment for two months, and denied the honours due to her high rank, before the final tragedy took place.

At the same time that she was removed from Naples, Charles caused her husband, Prince Otho of Brunswick, his prisoner-of-war, to be taken to the Castle of Altamura, on the extreme west of the Basilicata. Joanna asked one favour of her conqueror on reaching Castel del Muro, and that was not for herself, but the release of her husband, Otho of Brunswick; and this request Durazzo ultimately granted after Joanna's death, the account of which we must reserve for another chapter.

## CHAPTER XXIII

## The Final Tragedy

FOR two months Joanna dragged on a miserable existence in her gloomy prison, cut off from all her friends and from holding any communication with them, deprived of all the state and splendour to which her high rank had accustomed her, and equally deprived of the occupations the duties of her regal office afforded, and of the amusements for which her brilliant court had so long been famous.

Added to all these negative trials was the positive one of anxiety as to the fate of her husband, Otho of Brunswick, to whom she was deeply attached. Life had now little to offer her, for she knew her captivity was intended by her captor to be lifelong.

Her time was largely spent in the chapel, praying before the altar. She had always been famous for her love of devotional exercises and her strict observance of ecclesiastical feasts and ceremonies, but now she gave herself up almost entirely to prayer.

Meanwhile the final catastrophe was hastened to its ghastly consummation by the appearance of part of Louis of Anjou's fleet in the Bay of Naples. This arrived in the middle of May from Provence, where Louis had collected an army of 35,000 knights to drive out the usurper and seize upon the throne.

Urban VI. had by this time decided to depose Charles Durazzo, who had offended him, and daily the Neapolitan nobility were forsaking him for Joanna, to whom in her distress they now turned, and the universal desire among her subjects for her restoration became more and more evident.

The last straw which decided Charles to take her life was an embassy from her old enemy, Louis of Hungary, Charles's uncle, to congratulate him upon his success, and to demand the death of the Queen. Louis asked this as the price of his support of Charles's cause and as a reward for his past help.

Historians differ very much as to the details of Joanna's assassination, some even going as far as to excuse Charles from conniving at it; but there can be no doubt that he sent the four Hungarian soldiers who actually accomplished the foul deed

# The Final Tragedy

to Muro for the purpose of murdering his aunt and foster-mother, from whom he had received so many favours and benefits. He dared not trust its performance to any Neapolitan—he could not easily have found one so base as to attempt it—and so he chose four of his rude Hungarian soldiers, whose hatred of Joanna and of all Neapolitans was intense, and to whom the barbarous crime was a most congenial task, while their master, Louis of Hungary, who had always obstinately believed that Joanna had been an accomplice in the murder of his brother, Andrew of Hungary, looked upon it as a tardy act of just retribution.

"Let Joanna die the same death which Andrew suffered through her," he wrote to Charles.

Some accounts of the manner of Joanna's murder say that she was smothered in bed with pillows, others—and these are the most frequent—that she was strangled. The version we are about to give, which seems the most reliable, is taken from the works of Urban's secretary, Theodoric de Niem, who was at Naples during the time her remains were exposed to public view, and no doubt had ample opportunities for learning the truth.

It seems that on the morning of May 22nd, the captive Queen, who was now treated like a common prisoner, went to the chapel for her devotions, as was her habit at this time, when the four Hungarian soldiers secretly entered, and while two guarded the door the other two crept up to the kneeling Queen, and throwing a silken cord round her neck, strangled her instantly.

The only redeeming feature in this ghastly, cruel murder is that it was done quickly before the poor, helpless Queen had time to realise their intention; possibly before she even saw her murderers they had done their work.

Probably Joanna had during these seven or eight weeks at Muro prepared herself for death; her prayers had doubtless obtained her the pardon she sought for her past transgressions, and at the moment of death she was in the act of prayer. There can be little doubt she was well prepared to meet that great and most just Judge who alone knows the secrets of all hearts.

When the news of her death was brought to Charles, he ordered that her body should be taken to the Church of St. Clare in Naples, and placed in the choir there and exposed to the view of all her people, that they might see her for themselves that she was truly dead, and by that sad sight be convinced that any further efforts to restore her to her throne were in vain.

At the expiration of the eight days during which she lay in state, she was interred in this same church between the sacristy and the tomb of her late father, the Duke of Calabria. Round it is sculptured a Latin inscription to this effect:

*From an engraving by J. W. Cook.*

THE TOMB OF JOANNA OF NAPLES.
In the Church of St. Clair at Naples.

> "Here lies Joanna I., the illustrious Queen of Naples,
> Happy at first, afterwards exceedingly to be pitied.
> To Charles a daughter, tortured by another Charles,
> She suffered death before her husband."
> 1832. May XXVII.[1]

She was in the fifty-sixth year of her age, and the thirty-ninth of her reign, when she was thus done to death by her implacable enemy, Louis of Hungary, and her ungrateful adopted son, Charles III., whose name was execrated all over Europe as a matricide when the news of Joanna's murder transpired. The sad spectacle of her dead body in the Church of St. Clare had quite the contrary effect to that which Charles had hoped and intended to create. Even those who had before been indifferent to her fate were moved to compassion for her sufferings by the sight of her corpse, and so indignant at Charles's cruelty and ingratitude that they refused to submit any longer to his rule; while those who had ever been faithful to Joanna were now so exasperated against Charles that they swore vengeance against him, and joined the forces of Louis of Anjou.

Thus perished Joanna of Naples, one of the most beautiful and most maligned of women, whose praises, as we have seen, have been sung by the most

---

[1] Inclyta Parthenones, jacet hic Regina Joanna
Prima, prius felix, mox miseranda nimis:
Quam Carlo genitam mulctavit Carolus alter,
Qua morte illa virum sustulit ante suum.
MCCCLXXXII. XII. Maij V. Indict.
Camera. Giovanna I e Carlo III. Salerno, 1889.

celebrated men of her time, by Petrarch and Boccaccio, and who is known to this day to the Neapolitan boatmen, and has always been spoken of by Provençal historians, as "the Good Queen Jeanne I."

There will always be a difference of opinion among historians as to her merits, and the death of Andrew of Hungary will ever remain one of the unsolved mysteries of history; the only thing that seems certain about it being that Joanna had no part in it, as not only her acquittal at the court of Clement VI., but also her great grief at the time, and her great clemency to all conclusively show.

Her beauty, her majestic presence, her moving eloquence, her fascinating personality are now things of the past, as dead to us as last year's roses; but the spell which she cast in her lifetime over all who came in contact with her is immortal and still clings to her name, and, as we have endeavoured to show, makes her one of the most interesting characters in history.

It is not our purpose to describe the subsequent struggle between Charles Durazzo and Louis of Anjou, or the scarcely less bitter contest between the Pope, Urban VI., and his former protégé. We shall merely content ourselves with saying briefly what became of the principal persons who have figured in this historical tragedy, of which the central figure was the great Sicilian Queen.

Her husband, Otho of Brunswick, was liberated

## The Final Tragedy

by Charles two years after her death, and in reward for some advice which he had given Durazzo, Charles conferred upon him the principality of Taranto. Some years later, when Louis II. of Anjou grew up, Otho, with the aid of the Sanseverini, succeeded in placing him upon the Neapolitan throne; and when Louis refused to live in Naples, the Prince of Brunswick was offered the title and office of Viceroy, but he yielded it to Sanseverini. He died in Foggia in 1398, having survived Joanna fifteen years.

Joanna's lifelong enemy, Louis, King of Hungary, survived her only four months; he was surnamed the Great, and was deeply mourned by the Hungarians, who lost in him a good, brave, and wise king, as celebrated for his victories in the field of battle as for his private virtues, which together earned him this title. In his dealings with Joanna he allowed his natural affections for his brother Andrew to overpower his sense of justice.

In the year following the assassination of Joanna, Louis of Anjou, having in vain endeavoured to provoke Charles Durazzo to an engagement outside the walls of Barletto, withdrew with his army to Bari, where a fever of a pestilential character broke out in his camp, to which he succumbed on September the 21st, in his forty-seventh year. He left two sons, the elder of whom, Louis II., succeeded him, and for a short time occupied the Neapolitan throne.

Charles Durazzo was lying dangerously ill of fever at the time of Louis's death, but he recovered, and as soon as he had settled affairs in Naples, which Louis's death facilitated, he went to Hungary in answer to an invitation from some of the Hungarians to assume the crown. Here, after much plotting and scheming on his side and counterplotting on the part of the Dowager Queen Elizabeth and Maria, who had been proclaimed " King " of Hungary on the death of her father, whose only child she was, he was foully murdered on February 7th, 1386.

A soldier in the pay of the Dowager Queen Elizabeth struck him with a sword as he was in the act of reading a letter, half severing his head from his body. He lingered in great pain for two days, and was finally smothered, as he showed signs of recovering.

Thus retributive justice was dealt to the murderer of Joanna in the prime of his life, for he was just forty-one when the avenging angel overtook him. As his quarrel with Pope Urban VI. had led to his excommunication, he was denied Christian burial.

Charles III. was a little man, with fair hair and a ruddy and smiling countenance; he was affable and very popular; he was very generous to his partisans, and a great patron of men of letters. He had many good qualities; he was a very brave and most accomplished soldier. But his cruel ingratitude to his foster-mother, against whom, no doubt, his uncle,

# The Final Tragedy

Louis of Hungary, greatly prejudiced him, has made a blot on his fair name which can never be eradicated.

And here we take leave of this great but unhappy Queen, who has so often and so aptly been called the Neapolitan Mary Queen of Scots, whom she resembled so much in some respects, notably in her beauty and her misfortunes and in the mystery which surrounds the assassination of Andrew of Hungary and of Darnley. A parallel might also be drawn between the conduct of Charles Durazzo and the Earl of Murray.

Both these unhappy Queens will ever have their admirers and their detractors, for their beauty and their charm aroused envy among their contemporaries as well as admiration, and brought them both cruel enemies as well as enthusiastic friends.

May we venture to hope that our readers, as far as Joanna of Sicily is concerned, will rank among the latter?

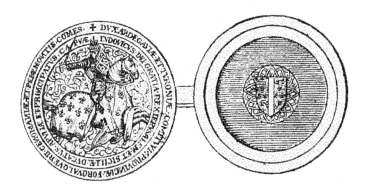

# Genealogy of the

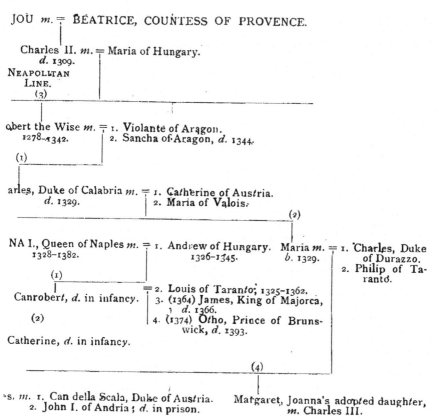

JOU m. = BÉATRICE, COUNTESS OF PROVENCE.
|
Charles II. m. = Maria of Hungary.
  d. 1309.
NEAPOLITAN
  LINE.
    (3)
|
Robert the Wise m. = 1. Violante of Aragon.
  1278–1342.        2. Sancha of Aragon, d. 1344.
    (1)
|
Charles, Duke of Calabria m. = 1. Catherine of Austria.
  d. 1329.                     2. Maria of Valois.
                                                (2)
|
JOANNA I., Queen of Naples m. = 1. Andrew of Hungary.   Maria m. = 1. Charles, Duke
  1328–1382.                    1326–1345.    b. 1329.           of Durazzo.
    (1)                                                      2. Philip of Ta-
|                                                               ranto.
Canrobert, d. in infancy.  = 2. Louis of Taranto, 1325–1362.
    (2)                     3. (1364) James, King of Majorca,
                                 d. 1366.
Catherine, d. in infancy.   4. (1374) Otho, Prince of Bruns-
                                wick, d. 1393.
                                          (4)
|
...s, m. 1. Can della Scala, Duke of Austria.    Margaret, Joanna's adopted daughter,
    2. John I. of Andria; d. in prison.            m. Charles III.

# Genealogy of the Ang

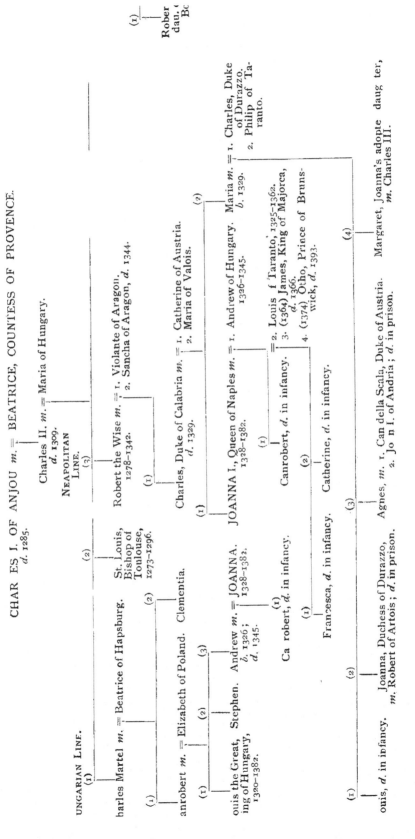

# SOURCES OF INFORMATION AND BOOKS CONSULTED IN WRITING THIS BIOGRAPHY

"Historical Life of Joanna of Sicily." Anonymous. London, 1824. 2 vols.

"Scenes in the Life of Joanna of Naples." Mrs. E. F. Ellet. Boston, 1840.

"La France et le Grand Schisme d'Occident." Valois. Vols. i. and ii. Paris, 1896.

"Giovanna la Regina di Napoli." Matteo Camera. Salerno, 1889.

"Joanna die Erste." Carl von Rotteck. Stuttgart, 1829.

"Crimes Célèbres." Dumas. Vol. ii.

"Storia del Regno di Napoli." Gravina. 1769.

"Vita Nicolai Acciajuoli, Rerum Italicarum Scriptores." Muratori.

"Della Prima e Della Secunda Giovanna." D. Crivelli. 1832.

"Vita di Giovanna, Regina di Napoli." Caraccioli.

*Quarterly Review* for 1824.

"Life of Petrarch." Mrs. Dodson. 1805.

"Revue des Questions Historiques." 1896. xlviii. and xxii.

"Queen Joanna I." An Essay on her Times. St. Clair Baddeley. London, 1893.

"Histoires des Reines Jeanne I. et II." Alex. T. Guyot. Paris, 1700.

"La Vie de Ste. Brigitte de Suède." La Comtesse de Flavigny.

Froissart's "Chronicles."

"Dictionnaire Critique." Bayle. Vol. iii.

"Histoire des Papes." L'Abbé Darras.
"Avignon, ses Histoires, ses Papes," etc. Joudon. London, 1842.
"Dictionnaire Historique." Bouillet. 1845.
"Ecclesiastical History." Mosheim.
"Harmsworth Encyclopædia."
"Encyclopædia Britannica."
"Middle Ages." Hallam.
"Papal Monarchy." William Barry.
"Mediæval Rome." Miller.
"Histoire de l'Eglise." Lavisse et Rambaud.
"Essai sur les Mœurs." Voltaire. iv.
"Old Provence." Cook.
"European History." Lodge.
"Les Papes." Marin de Boylesve, S.J. Tours. 1893.
"Rulers of the South." Marion Crawford.
"Italian Republics." J. C. L. de Sismondi
"Clemens VI." Baluzio. Vol. ii.

# INDEX

## A

Acciajuoli, Angelo, Bp. of Florence, 138 *et sqq.*, 148, 151
Acciajuoli, Nicholas, 123, 125, 138, 151, 197, 223, 228 ; his birth and position, 39, 40 ; and Joanna and Andrew, 51 ; his promotion to be Grand Seneschal, 79 ; and Andrew's murder, 83, 93 ; and Joanna's captivity at Aix, 141 ; has audience with Clement VI., 148, 156 ; and the invasion of Louis of Hungary, 169 ; and Petrarch, 195 ; and the war in Sicily, 200, 203 ; and the truce with King Frederick, 211 ; his death foretold by St. Bridget, 225 ; his death, 226-7 ; and Boccaccio, 251
Adrian IV., Pope, 117
Agnes of Durazzo (Princess of Verona), 135 *et sqq.*, 242-3, 289, 303, 318-19
Alferino of Salerno, 272-3
Americus, Cardinal, 69-70
Andrew of Hungary (Joanna's first husband), 4, 67 ; his murder, 3, 79, 84 *et sqq.*, 100-1, 109, 110, 184, 186, 209, 223, 329 ; his early marriage, 23 *et sqq.* ; his imbecility, 24-5, 28, 31, 64 ; and King Robert's will, 40 *et sqq.* ; his coarseness, 45, 51, 78, 90 ; ascends the throne with Joanna, 48 ; and Friar Robert's plotting, 49 *et sqq.* ; and the Court of Love, 62-3 ; and the Pipini brothers, 63 ; and Joanna's coronation, 69 ; stays at Aversa, 80 *et sqq.* ; his burial in Naples Cathedral, 89 ; his death avenged by Louis, 130 *et sqq.*
Andrew of Isernia, 233
Andria, Francis de Baux, Duke of : his marriage to Louis of Taranto's sister, 173-4, 246 ; his rebellion against Joanna, 263 *et sqq.*, 279, 280 ; and Charles of Durazzo, 287, 299 ; returns to Joanna's cause, 319, 320, 325-6
Angelo of Perugia, 94, 233
Anselmo, 269
Ariano, Count of, 310-11, 320
Artus, Charles, 41, 79, 84, 92, 106-7, 132
Austria, Duke of, 5
Aversa, Castle of, 80-1, 133, 261
Aversa, Count of, 321
Avignon, Petrarch at, 34 *et sqq.* ; Papal Court at, 72 *et sqq.*, 138 *et sqq.*, 210, 224, 236, 244, 291 ; the plague at, 161 *et sqq.*

## B

Baddeley, Mr., 230
Baldassero of Brunswick, 310-11
Baldus of Perugia, 94, 233
Balliol, Edward, 76
Barbatus of Sulmone, 37, 43, 99
Barrili, John, 37, 227
Barruto, Abbot (Archbp. of Naples), 291, 295
Baux, Hugh de, 101, 103
Baux, Raimond de, 125, 197, 200, 265-6
Baux, Rinaldo de, 182

# Index

Benedict XII., Pope, 75, 115
Beni, Duc de, 148
Bernard of Rhodes, 295
Bianca of Sicily, Princess, 199, 200
Bianchi, the, 30
Birel, John, 193
Birger of Sweden, Prince, 252 et sqq.
Blanche of Dampierre, Princess, 24
Blanche, Queen of Sweden, 223
Boccaccio, Giovanni, 2, 4, 19, 37, 43, 79, 196, 208, 235, 332; meets Maria of Sicily, 38; his birth, 39; his works, 39; his account of Joanna, 106, 233; his account of the plague in Florence, 167; and the brigands, 231; his "Decameron," 247 et sqq.; warned by Father Ciani, 249; becomes a priest, 250-1; and Nicholas Acciajuoli's treatment of, 251; his death, 252; his commentary on the "Divina Commedia," 252
Bondone, Giotto de, 207-8
Boniface IX., Pope, 274
Braganza, Bp. of, 189
Brantôme, 221; his account of Joanna's beauty, 43-4
Bridget of Sweden, St., 78, 193, 236, 271-2; her piety, 223-4, 270; works miracles, 225; and Nicholas Acciajuoli's death, 225-6; and Pope Urban's return to Avignon, 244-5; her second visit to Naples, 252; and her two sons, 253-4; received by the Queen, 254-5; and Prince Charles's infatuation for Joanna, 255 et sqq.; and her son's death, 258; goes to the Holy Land, 258; and the Plague at Naples, 258-9; her letter to the Queen, 259, 260; receives a present of money from Joanna, 261; her death at Rome, 261-2; her canonisation, 274-86
Brunelleschi, 207
Buondelmonte, Countess, 223

Bury, Richard de (Bp. of Durham), 37
Byron, Lord, 78

## C

Cabassole, Bp. of Cavaillon, Philip de, 41, 71-1, 79, 96 et sqq.
Cajetano Onerato, 281-2, 295
Canrobert, King of Hungary, 6, 23 et sqq., 40-1, 108
Canrobert, Prince (son of Joanna), 98 et sqq., 122, 124, 130, 134, 181
Caraccioli, his Life of Joanna, 19, 130
Casimir, King of Poland, 193
Catania, Raymond of, 85
Catherine of Austria (first wife of Charles, Duke of Calabria), 18
Catherine of Siena, St., 78, 221-2, 224-5, 252, 270 et sqq., 285 et sqq., 293-4
Chabannes, Raimond de, 18
Charles I. of Anjou, 5
Charles, Duke of Calabria (father of Joanna), 17, 331; his justice, 8, 9, 206; his journey to Florence, 10, 11; his death, 14
Charles, Duke of Durazzo (nephew of King Robert of Naples), 74, 179; his marriage to Maria of Sicily, 66 et sqq., 7 and Andrew's murder, 83, 92, 102, 117; rebels against Joanna, 107, 120; and Joanna's second marriage, 113; murdered by Louis of Hungary, 129 et sqq., 137, 187
Charles, Duke of Durazzo (son of Prince Louis), 267; adopted by Joanna, 202-3, 239; his marriage to Margaret of Durazzo, 203, 242 et sqq.; joins Louis of Hungary, 239, 266, 279, 292; and Joanna's second marriage, 269; his attempts to depose Joanna, 287, 293, 295-6, 298 et sqq.; his entry into Naples, 301,

# Index

304 et sqq.; and Prince Otho's strategy, 306-7; his assurances to Joanna, 308, 312 et sqq.; enters Castel NuoVo, 311; and Joanna's appointed successor, 317-18; crowned King of Naples, 319; his difficulties, 320; his treatment of Joanna, 324 et sqq.; and the murder of Joanna, 328 et sqq.; liberates Otho, 333; his murder, 334; his excommunication, 334; his appearance, 334
Charles V. of France, 292, 296-7, 318, 320
Charles IV. of Germany, 74-5, 195
Charles Martel (son of Charles II.), 6-7, 64, 71, 119
Charles II. of Naples, 213, 239
Charles of Sweden, Prince, 252 et sqq.
Ciani, Father Joachim, 249
Cicely, Duchess of Turenne, 146-7
Clare, St., Church of (AVignon), 34
Clare, St., Church and Monastery of (Naples), 15, 20, 38, 42, 64, 65, 67, 206 et sqq., 282, 323, 330-1
Clement IV., 5
Clement VI., Pope, 131, 211, 235, 241, 246; his belief in Joanna's innocence, 4, 42, 93 et sqq., 115, 169, 171; and Maria's marriage, 67; and Joanna's coronation, 69, 72; and Joanna's wish to goVern, 70, 71; his loVe of pomp, 73; and the Jews, 74; his court at AVignon, 142, 145 et sqq.; his attire, 153; Joanna pleads her cause to, 155 et sqq., 315; and the Mendicant Friars, 164-5; and the Flagellants, 166; and Louis of Taranto's coronation, 170; and Louis of Hungary, 184-5; and the Neapolitan succession, 185; his death, 191; his character, 192-3
Clement VII., the anti-Pope, 315, 322; Joanna's partisanship for, 3, 281, 285, 290, 307; at war with Pope Urban VI., 286, 288; goes to Castel del Ovo, 288 et sqq.; his reception by Joanna, 289; flees to Gaeta, 291; and Louis of Anjou, 298; Durazzo consults with, 321
Collennucci, Clemence di, 325
Colonna, Cardinal, 34, 52-3, 163-4
Conradine, 5
Constantinople, Empress of. See Princess of Taranto
Convulsionnaires, the, 143
Costanzo, 30, 51, 86, 269
Crillon, 142-3
Crispano, Landolpho, 255

## D

Dancers, the, 144
Dante, 8, 38, 196, 248
Darnley, Lord, 335
DaVid II. of Scotland, 76
Durazzo, Duke of (son of Charles II. of Naples), 6, 10, 66.

## E

Edward III. of England, 75-6, 150
Edward Prince of Wales, 216 et sqq.
Evoli, Count d', 49, 84-5, 91, 103

## F

Faliero Marino, 78
Flagellants, the, 165
FlaVio, Gioja, 235
Folard, CheValier, 143
Fondi, Count of, 320
Francesca, Princess, 181-2, 190
Frederick Barbarossa, 117
Frederick of Sicily, 196 et sqq., 211, 246
Frederick II. of Swabia, 5
Froissart, 215 et sqq., 230

## G

Galeazzo of Mantua, 219
Ghibellines, the, 29, 77, 165
Giannone, 4, 324
Giffone, Cardinal de, 323
Giovanni of Pisa, 207
Gravina, Bp. of, 246
Gregory XI., Pope, 246, 252, 254, 265-6, 270-1, 273 et sqq.
Guelphs, The, 29, 77, 140, 165
Guinguéne, 248

## H

Hawkwood, Sir John, 295
Henry IV. of France, 143
Henry of Transtamare, 217

## I

Innocent VI., Pope, 194-5, 210
Innocent VII., Pope, 75
Isolda (Andrew's nurse), 82, 85 et sqq.
Itro, Cardinal d', 323

## J

James I. of Aragon, 213
James II. of Aragon, 213
James I. of Majorca, 213
James II. of Majorca, 213-14
James III. of Majorca, 226; his descent, 213; his marriage to Joanna, 215, 223; his military exploits, 215 et sqq.; his death, 230
Jerome, St., 250
Joanna, Duchess of Durazzo, 135 et sqq., 287, 289, 303, 305-6, 318-19
Joanna, Queen of Naples:
her biographers, 1, 3, 4
her beauty, 1, 2, 30-1, 43 et sqq., 106, 122 et sqq., 233, 332
her birth, 12 et sqq.
her attendants, 17 et sqq.
her early years, 19 et sqq.
her education, 22, 30
oaths of allegiance to, 22, 31-2
her marriage with Andrew of Hungary, 23 et sqq.

Joanna, Queen of Naples (*cont.*):
and King Robert's will, 40 et sqq.
and King Robert's death, 42
her supposed portrait, 44-5
proclaimed Queen, 48
and Friar Robert's plotting, 49, 50
and Louis of Taranto, 51-2
her talent and learning, 55
and the great tempest, 59
her "Court of Love," 61 et sqq.
and Andrew's boorishness, 62-3, 78
and Maria's marriage, 69
her wish to govern, 70-1
her coronation, 72, 84
stays at Aversa, 80 et sqq.
and Andrew's murder, 86 et sqq., 100-1, 103, 109 et sqq., 184, 186, 209
her letters to King Louis, 88, 93, 101
gives birth to a son, and the execution of Philippa, 104 et sqq.
her queenly bearing, 106, 211, 333
and the civil war, 107
her second marriage, to Louis of Taranto, 114-15
calls a council, 120-1
her speech, 121-2
taken prisoner to Aix, 125 et sqq., 148-9
and her governors, 128
receives Maria and her children, 137-8
and the Papal Court, 138, 141
her release, 148
her triumphant entry into Avignon, 149 et sqq.
her reception by the Pope, 155 et sqq.
her gift of oratory, 159, 315
her defence, 159
her acquittal, 159, 160
receives the Golden Rose, 160-1, 241
her subjects invite her to return to Naples, 168 et sqq.
her reception at Naples, 172
and her sister-in-law's marriage, 173-4

# INDEX

343

Joanna, Queen of Naples (*cont.*):
rewards Nicholas Acciajuoli, 174
her gay court, 175, 203
birth of her daughters, 181
and de Baux, 182–3
her second trial, 184
and the succession, 185, 238–9, 243–4, 292
her coronation, 186 *et sqq.*, 196
death of her little daughter, 190
and death of Clement VI., 197
crowned Queen of Sicily at Messina, 197
and the King of Sicily's sisters, 199, 200
and the civil war, 200–1
pardons Louis of Durazzo, 202
adopts Charles of Durazzo as her heir, 202
adopts Maria's daughter, Princess Margaret, 203
and Louis' death, 203
her widowhood, 204 *et sqq.*
builds churches and institutions, 206–7
her piety, 206, 309, 327 *et sqq.*
as a ruler, 208, 232
and Philip of Taranto, 211–12
her suitors, 212
her third marriage to James of Majorca, 214
her husband's absence, 215 *et sqq.*
and Galeazzo's admiration for, 219
and Galeazzo's knights, 220
receives St. Bridget of Sweden, 224
her piety, 224
sends out an army against Ambrose Visconti, 229 *et sqq.*
and the death of her husband, 230
suppresses brigandage, 231
her advisers, 233
celebrities of her reign, 235
visits Pope Urban V. at Rome, 238 *et sqq.*
and Charles of Durazzo's ingratitude, 239, 266, 287
favoured by the Pope, 240 *et sqq.*

Joanna, Queen of Naples (*cont.*):
and Peter of Lusignan, 242
her affection for Charles of Durazzo, 243
and the independence of Sicily, 246
and Prince Charles of Sweden's admiration for, 252 *et sqq.*
and Prince Charles's funeral, 258
St. Bridget's letter to, 259, 260
her present of money to St. Bridget, 261
and St. Bridget's death, 262
and Duke of Andria's rebellion, 263 *et sqq.*
her fourth marriage to Prince Otho of Brunswick, 267 *et sqq.*
and St. Catherine, 272, 286–7
her regard for Urban VI., 278–9
and Cardinal Orsini, 280
supports the anti-pope, Clement VII., 281, 288, 294
Urban VI.'s enmity to, 280, 282
her mission to Rome, 282
her anger at Urban's insults, 284
receives Clement VII. at Castel del Ovo, 288 *et sqq.*
excommunicated by Urban VI., 294
elects Louis of Anjou as her successor, in place of Charles of Durazzo, 296, 298
and Charles Durazzo's advance on Naples, 295 *et sqq.*
retires to Castel del Nuovo, 303 *et sqq.*
her privations, 304 *et sqq.*
and Joanna of Durazzo's offering, 306
her surrender to Charles, 311 *et sqq.*, 319
her speech to Charles, 312
her speech to the Provençal barons, 315 *et sqq.*
removed to Castel del Ovo 318
taken to Castel del Muro, 324
and her maid of honour, 325

Joanna, Queen of Naples (*cont.*):
 her affection for her husband, 326–7
 her murder, 329 *et sqq.*
 her lying-in-state, 330–1
 her epitaph, 331
 compared with Mary, Queen of Scots, 335
John of Bohemia, Prince, 24
John I. of France, 126, 194, 212, 228
John XXII., Pope, 7, 20, 23, 31, 192

## L

Landuccio, Neri di, 287
Laura. See Laura de Sades
Louis of Anjou, adopted by Joanna as her heir, 287, 292, 296, 305, 314, 316; declared Regent of France, 297, 320–1; Joanna seeks his aid, 299; his valour and costly collections, 318; his fleet in the Bay of Naples, 328, 331; his struggles with Charles of Durazzo, 332 *et sqq.*
Louis, Prince of Durazzo, 200 *et sqq.*
Louis XIV. of France, 143
Louis IV. of Germany, 74 *et sqq.*, 115, 191
Louis, King of Hungary, 149, 228, 239, 242, 244, 266, 279; his proposed marriage to Princess Maria, 40, 64, 66 *et sqq.*, 109; and his brother Andrew's murder, 88, 92 *et sqq.*, 130 *et sqq.*, 185–6, 329, 332; Joanna's letters to, 88, 101–2; invades Joanna's dominions, 108, 116 *et sqq.*, 128; his letters to Joanna, 109, 111; demands Naples, 115; accuses Joanna, 115; his treachery, 129; murders the Duke of Durazzo, 132–3, 135; abducts Prince Canrobert, 134; his ambassadors at Avignon, 155; retreats from Naples, 168; enters Apulia, 180; challenged by Louis of Taranto, 180; and the siege of Aversa, 181; enters Naples, 183; and the Pope's commands, 184; and the Treaty of Peace, 185 *et sqq.*; and Joanna's death, 328–9, 331; his death, 333
Louis, Prince of Taranto (Joanna's second husband), 3, 40, 52, 62, 83, 107, 125, 131, 148, 160, 195, 229; his personal appearance, 51, 112, 175; and Andrew's murder, 92; his love for Joanna, 113; his marriage, 114 *et sqq.*, 223; fights against Louis of Hungary, 118 *et sqq.*; forbidden to enter Florence, 140; sails for Provence, 141; enters Avignon in state, 151, 161; received by the Pope, 156; his coronation, 171, 186 *et sqq.* returns to Naples with Joanna, 171; his popularity, 175; his profligacy, 175; and Warner and Wolf, 176 *et sqq.*; kills Rinaldo de Baux, 183; and the succession, 185; thrown from his horse, 189, 190; crowned King of Sicily, 197; returns to Naples, 201; his vices, 203–4; his death, 203, 209 *et sqq.*
Louis, St. (Bp. of Toulouse), 6, 7
Ludovico, Antonio, Count of Caserta, 313 *et sqq.*, 317, 321
Luke of Isernia, 233

## M

Magnus II. of Sweden, 24, 223, 245
Malateca, Giovanni, 229
Manfred, 5
Margaret of Durazzo, Princess, 203, 243, 269, 289, 293
Margaret, Queen of Sweden, 24
Margaret of Taranto, Princess, 246, 263, 279
Maria, Duchess of Calabria (mother of Joanna), 10 *et sqq.*; her apartments, 12 *et sqq.*; birth of a second daughter, 15; her death, 16
Maria, Duchess of Durazzo (Joanna's sister), 43, 173, 182,

242, 287; her birth, 15; and the succession, 22, 40; her proposed marriage to the King of Hungary, 40-1, 64, 133; her marriage to the Duke of Durazzo, 67 et sqq., 72, 79, 109; and the throne of Naples, 113, 120; informed of her husband's murder, 135; flees to Santa Croce, 135-6; goes to Joanna, 136 et sqq.; marries Prince Philip of Taranto, 203; her death, 238
Maria of Hungary (wife of Charles II. of Naples), 6
Maria of Sicily (daughter of King Frederick), 282
Maria of Sicily (King Robert's natural daughter), 38
Martini, Simon, 208
Mary, Queen of Scots, 1, 43, 335
Masuccios, the Two, 207-8
Milan, Duke of, 215
Minervino Count de, 116, 172, 178, 201-2
Mirazzano, Michael de, 84, 102
Molta, Bertram della, 188
Montferrat, Marquis of, 282
Montoni, Countess of. See Phillipa the Catanese
Moriale, Fra (Montreal d'Albano), 179, 180
Muratori, 87
Muro, Castle of, 94, 324 et sqq.
Murray, Earl of, 335

N

Neri, the, 30
Nericia, Princess of. See St. Bridget of Sweden
Nicholas of Hungary (governor of Andrew), 27, 49, 62, 91, 108, 116
Nicholas of Naples, 233
Nicholas of Pisa, 207
Niem, Theodoric de, 329
Nuovo Castel, 288; the siege at, 303 et sqq.

O

Orlando, Prince of Aragon, 198-9

Orsini, Cardinal, 277, 279, 285
Orsini, Giovanni, 295, 297
Orsini, Rinaldo, 295, 297
Orsini, Robert, 273
Orsini, the, 30, 52
Otho of Brunswick, Prince (Joanna's fourth husband), 271, 297, 312; meets Joanna, 267; his marriage, 268; and Pope Urban VI., 280, 283-4; his bravery, 298; fights against Charles of Durazzo, 298 et sqq.; and the besieged Queen 306 et sqq.; taken prisoner by Charles of Durazzo, 326; liberated by Charles, 333; his death, 333
Ovo, Castel del, 124, 254, 268, 288 et sqq., 296, 318

P

Pace, Jacobo de, 84, 92, 102
Paris of Pozzuoli, 235
Paul of Perugia, 7, 37-8
Pedro III. of Aragon, 213
Pedro IV. of Aragon, 213
Pedro I. of Spain (the Cruel), 77, 195, 216 et sqq.
Peter Damien, St., 47
Peter of Lusignan, King of Cyprus, 240-42
Petrarch, 2, 4, 28, 31, 50, 83, 150, 196, 235, 332; his writings, 33 et sqq.; his appearance and accomplishments, 33-4; his love for Laura, 34 et sqq., 162-3; his great learning, 36; wins the laurel crown, 36; his "Africa," 37; and King Robert's death, 42-3; his description of Naples, 53-4; his preferment, 55; and the great tempest, 55 et sqq.; and the gladiatorial combats, 60-1; and the Court of Love, 62; his epitaph on King Robert, 65; and Clement VI., 73; and Andrew, 90; and Joanna's innocence, 94, 99; visited by the Bp. of Florence, 138 et sqq.; and the Papal Court, 145, 193; and

Pope Innocent VI., 194; and Zanobi's laurel crown, 195; and the quarrel between Acciajuoli and Barrili, 227; his admiration for Joanna, 247; and Boccaccio's library, 250; his death, 252
Petroni, Father, 249, 250
Philip de Valois (King of France), 16, 75, 126
Philippa the Catanese, 3, 50, 68; her origin, 17, 19, 22; takes charge of Joanna, 17 et sqq.; her second marriage, 18; promoted by Joanna, 48; and the Princess of Taranto, 51, 69; and the murder of Andrew, 83, 91, 103; her execution, 104-5
Philip of Taranto (Louis of Taranto's younger brother), 203, 263
Philip, Duke of Tours, 212, 228
Piero, Cardinal, 277, 285
Pierre de Luna, Cardinal, 277
Pipini, the, 52, 63, 90, 201-2
Pius V., Pope, 153
Prignano, Francisco, 280, 282, 296, 299

R

Raimond of Capua, 286
Raimond the Moor (second husband of Philippa the Catanese), 18
Rastrelli, 86
Ravignano, 291
Richard II. of England, 216
Rienzi, Cola de, 74-5, 115-16
Robert of Artois (afterwards Duke of Durazzo), 76, 287, 310-11
Robert, Friar, 31, 69, 70, 78, 81, 84, 91; his characteristics, 27-8, 43, 50; plots against Joanna, 49; and the Pipini brothers, 63; his power, 82, 110; returns to Hungary, 108
Robert, Prince of Taranto, 107, 113, 123
Robert the Wise (King of Naples), 6, 12, 14 et sqq., 79, 91, 100, 107, 121, 139, 185, 208, 232; his ascent to the throne, 7; his learning, 7, 32; and the Duke of Calabria's death, 14; and the church of St. Clare, 15, 206-7; and Philippa the Catanese, 17 et sqq.; and Joanna's early training, 19 et sqq.; arranges a marriage for Joanna, 23 et sqq.; and the oath of allegiance, 22, 31-2; and Petrarch, 36-7; his will, 40 et sqq., 70; his death, 42; Petrarch's epitaph on, 65
Rosarno, Angeluccio di, 313

S

Sades, Laura de, 34-5, 38, 43, 142, 162
Sancha (King Robert of Naples's second wife), 16 et sqq., 41, 48, 50, 64, 67-8, 70, 103, 206
Sancha (Philippa's granddaughter), 3, 79, 92, 103 et sqq.
Sangro, Gentilis de, 299, 322
Sanguineto, Philip of, 41
SanseVerino, Ugo de, 308
SaVoy, Duke of, 215, 266, 322
Simon, Count of Chiaramonte, 196, 199
Soult, Count de, 125
Spinelli, Nicholas, 280, 282-3
Squillazzo, Geoffrey, Count of, 41
Stephen, Prince, 178-9
Strada, Zanobi de, 195
Swinburne, Algernon C., 78

T

Talleyrand, Cardinal, 66-7, 193-4
Taranto, Prince of (Louis' elder brother), 201, 211-12
Taranto, Prince of, 10, 22
Taranto, Princess of (mother of Louis), 40, 51, 67, 79, 83, 93, 107
Taranto, Princess of (wife of Robert), 123, 125, 246
TrasteVera, Henry of, 77
Trelice, Count de, 85, 105
Tropea, Bp. of, 108
Turinga, Camiola, 197 et sqq.

## U

Urban V., Pope, 153, 161, 235, 273; and Petrarch's marriage, 35; his friendliness towards Joanna, 211; and Joanna's third marriage, 212; and St. Bridget, 224; and the Viscontis, 228-9; decides to return to Avignon, 244; his death, 245-6

Urban VI., Pope, 322, 329; his enmity towards Joanna, 4, 94, 279, 250, 295; his character, 278; his haughtiness, 281; his treatment of the Cardinals, 281; and Joanna's embassy, 282-3; insults Prince Otho, 283-4; creates twenty-nine new cardinals, 284-5; and Clement VII., the anti-pope, 286 *et sqq.*; his unpopularity, 293; excommunicates Joanna, 294, 298; supports Charles of Durazzo, 295-6, 307, 319; tortures the rebellious Cardinals, 323-4; now opposes Charles of Durazzo, 328, 334

## V

Verona, Princess of. See Agnes of Durazzo
Vico, Francesca de, 285
Villani, Matthew, 29, 93, 95, 114, 117, 164
Vinci, Leonardo da, 44
Violante (wife of King Robert of Naples), 8, 17-18
Violante of Sicily, Princess, 199, 200
Virgil, 36
Visconti, Ambrose, 228 *et sqq.*, 257, 268
Visconti, Barnabas, 228 *et sqq.*

## W

Warner, Duke, 176 *et sqq.*
Wolf, Conrad, 176 *et sqq.*, 184

## Z

Zurlo, Jacimo, 310-11

CPSIA information can be obtained
at www.ICGtesting.com
Printed in the USA
BVOW04s1007171216
471117BV00028B/592/P